THE REFORM OF PLANNING LAW

The Reform of Planning Law

A Study of the Legal, Political and Administrative Reform of the British Land-use Planning System

NEAL ALISON ROBERTS

Assistant Professor, Osgoode Hall Law School,
York University, Canada
Lecturer, 1972–4, in the School of Law,
University of Warwick, England

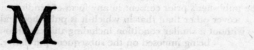

First published 1976 by
THE MACMILLAN PRESS LTD
London and Basingstoke
Associated companies in New York Dublin
Melbourne Johannesburg and Madras

SBN 333 18007 0 (hard cover)
333 18821 7 (paper cover)

Printed in Great Britain by
THE BOWERING PRESS LTD
Plymouth

DEDICATED TO
BEDE

Contents

CONTENTS

Swedish land storage – the tools available, the fruits of the storage system. The Labour proposals for land storage. A model scheme for British land storage.

Foreword

FOREWORD

study of English planning and local government. If others to

The system of town and country planning, created in 1947, has undergone major changes since then, not least when structure and local plans were substituted for development plans in 1968 and structure and functions, though not, mistakenly, the finance of local government, were reorganised in 1972. The creation, administration and reforms of planning have been brought about by law, hundreds and hundreds of pages of it. Until comparatively recently, however, this mass of law has not been regarded as a fit subject for academic digestion by lawyers, who have contented themselves with nibbling fastidiously at those bits that have found their way into the law reports. The only significant pieces of legal research into the English planning system which have been published have been by American lawyers: Charles Haar's *Land Planning Law in a Free Society* and Daniel Mandelker's *Green Belts and Urban Growth*. These two works are now joined by this one by my former colleague Neal Roberts, and together they make up a worthy and, from an English legal point of view, slightly shaming trio.

Professor Roberts, now at Osgoode Hall Law School, was a member of Warwick University's School of Law from 1972 to 1974. He came with some considerable experience of American urban law and at the best possible time to observe the English planning and local government system undergoing a major transformation. Or was it? And if it was, why, and if not, why not? With characteristic American panache Professor Roberts set out to try and find the answers to these questions. He has also given a close examination to that recent addition to the armoury of the planners – the public examination – as he was able to witness its first use in the engagement between the planners and the public in the Coventry–Solihull–Warwickshire Structure Plan Examination in November and December 1973. His report from the front lines repays careful study.

I hope this work will be widely read, and not only by non-lawyers. It might not be thought perfect; some lawyers will argue that two years is too short a time to write an adequate study of English planning and local government. If that is so, let them try and do better. At any rate, I hope that, unlike the other American legal works on our system of planning law, this one does spark off English competitors; it will not be before time.

School of Law,   PATRICK McAUSLAN
University of Warwick

Preface

This book may strike the reader as the work of either a rude visitor or at least a presumptuous guest. I would hope that the reader will find the piece interesting even if some of the conclusions are not entirely complimentary, and I would like to extend my apologies at an early point to any of my host country's citizens who might be unusually sensitive. Hopefully, the work will be useful not only to students of the planning-law system but also to government officials, practising lawyers, and their counterparts in the United States and Canada, who are facing similar situations.

Since the intelligent reader usually reads a preface in order to glean an idea of the possible bias of the author, I should perhaps begin by exposing my academic background. Although I am a law teacher I was trained as a political scientist as well as a lawyer, and the reader will find that the work is written from a number of viewpoints.

A few notes are in order: those readers interested primarily in Northern Ireland or Scotland should be forewarned that this work deals primarily with England and Wales. Also, readers of the *Urban Lawyer* and the *Modern Law Review* will recognise sections of Parts One and Three as being based on articles which appeared in those esteemed publications.

I am extremely indebted both to the U.S. Department of Housing and Urban Development and the School of Law at the University of Warwick, for supporting this project. I would like to thank Gwen Bevan, Paul Davies, Malcolm Grant, Jeffery Jowell, George Lefcoe, Geoffrey Little, Patrick Mc-Auslan, Martin Partington, Susanne Roberts and Larry Taman, whose confidence, analysis and thought helped this book see the light of day. Lastly I should like to thank my property students who coped with a great many Americanisms in both speech and thought and who helped immensely in my understanding of English land use and property law.

1 The Perspective and the Governmental Structure

THE PERSPECTIVE: AN INTRODUCTION TO THE APPROACH AS WELL AS THE GARDEN MENTALITY *et al.*

That 'daring experiment in social control of the environment' as Professor Haar described the 1947 Town and Country Planning Act in Britain, has now been in force for over a quarter of a century (HAAR, 1951, p. 1).* The elaborate scheme which had as its goal the protection of the communities' rights in that most unique form of private property, land, has now been in existence a sufficient time to have spawned dramatic reforms in its character. It is those changes, more especially the changes in the administrative units administering the system, and their procedures and approach, which will be the major focus for this book.

The purpose of this enquiry is to explore how the changes and reforms have affected the process, and in particular the fairness and efficiency of the administrative procedures involved. First, we will look at the reform of the local government administrative structure, both in terms of the provision of services, and of finance. Second will come a discussion of the changes in the form of planning: the introduction of a two-tier planning approach, the creation of new administrative review procedures, and an analysis of possible changes in the day-to-day system of planning-application review. Finally, in Part Three, we will turn to the conclusions that can be drawn from the reforms and the possibilities for a more effective change in the rules of the game through the mechanism of public ownership rather than public regulation of land.

Before rushing headlong into these changes in the planning system we must first have some idea both of the goals underlying the system and its framework. The first enquiry concerning goals must begin with the perennial land-use problems facing

---

*References in small capitals in parentheses refer to the Bibliography, pp. 281–93.

the British Isles and from there explore the firmly felt but often conflicting values held by most members of the public or at least by the governing elite.

THE PROBLEMS WHICH PLANNERS HAVE TO FACE

The problems faced sound very similar to those reverberating on both sides of the Atlantic, or for that matter throughout the industrialised world. In a small island with a large population they are magnified because England has been industrialised longer than any other country. The first problem is what is known as the housing crisis, or more conveniently the problem of slums and housing shortage.

It might more easily be labelled a condition rather than a problem, for it seems to be, like other problems, a fixed variable within which land planning must work. The 1848 Public Health and Housing Act and its successors in the nineteenth century were designed to eliminate substandard housing and urban decay; and modern legislation is still facing the same problem. According to a recent Shelter Report, of the 16 million dwellings in the country some 1·8 to 2 million are officially slums with another 5 million houses in an unsatisfactory condition (SHELTER). The newspaper headlines of 1867 or 1947 bear striking resemblance to present-day accounts of the urban homeless and squatter population. 'We have repeatedly asked for the demolition of the property. . . . One of them collapsed. Fortunately the old people who lived there weren't injured. The other had begun to collapse so that was vacated . . . I fell through the floor there.' (SHELTER)

Linked with this deterioration of urban dwellings is an increase in the cost of residential land at a rate higher than other prices, which seems to be a permanent fixture. This occurred in various periods, but the late 1960s and early 1970s again saw a tremendous rise in housing prices. The point is, that unlike earlier investigators in 1960, who might point to 'skyrocketing land prices' (MANDELKER, 1962) as a unique strain under which the planning system must operate, by the mid-1970s it is perhaps wiser to view such problems as a part of a continuing process within which the planning-law system must deal. While prices may occasionally stabilise, long-range rises would seem the norm rather than the exception.

The second problem, similarly, is one that has been on the

English scene for a long time, although it has become a matter of extreme, almost fetishistic, importance in the last few years, and that is the quality of life, which is threatened by the kindred demons of pollution, lack of open space and lack of recreational amenity. Dating from the eighteenth century there has been tremendous concern for preserving the beauties of nature and a 'healthy use' of land. England is a country where almost half of all existing structures have been built since the Second World War, where the historic cities of Bath and York are in severe danger of partial elimination, and where there is an almost constant series of protests over pollution crises, whether they be over North Sea Oil in Scotland or mining operations in Snowdonia National Park. Since these disputes are a function of economic and technological advances, the question is not whether environmental problems have been eliminated, but whether the planning system helps to settle or merely reifies these problems, and whether other alternatives are available.

The third major problem with which land planning must deal is that of transport. The congestion of transportation networks, if anything, seems to have become worse in the past fifteen years. With only a fairly rudimentary system of motorways (although it is perhaps as comprehensive as some would wish) and diminishing investment in public transportation, the problems of how to move about on this rather small space have proved to be substantial. The most notable rapid change with which planners have had to deal is the phenomenal increase in the use and ownership of cars. Since 1957 the number of cars has increased from 4 to 14 million and, the energy crisis notwithstanding, shows few signs of decreasing. (TETLOW and GOSS)

The final major condition is perhaps the most important in terms of the disparity in standards of life between areas, whether they be towns and cities or whole regions, and that is the question of income and productivity imbalance. Britain's great wealth in the eighteenth and nineteenth centuries was based on the mineral wealth of certain parts of the country and the industrialisation of other parts. By the mid-twentieth century the great industrial areas still dominated the country (principally Greater Manchester, the Midlands, and London and the South East) in terms of incomes and salaries. There are whole areas where the mineral resources have been depleted and

3

prosperity has moved on, leaving behind derelict towns, countryside and people. Coupled with this are areas such as the Scottish Highlands or parts of Wales which never were included in the process of economic development. This same type of disparity also exists at the local level where large urban areas contain significantly higher proportions of the old, unemployed and poor, compared to the smaller city and country areas.

THE COGNITIVE LENSES THROUGH WHICH THE ENGLISH-MAN LOOKS AT LAND

Set against these conditions are the popularly held land-use goals which serve as a guide to how the planning system was established and at least how it was thought to have worked in practice. The first perception which significantly colours the English view of planning seems to serve as a basis for a great deal of official 'discretion' on the part of public officials but is wholeheartedly endorsed even by people whose economic interests are directly at stake. This is, for want of a better term, the garden mentality. Perhaps a quote from Ebenezer Howard, the father of the garden-city movement and grandfather of the New Town movement, will give some sort of idea of the flavour of the English approach to gardens, countryside and urban development:

> The country is the symbol of God's love and care for man. All that we are and all that we have comes from it. Our bodies are formed of it: to it they return, we are fed by it, clothed by it, and by it we are warmed and sheltered. On its bosom we rest. Its beauty is the inspiration of art, of music, of poetry. Its forces propel all the wheels of industry. It is source of all health, all wealth, all knowledge. But its fullness of joy and wisdom has not revealed itself to man. Nor can it ever, so long as this unholy, unnatural separation of society and nature endures. Town and country must be married, and out of this joyous union will spring a new hope, a new life, a new civilisation. (HOWARD, p. 48)

Perhaps taking its beginnings from the eighteenth century, and the chiefly aristocratic movements centring on landscape agriculture, there is in Britain a pronounced, almost fanatically held, interest in a bit of greenery, a flower pot, or a landscaped traffic roundabout. Those who make public decisions seem to

4

have a certain uniformity of feelings about the need to preserve the countryside, to let everyone have some green space and to provide for garden-type public amenities, whether they be city gardens or public footpaths. The same perceptive lenses which led to the model private cities of Crewe or Bournville likewise led to the amenity side of public planning and most notably the New Town and green belt.

The second cognitive lens through which the Englishman views land is coloured by the limited amount of the commodity. Land has a different character where you have 56 million people in an area less than the size of Wisconsin and where the 'frontier', if it existed at all, was closed in the time of William the Conqueror. In a nation where feudalism originally pre-supposed a 'public' character to private use of land there has always been a realisation that the allocation of this particular unique resource has far-ranging effects. In one sense the whole history of the common law of property in England, whether it be that horrible morass known as future interests, or the comparably more recent inventions of covenants running with the land and actions for nuisance, can be seen as a legal recognition of the social character of this particular resource. This development has accented the need for special legal apparatus to deal with both land's use *vis-à-vis* the interests of neighbours and its use over time.

The third perception is one that differs, if not in kind, at least in substantial degree, from that held by the majority of citizens elsewhere; it is the widely held commitment to the belief that every citizen has the right to have a pleasant house. More significantly, coupled with this is a feeling that if the private market does not fulfil this aim then the government should. With over 28 per cent of the entire housing stock in England and Wales owned by local government, and with a plethora of mechanisms continually being developed to try to create more housing, land-use policies must obviously try to accommodate these widely held goals.

The fourth perception of land which governs British thought towards land-use is the 'private property' aspect of land. Running throughout the British scheme of things is a notion of the exclusiveness of land-use, which is, of course, diametrically opposed to the social character of that use. There is a stream of thought, again dating from the times of incipient capitalism,

5

which presupposes that 'owners' of land can do what they want and can do it as well or better than the government could. They feel that they are entitled to the monetary gains that ensue both from that use and from the value given to the land, due to either public or private action beyond the land. While this perception is, perhaps, not as great an ideological force as it is in, say, North America, it is still a very strong one, even at the present time, almost a quarter of a century after the passage of the 1947 Town and Country Planning Act.

The final lens through which the Englishman looks at his land, and the use to which it is put, is the most distorting in terms of designing a land-use system, and that is the belief that the various land-use problems, which seem to block the attainment of his land-use goals, are caused by a particular and easily identifiable group of social factors (or, more correctly perhaps, devils). A survey of *The Times* or the *Guardian* today reveals these devils to be either property 'speculators', who hoard land and cause its price to increase, or traffic engineers, who deliberately seek to destroy the central section of every historic village and town in England. Twenty years ago the devils were either private landlords, who deliberately, and one would think from reading the debates over the rent-control legislation extensions after the war, collusively increased private rentals, or else any owner of property in an area which could conceivably be classified as a slum. The problem with this devil's approach is that it tends to create specific measures which, while perhaps helping to eliminate particular problems, tend to fragment the approach to the planning of land use.

AN INTRODUCTION TO THE GOVERNMENTAL AND PLAN-
NING FRAMEWORK

Once we have the British conception of land in mind, we can proceed to the legal machinery which governs the. land-planning system. Although there was a Town Planning Act as early as 1909, the basis for the modern system of land-use control is the 1947 Town and Country Planning Act, which, although it has undergone a number of reforms with which we will deal, is still the pillar of English planning. What this elaborate piece of legislation did was to require local governments to draw up land-use plans and also give them the power to ensure that development followed the plans through a system of development control, which guarantees that each and every 'development' or new 'use' (except a tightly drawn list of exceptions) will have to receive specific planning permission, and those that do not can be, and sometimes are, knocked to the ground.

To give a thumbnail sketch of the government infrastructure, starting at the bottom, local government in England is dependent entirely upon central government for its existence, and draws its powers only through specific legislation. There are no generally reserved powers vesting areas of law-making discretion to other than the central government, so local governments must rely entirely on national legislation for their governmental being. This means that not only must they not go beyond often very carefully delineated statutory language, but often that statutory instruction is of a mandatory, not a permissive character. There is no question of whether central government has the power to carry instructions to the lowest level, so questions of national land-use policy tend to focus on the extent to which national control is politically felt to be acceptable, and more important, what is administratively and economically possible.

The local governments which were charged with the original administration of the 1947 Act had been in existence more or less in their same form since the great reform movements of the 1880s. They consisted of a top level of counties or shires, below which were the districts, both urban and rural. These two levels divided between them the making of decisions and the provision of services. There were also some urbanised areas called county boroughs, which had a unified structure and carried out the duties of both the upper and lower tiers. There was a lower tier in most rural areas, the parish, which had few duties other than the maintenance of footpaths and the holding of various celebrations. Each of these bodies is based on an elected council, which has its staff of administrative officers.

The upper-tier counties were vested under the 1947 Act with the exclusive power to draw up the plans for the areas within their boundaries. The second tier was only to be consulted. The second stage, namely the control to ensure conformance, was similarly intended to only be within the purview of the upper tier. However, often what was originally intended in the Act did not exactly take place and, under a series of separate and often

7

differing delegation agreements, the lower-tier districts began to take over part of the day-to-day administration of development control. Over time, the local government units charged with the administration of the planning process became antiquated and their boundaries came to bear no rational relationship to any of the services, including planning, which they were supposed to deliver.

To fill out this brief description of the government units charged with carrying out this planning system, there is the central government. Land-use planning is just one tool in the central government's potpourri of means to affect local allocation of economic resources. In a country which has had a tradition of Fabian socialism since the beginning of the century, land-use planning from the centre should be seen as just one of the many mechanisms for making national policies at the local level. Britain has a high degree of economic centralisation, and major industries (such as steel and coal) and major transportation schemes (such as the rail, roads and bus networks) are all nationally owned, as are the major communications and mail networks. Turning to actual land-use systems the government has, separate from the land-planning system, a system of regional policies which include the financing of New Towns, a series of permissions in order to build factories or office buildings, and grants for developments in certain regions of the country.

The central government is supposed to supervise local planning. The idea was that the central government could review the development plans together and co-ordinate national policy by not approving deviant plans. The central government was to keep track of local priorities by reviewing amended plans every five years. It is the problems with this system in reality (principally that central government had a difficult time reviewing the first plans for a number of years and, with few exceptions, there was no local review) which have led to the new planning reforms, with which we shall deal at some length. At the outset it is important at least to understand the role the central government was supposed to play, which was one of a national co-ordinator, who by both the review of plans and by regulations and circulars, could orchestrate a unified and complete approach to land-planning.

The central government was also charged with the task of

being the final arbiter, on the control side of the planning equation, of the fairness of local decisions denying permission to develop. The government, through a series of mechanisms such as planning appeals, inspectors' decisions and ministerial review, was to serve as the final review body for situations where local landowners felt that permission had been wrongly declined.

Turning from the government units to the plans and control itself, the original idea was that the counties were to draw up development plans. These plans were to be proposed at a public hearing, and the various comments from the public and interested groups were then to be taken into account and a final, integrated, all-embracing document was to be sent to the central government. This document was to consist of a development map with specific uses delineated for each area, and a written statement which originally was not meant to contain any reference to specific parcels of land. The fact that the original plans took some fifteen years to come into being, from promulgation to review and approval, caused numerous difficulties. The plans no longer reflected current land-use and were not a dependable guide for future development. This made the reality of policy-making focus on the permission system of development control, and the exceptions to the development plan came to determine future land-use policies. The *ad hoc* approach lends itself much less easily to a systematised system of planning. The most interesting aspect of the English system of control, and one that has been explored at some length by other American investigators, is that even as originally designed, the system placed a great deal of discretion in the lands of local officials. The basic check, the public inquiry, is internal within the central government Ministry, and the amount of judicial interference is extremely limited. Although the central government can call in decisions on important issues, central-government review of the 80 per cent of all applications which are approved at the local level is very difficult, because – except in cases of major disagreement with the development plan – such decisions are rarely brought to the attention of the Minister. This is exacerbated by the fact that third parties are not allowed to appeal against permission approvals. It was this situation – with the fear that a great deal of official discretion was being exercised in the dark, perhaps fairly, but without any

9

up-to-date plan, much less a unified approach based on a national integration of priorities – which led to the reform of the approach to planning with the addition of the strategic or structure plan and the attempt to introduce further access through additional public participation.

THESIS

It is perhaps wise to warn the reader at this early stage about my intentions which, while honourable, may not be entirely well-received amongst those government employees who call themselves planners. This study has an overriding theme, which, put in its simplest form, may be a bit unnerving for those who have made a career in 'planning'.

The following discussion of the tremendous intellectual and administrative energy that has been devoted to the reform of the planning system will tend to show that often those changes have had very little effect, and, more importantly, that the documents, studies, plans, expertise, and 'scientific approaches' often bear very little relation to the final end-product of how the land is used. As we shall see, the lack of success in some areas has led to more grandiose attempts to make bigger systems, more documents and more reforms.

What is being suggested here is that the idea of planning the way communities are to grow and change is, by its nature, too complex for any single, rational, administrative system, reformed or unreformed, to deal with. The range of possible factors and the diffusion of conflicting values perhaps makes the ideal of a viable, reformed planning process which can actually control future land-use an unattainable one. This is not to say that the ideal should be abandoned, but simply that our intellectual energies might be put to better use.

There are basically two avenues of reform and analysis which may lead to more fruitful results. The first will be a basic premise of the changes to date and will form the core of the concluding section, Part Three, of this book. It is that the realities of the process lie in the procedures for drafting the plans or granting the permission, not in the plans themselves. Thus administrative energies should focus on the methods, types and ways of settling specific land-use disputes or policy arguments as they arise: who can appear, how various parties can best be represented, what methods are available to citizens to obtain knowledge of specific decisions or to contest them.

Such a concentration on procedures will carry with it changes of emphasis which may cause no little amount of professional insecurity. For the government officials called planners it may mean that they will have to drop the mantle of scientific or professionalised decision-making, and in many instances go out of their way to defer to elected and more politically responsible decision-makers. This may entail a redefinition of their task from one of planning, in the sense of attempting to order the future, to one of simply bringing disputes out into the local political or public arena, marshalling the various conflicting facts, and groups and values, and then deferring completely on the question of what choice is best 'from a planner's point of view'.

For lawyers such a concentration on procedures will have similar problems, for, while they have shown themselves extremely adept at handling and fashioning procedures for one compartment of planning law (that is, planning-permission refusal appeals), they have been shown to be woefully lacking in ability to devise procedures to represent different parts of the affected public. If the legal, intellectual energies were focused on the procedures of settling the particularised land-use dispute there might be a more thorough airing of all the various interests involved. However, it might also be the case that lawyers would have to devise procedures which eliminated their own role in the process.

There is a second avenue of reform which may have a great potential for results, and it is this alternative with which we shall close this discussion in Chapter 12. Without giving away too much at this early point the second possible pathway to ideal land-use is simply to have the local governments own the land and develop it themselves rather than attempt what often seems to be a futile task of 'planning' the various private owners' use of it. As we shall see, such a radical change in ownership may give the planners more chances to integrate the various factors and values, but it will make the original worry about procedures doubly important.

With this brief sketch of the setting, with the form of planning and government in mind, and with a forewarning of the conclusions to be drawn, it is hoped that the appetite is

11

sufficiently whetted for a discussion of the administrative units which deliver the planning service. For those readers well acquainted with the reform of local government and the local taxation system, Part One may not add greatly to their knowledge, since it is by no means exhaustive and is based to a large degree on the literature in the area. Such knowledgeable readers may wish to proceed directly to Part Two, which is based on the author's own original research through a series of interviews stretching over the two years which saw the introduction of the first fruits of the reforms of the methods of plan-making. For the remainder, however, the following discussion provides the trellis against which the growth, change and reform of the planning system can be seen to have developed.

PART ONE

Setting the Scene: The Reform and Reorganisation of the Government Units (Tweedledee or Tweedledum)

2 Problems in the Planning Entities and the Attempts at Change

Most studies of land-use planning take the existing government framework as the basis for various planning systems or reforms. In this book we start from the opposite premise, namely that the character of the units, their finance, and the way they have been reformed explain a great deal about the efficacy of the planning system. The make-up of the local government units and their overseeing central government ministries will, to a large extent, determine the type and quality of the planning administration.

In order to judge the worth of the planning system, its efficacy and fairness, both to members of the public and affected property-holders, one must understand the political and administrative reasons for the shape and character of the government entities. Running throughout the discussion of how best to operate and design government units at the local level are the same threads that appear in a detailed analysis of one local-government service: land-use planning. The problem of how to create an efficient local-government unit which has jurisdiction over many of the interrelated social problems, without creating a remote body immune from local access, mirrors the planning problem of efficiency and access. Similarly, the contradiction between an autonomous, independent group responsible to local citizens, and the need for nationally co-ordinated standards of service, parallels the problem of local control of land-use developments of national consequence. With this relationship in mind we can begin with the framework of central and local government, and then proceed to problems which the units faced by the mid-1960s.

BACKGROUND: CENTRAL GOVERNMENT

In central government the executive is divided into various ministries, and from 1947, when the Town and Country Planning Act was passed, until 1970, the ministry in charge of overseeing planning changed its name and function twice. Initially, the Ministry of Town and Country Planning was established to oversee the 1947 Town and Country Planning Act, and it had a fairly limited brief, namely to review development plans and handle planning-refusal appeals. In January 1951 the Ministry was enlarged to encompass various functions previously under the Minister of Health, such as local government, housing, rent control, burials and coast protection (Transfer of Functions Order, 1951 Statutory Instrument, no. 142), and its name changed to that of the Ministry of Local Government and Planning. Later in that same year further functions were transferred to the Ministry (that is local government finance, water, sewerage, civil defence, 1951 Statutory Instrument, no. 753), but the powers of compulsory purchase for the improvement of highways, and thus highway planning, were hived off to the Minister of Transport (1951 Statutory Instrument, no. 751). With this, the Planning Ministry's name was changed again to the Ministry of Housing and Local Government.

The Ministry existed in this form through the two decades of the 1950s and 1960s. The major problem that existed throughout this time was that the separation of highway planning from the remainder of land-use planning caused great institutional rivalry between the Ministries, on what came to be politically sensitive environmental disputes.

By the end of the 1960s the Ministry of Housing and Local Government was supposed to be looking after the provision of council housing, private-housing finance, land-use planning and environmental protection. The sister departments, the Ministries of Transport and Public Works, were in charge of the provision of the related infrastructure of communication, and in particular roads and road services. The difficulty was that the broad environmental aims in one ministry were often in direct conflict with the projected traffic demands of the engineers in the Ministry of Transport. What was correct for transport, when viewed alone, was not necessarily correct for the rest of the planning decisions on residential location and industrial siting. Paralleling this conflict between central-government ministries, there was a problem common to both departments – the affected local governments always had to go all the way to London to deal with central-government officials, and the officials in charge of a particular area's programmes were often very unfamiliar with the area and the setting of the problem.

If central-government ministries had difficulties gearing their administrative procedures to the problems, they did have one distinct advantage, which was that they could rather easily change their own department's size and jurisdiction. In contrast the local-government units, who were in charge of the delivery of a wide range of services, and most important for us, the day-to-day administration of the planning system, had remained virtually fossilised for almost a hundred years.

BACKGROUND: LOCAL GOVERNMENT

Turning to local government, while the basic form of local government in Britain, namely the county or shire, was in existence at the time of the Norman Conquest and has its basis in the initial settlement areas of Anglo-Saxon tribes, the important developments for modern purposes began in the last century. The Local Government Acts of the late nineteenth century (1888 and 1894) created a system that had two distinct purposes, to create a democratically responsible local government, and to establish different local bodies to govern the then very different rural and urban areas. The nineteenth-century system created two tiers of government, the counties and the districts, and then separated urbanised areas into their own self-contained units. Large urban areas had a special status, that of county borough, completely beyond the control of neighbouring counties. Smaller towns became urban districts (or non-county boroughs) under the control of the counties within whose territory they came.

The boundaries of these local government units over time came to bear little relationship to population or the needs for services in the area. In the late nineteenth century it had perhaps been logical to separate the town from the country, but with population growth, greater freedom of travel, and economic dependence between the two types of areas, the distinctions became less and less logical. The legislation which established this two-tier, rural–urban machinery was not designed to effectuate efficient local service delivery or the co-ordination of the efforts of the various local governments.

The system created in 1888 and 1894 was the basis of local

government which remained in existence until the new reform went into effect on 1 April 1974. Although the total number of units grew by almost one-half through annexation during the first quarter of the century, the form remained essentially the same. Under this system there were (REDCLIFFE-MAUD COMMISSION REPORT, vol. I, p. 21):

58	county councils	
82	county borough councils	
276	non-county borough councils	Total of
548	urban districts	1298 local
474	rural districts	governments
7500	parishes	
3400	parish meetings	

The system was basically a two-tier system, with a virtually moribund third tier consisting of parishes whose sole responsibility was such functions as the creation of public footpaths or the maintenance of a public clock. The top-level authorities were the county councils; these were the basic administrative units with three different types of lower-tier structures below them – two urban, the non-county boroughs and the urban districts, and one rural, the rural district. The county borough councils were unitary authorities which had county administrative powers over an entire urban area. These different units shared, or more often competed for, different degrees of responsibility for local services. Often the amount of lower-authority responsibility in a given area depended on the specifics of a delegation agreement for a specific function.

While a number of services are administered directly by the central government (for example, major highways, the National Health Service, welfare payments), the majority of personal services are delivered by local governments. The local authorities are in charge of education, social-service counselling, and children's services. They also provide the basic police and fire protection. The councils deal with all local roads and minor highways, and are in charge of such services as public health, public recreation (parks and swimming pools), and the entire programme of local planning and urban renewal. Often the service, which is nominally a local one, will have very strong central-government supervision. For instance, while there is no national police force in the United Kingdom, there has been an amalgamation of local forces to streamline central control, and the support facilities offered by central government are quite extensive. There are not only a number of on-the-spot central government inspectors, but also regional research officers, and even a series of Regional Crime Squads to deal with specific types of criminal behaviour. (REDCLIFFE-MAUD COMMISSION REPORT, vol. 1, p. 88)

In 1890 local governments spent only 3·3 per cent of the gross national product. With the great migrations of rural residents to the towns and cities these local governments suffered a tremendous increase in their population. In the initial stages of fluid urban living the growing metropolises, by means of voluntary annexation, enlarged their boundaries to encompass the urban growth. In the years from 1888 to 1926 the population grew by fully one-third and the number of county boroughs grew from 59 to 78 (JACKSON). Institutionally, the two sets of local governments were in a continual race for the favour of central-government ministries. By 1930, however, the process of annexation virtually stopped, and the boundaries became fixed. Linked with this rigidity of boundaries was a great expansion in the functions being thrust onto local governments. A great many social services began to be required. Along with them came local interest in economic planning and, most importantly for us, in land-development control and the delivery and maintenance of housing. Often the need for special local control of specific service planning was thrust on multi-unit, *ad hoc* authorities such as regional water, sanitary or sewage boards. (ROBSON, 1968, pp. 20–8)

There emerged a central-government concern for the running of what traditionally had been a local affair and also a transfer of many of these decisions to different bodies. For instance the central government took over direct control of local governments' major roads in the 1930s and 1940s (Road Traffic Acts), their hospitals in 1946 (National Health Service Act), the poor (Unemployment Act, 1934; National Assistance Act, 1948), public utilities (Transport Act, 1947 – Buses; Electricity Act, 1947) and, as we shall see in Chapter 3, the valuation of property for purposes of local property taxes. All these functions were taken over by central-government ministries themselves, or special, non-elected bodies established by central government.

The result of all this was that the urban local authorities

19

(urban district or non-county boroughs) would be in a continual fight with the county council. Similarly the unitary county boroughs (again urban) were closely contained by the neighbouring county authority. This urban–rural animosity continued as the urban areas grew and thus became more closely contained by their neighbouring rural areas. As Redcliffe-Maud and Wood summed it up: 'A cold war between authorities (particularly between counties and county boroughs) continued to develop until it could be checked only by the creation of a new structure of local government' (REDCLIFFE-MAUD AND WOOD, p. 3). Concomitant with this urban–rural friction a serious problem grew up about the efficiency of the delivery of local services. The calibre and method of operation of the public administration of the local units began to deteriorate appreciably *vis-à-vis* the central government. The quality and job satisfaction of administrators decreased (some 48 per cent in a recent survey would like to find other work – BUXTON, p. 81) and the public came to be less and less concerned with local government (in one survey less than 20 per cent of those interviewed could name a single local official) except as deliverers of nationally decided services (REDCLIFFE-MAUD COMMITTEE REPORT, vol. 3, table 3). The local-government method of government by committee and excessive reliance upon detailed (as opposed to policy) decision-making further exacerbated this decline. The vast network of small artificial grouping and inefficient administrators (some 1200 governments in all) meant that some type of reform had to be considered.

The political and constitutional setting within which local government operates should be kept in mind when approaching these reforms. Since the United Kingdom has a unitary as opposed to a federal form of government, the basic policy decisions have always tended to be more central-government matters than local matters. There is a political homogeneity which means that there are few local maverick political parties and little sense of local autonomy (STANYER). While the occasional group may form on a local issue, such groups are almost universally short lived. Also it is a firmly held belief amongst local politicians that matters of national party policies are out of place in local politics. Coupled with this are numerous studies which show that national, not local, political party identification is the major determinant in local council elections

(SPENSER). Thus there are usually strong parties but little consideration of political policies in local councils.

The basic fact is that the constitutional framework presupposes central decision-making in the national legislature. This framework tends to accentuate the lack of importance of local governments. It is best to keep in mind that there is no tradition of existing regional legislatures, or institutional focuses for regional interests. On the other hand, it is easier to institute local reform when the power of decision-making, both ideologically and legally, resides in the national government. In a practical way this autonomy is expressed in the very structure of local-government institutions. If Parliament has not authorised the local government to do something, it is beyond the powers of that unit to do so. This results in a continual reliance upon the centre to make decisions of policy, or at least the decisions as to which level of government will make such decisions. This centripetal tendency is further reinforced by the catholic nature of political parties in Britain (JONES). Local government's elected councils are run by the majority party. While this often reflects the national government, especially in years when councils and national governments both go to the polls, this may not be the case in the interim years between national elections, when local elections frequently go against the party in power in Westminster.

At least in public, party loyalty, combined with the legislative control of the programmes and Acts under which the local governments have the power to survive at all, means that there are few disagreements between local and central government on matters of policy, for at the end of the day the central government will usually prevail. Since the central government ministry through its directions and circulars can set the rules and conditions of how local governments should function, and enforce those rules through personal levies against councillors making unauthorised expenditures, the disagreements are kept to a minimum.

Coupled with this centralising tendency of party politics is a method of legislative decision-making on local councils which, while natural in the face of the large amount of central discretion on policy, nevertheless results in even less efficiency on the councils. The various political studies done on local-government decision-making point out that most matters are considered by committees and that the councillor's self-image demands a thorough investigation of the detail rather than the policy of local governments' decisions (BUXTON, p. 37). The councillors generally are older and less educated than central government politicians. The reliance on detail often coupled with lack of competence in the subject-matter area causes both stagnation and lack of political respect from the electorate. (REDCLIFFE-MAUD COMMITTEE REPORT, vol. 5, ch. 4, para 37)

We now have a clear enough idea of the problems inherent in the central and local administrative structure to understand why major reforms were necessary. However, as is often the way with the reform of political institutions, the impetus for the changes came not from a reasoned analysis of the myriad problems but from a series of immediate political pressures. For instance, the reform of the central-government ministries was caused by the Labour and Conservative Parties' wooing (or perhaps fear) in 1969–70 of the then blossoming ecology movement. Similarly, the Labour Government in the late 1960s saw local government reform as a means of strengthening the urban, and thus Labour, constituencies, *vis-à-vis* the rural county, and thus Conservative constituencies. They established a vast and expensive Royal Commission, whose recommendations (which generally strengthened the urban areas) were immediately ignored to a large extent by the new Conservative Government, who instituted their own particular type of local-government reform. Likewise, the corruption in local-government planning, permission approval, and public-works contracting, unearthed in the early 1970s, led to more openness in local officials' decision-making. In the following section we will look at these various decisions and reforms and attempt to distil the general pattern of changes and their effect upon the units that are entrusted with the land-use planning responsibility.

CHANGING CENTRAL GOVERNMENT

Starting at the top the overseeing central-government Ministry of Housing and Local Government came into institutional jeopardy as the environmental idea became of political importance in 1969. The then Labour Government began to restructure its various departments in order to concentrate on the popular enthusiasm for the elimination of pollution – which could mean a great many things to a great many people. First there was to be a reorganisation of the industrial overseeing agencies such as the Board of Trade and the Ministry of Power. Secondly the Prime Minister, Harold Wilson, called for a new Secretary of State for Local Government and Regional Planning, who would be in charge of the Housing, Local Government and Transport Ministries. However, in the initial reshuffle,* the supposedly subservient Ministries of Housing, Local Government and Transport continued to be statutorily responsible directly to Parliament for their own portfolios and the exact nature of the new Secretary of State's duties (Anthony Crosland) were not entirely clear. (JOHNSON, 1970, p. 98)

By the first months of 1970 the political party leaders had made their concern for the environment a hotly debated issue, and it was hoped that the forthcoming election would result in a vigorous analysis of the government institutions responsible for the environment. When the election actually came such a discussion failed to materialise (JOHNSON, 1970, p. 125), and thus it came as somewhat of a surprise that, in the autumn of 1970, the new Conservative Government introduced a White Paper on the reorganisation of central government (CENTRAL GOVERNMENT REORGANISATION WHITE PAPER), which contained major institutional changes. A new department was to be created which would, in the White Paper's words, be:

> responsible for the whole range of functions which affect people's living environment. It will cover planning of land – where people live, work, move and enjoy themselves. It will be responsible for the construction industries, including the housing programme, and for the transport industries, including public programmes of support and development for the means of transport. There is a need to associate with these functions responsibility for other major environmental matters: the preservation of amenity, the protection of the coast and countryside, the preservation of historic towns and monuments, and the control of air, water, and noise pollution; all of which must be pursued locally, regionally, nationally and in some cases internationally.

Hansard (13 Oct. 1969) vol. 788, col. 31.

The overseeing central-government Ministry of Housing and Local Government was merged with the Ministry of Transport and the Ministry of Public Building and Works, to form one mega-ministry, in the autumn after Edward Heath's Conservative Government came into office in 1970 (1970 Statutory Instrument no. 1681). This new Ministry, whose appellation, the Department of the Environment, showed the breadth of it's progenitors' vision, was to control something very near to the entire physical quality of life. In an article in the *Spectator* the wide brief of the new Ministry was eloquently described:

> It is within the framework of a regional strategy, one which looks after the town as well as the countryside, which the bits and pieces which go to make up a policy for the environment will be fitted. . . . It seems clear that, under the new management the focus of the debate will not be on conservation *per se*, but rather on the potential of long-term planning as a tool for good housekeeping. (JOHNSON, 1970, p. 494)

And the new Secretary of State for the Environment, Peter Walker, emphasised that the entire 'quality of life' would be considered when planning and road design matters arrived at his desk. He said that the major priority of his new department would be 'to develop, as no other nation has previously developed, a total approach to our urban problem' (quoted in JOHNSON, 1970, p. 140).

In the four years since its creation the D.O.E. has regionalised its planning-review sections to six regional planning offices, and decentralised the decision-making on the administration of road construction to a series of regional construction units. While of course the most controversial issues wend their way up the civil service and arrive at the politically responsible Secretary of State's desk, the day-to-day liaison with local-government units has, to a large degree, been moved to the regional offices. In interviews with local-government officials, it was often mentioned that the D.O.E. is more easily approached than were its parent ministries, centred only in London.

We will go into some detail as to the workings of the D.O.E. in the areas of plan-making review in Chapter 9, but at this point it should be mentioned that thus far the hopes for a central-government ministry that would merge land-use considerations with transportation decision-making and public-works expenditure has not been viewed universally as a success. The officials in 'Plans and Planning' at the D.O.E. still complain that their brothers in the road-building units ignore a great many considerations brought to their attention. Similarly the environmental pressure groups have not greeted the first years under the super-ministry as particularly different from the previous ones. Tony Aldous, writing in *The Times*, commented that:

> All over the country there are amenity groups and individuals fighting road schemes that are both barbaric in their environmental and social effects and of dubious economic worth, from whom those words of Mr Walker (as to the quality of life being considered) would evoke bitter, ironic laughter.

We shall go in some depth into the way in which central government decides land-use disputes and attempts to co-ordinate the policies of local government, but with central government the problem is not whether it has jurisdiction over the various programmes and geographical areas, for it does, but whether it can co-ordinate the various sub-parts within its own administration. With some eight ministries and sub-ministries, and over 70,000 staff members, the Department of the Environment had no small job of co-ordination. While this presents problems of intra-departmental communication, and problems of priorities among competing interests, the central government at least has legislative, financial and for that matter geographic control over land-use disputes. On the other hand the local governments who have the day-to-day responsibility for deciding whether development can take place within their local areas must function within the boundaries of the national legislation, and most importantly the geographical boundaries which frequently separate problems (for example housing shortage, lack of open space) from solutions (for example undeveloped land, financial resources). It is to the attempt to reform the local authorities, the workhorses of the planning system, that we shall now direct our attention.

CHANGING LOCAL GOVERNMENT

No one ever seems entirely pleased with the state of local government or planning, either before reforms or reorganisations are attempted or after. Alisdair Fairley, writing in the *Listener* in 1973, started an article with the depressing statement that:

> Local Government is now one of the most powerful industries in the country. . . . Its most powerful intervention in our lives is through planning, and planning is corrupted – by neglect, by inefficiency, and by a peculiar form of legally permitted bribery which must be unique to this country. (FAIRLEY)

And this statement was made after a very lengthy and expensive Royal Commission investigation into the form and responsibility of local government, and after government plans had been aired for the greatest reorganisation of local government in the history of the country.

Attempts to change local government are not novel in Great Britain. The first major investigation of the problems of the governmental structure was generated by the Ministry of Health in the 1920s in the hope of facilitating the delivery of health services. The Royal Commission on Local Government (1923–9), rather than suggesting a new type of system, merely sought to limit the proliferation of the smaller districts and to amalgamate some of the counties into larger bodies within the same two-tier structure (ROYAL COMMISSION, 1929). While there were some governmental murmurings of radically changing the local government structure and regionalising some of its functions (see BARLOW REPORT), the succession of governments seemed singularly uninterested in fundamentally changing the character of local government.

It was not until the late 1950s that attention once again turned to local government. However, once the successive governments became interested there was no lack of official concern, and in the period from 1957 to 1974 there was a virtual deluge of committees and inquiries. First came a Royal Commission on Local Government in Greater London (1957–60, the Herbert Commission), which instigated a reform of London. Then a Local Government Commission for England (1958–66, HANCOCK REPORT) was established to look at local government outside London; it was superseded by the Royal Commission on Local Government in England (1966–9, REDCLIFFE-MAUD COMMISSION). There was also a Commission on the Constitution (1972–3, the KILBRANDON COMMISSION), which looked into regional government. Each of these bodies, as we shall see, recommended major structural reforms in the make-up and type of local government. To help implement the changes suggested a further series of committees was created to look at various aspects of local-government functioning. A permanent body was established to review boundaries under the 1972 Local Government Act (Local Government Boundary Commission), and there was a series of reports on local government administration. These included the Maud Committee on management, the Mallaby Committee on staffing, the Bains Report on management structures, and the Seebohm Committee on social-service delivery.

In 1957 and 1958 the central government instigated a review of local government both in London and in the west of England. The task of the Local Government Commission for England was to review local government structure and boundaries both within the five major urban areas (excluding London), and the remaining county areas. The Commission was authorised to draw new boundaries, but it was presupposed that it was to to take the existing urban–rural pattern of government and attempt to mould it to the new population configurations. It was singularly unsuccessful, due both to its lengthy procedures of consultation with the existing local authorities and the extreme intransigence of any local authority called upon to give up its land or administrative powers to a neighbouring authority. The Local Government Commission, during its seven years of existence, only managed to create three county boroughs out of highly urbanised urban districts or non-county boroughs, and only changed the boundaries in twenty-five varied circumstances. The Commission did not, however, make any large, sweeping changes, nor did it manage to relegate any under-populated county borough to district status.

Meanwhile, the second major commission, the Herbert Commission, was having more concrete results. It reported in 1960, and suggested a Greater London Council which would cover some 620 square miles of land and over 8 million people, beneath which would be a network of some 52 lower-tier boroughs. The government accepted its recommendations in general, and the G.L.C. was created to deal with upper-level environmental services such as transport and planning, and such non-personal services as drainage and refuse disposal. Beneath this behemoth were the London Boroughs, charged with housing and social services. Education was parcelled out partly to the Inner London Educational Authority and partly to the various Outer London Boroughs.

These changes were generally viewed as a success, the transition in the early 1960s had gone smoothly, and there had been few catastrophes except in the highway transport area where the central government had to intervene continually. There were those critics who said that the upper-tier G.L.C. was impotent, and there were those who pointed to the lack of clear definition of authority in areas of joint functioning. Similarly, some critics pointed out that there had been no proof of savings or efficiency under the structure. There were, however, actual changes in boundaries and functions, which is more than could be said for the results of the Boundary Commission. (RHODES)

The Labour Government of the mid-1960s saw the supposed successes of the London reform and chose to establish a review of local-government structure for the rest of England which would have a wider mandate than that of the Local Government Commission. It is not a coincidence that one of the major difficulties with the local-government structure existing in 1966, namely the separation of town from country and the dominance of the urban areas by the rural county interests, reflected a political problem for the Labour Party. An investigation which might suggest a reform leading to urban dominance of local-government machinery was an investigation that suited the interests of the Labour Party. In 1966 the Government established the Royal Commission on Local Government. This body, the Redcliffe-Maud Commission, sat for almost four years, and its published reports take up twelve volumes of fine print. It was one of the most thorough and certainly one of the most expensive commissions ever undertaken anywhere. Perhaps the best approach to both its findings and conclusions is first to analyse what were seen to be the problems, and then to look at the various solutions proposed to meet those problems.

THE REDCLIFFE-MAUD ROYAL COMMISSION REPORT

1 *Their View of the Problems*

While Lord Redcliffe-Maud and Bruce Wood's own book is certainly the best discussion of the Report, the following account gives the basics of the report (REDCLIFFE-MAUD AND WOOD). The Commission established that there were essentially five basic problems facing local government. The first was that the demographic and technological changes of the past fifty years had made the existing configurations essentially meaningless. In terms of the problems of roads or houses, or the everyday life of citizens, there was a tremendous overlap of various sub-units. Similarly the disparity in size between the smallest and largest units with the same powers seemed to make little sense.

The second problem was that the existing units overlapped in terms of functions and geography, with no clear demarcation of powers. Not only did the towns versus suburbs conflict arise, but the administration of particular joint programmes, such as planning or housing, caused serious friction between the upper and lower tiers. This necessitated the frequent intervention of central government to settle these disputes.

Thirdly, the local-government structure was viewed as being politically unresponsive and remote from the local citizens. This resulted in weak turnout at elections, poor attendance at meetings and a general sense of apathy among the electorate. As mentioned, the studies done both by the Royal Commission and the previous Committee on Management showed a surprising lack of awareness of local government. Less than 1 per cent have ever been to any type of local-government meeting. (REDCLIFFE-MAUD COMMITTEE REPORT, vol. 3, table 3, and REES)

The fourth problem which was mentioned was that the units did not have a sufficiently broad-based financial foundation to deal with the problems of modern social services. This was particularly true of the smaller authorities in terms of such specialised services as housing counselling, planning of renewal projects, or special educational facilities for the deaf or emotionally retarded.

The last concern of the Commission was a thread which ran through each of the particular problems, namely the dominance of central-government administrators in even the most minor affairs. Throughout the inquiry it became apparent that not only did the local authorities resent the presence of the central government, but often the central government intervention in some minor affair merely slowed down the central bureaucracy and did not appreciably improve the functioning at the local level. (REDCLIFFE-MAUD COMMISSION REPORT, vol. I, pp. 30–2)

2 *The Difficulties of Knowing what is the 'Best Size' of Local Unit*

The Commission instituted a series of studies of these problems to investigate what possible factors, particularly in terms of optimal size of units, should be taken into account in arriving at a new government framework. Clearly the most dramatic finding of these survey and study groups was that there simply are no hard-and-fast rules as to what is the best size of unit (see REDCLIFFE-MAUD COMMISSION REPORT, vols II–IV, studies 1–10).

For one thing there is the question of how one defines optimum, for what might appear extremely functional to a central-government bureaucrat, who is trying to co-ordinate a programme over a wide area, may appear unresponsive and unwieldy to the citizen who is trying to gain access to the same institution.

Turning for instance to the question of political responsiveness, the Government Social Survey did a rather involved study of the day-to-day functioning of the local elected representatives in their role as watchdog over the administration of governmental services (REDCLIFFE-MAUD COMMISSION REPORT, study 9). The problems discovered were that in terms of local status and the personal quality of representation, the voter could only feel a sense of political community in a very small unit. Where the population of a town exceeded 60,000 people the sense of participation and cohesion necessary for a viable watchdog effect was lost. And political and social loyalty extended only to neighbourhood areas. The obvious result of this type of representation is that it is virtually impossible to base service delivery on a political notion of civic community. The question then is whether political lines should be drawn in terms of administrative efficiency.

The problem, however, of what one could define as being an administratively efficient unit for the delivery of various services is again an impossible task. The studies done by the Greater London Group, the London School of Economics, York and Leeds Universities, and the Government Social Survey, all point out that it is extremely difficult to generalise as to the optimum size of a unit even for the delivery of one type of service, and virtually impossible to define a unit which would be efficient for such varied services as schooling, land-use planning,

30

garbage, water and housing. (REDCLIFFE-MAUD COMMISSION REPORT, studies 1–10)

Typical perhaps of these findings is the study done on southeast England by the London School of Economics and the Greater London Group (REDCLIFFE-MAUD COMMISSION REPORT, study 1). Here is a densely populated area, which has a great disparity of size between the smallest and largest authorities. The correlation between the major variable of size and the performance of the authorities was investigated. The social scientists looked at the four service areas of child care, education, welfare, and housing. While it is difficult to entirely trust their quantifications of the performance levels, some interesting results were shown.

The quality of the authorities studied varied immensely both between each other and also within the same authority. Thus one might be brilliant in education, poor in housing, another poor in both. After a statistical analysis discovered the basic fact that there was not a consistent pattern of correlation between size and efficiency, a number of interview samples were taken which produced some very interesting results. Often the smallest authority which, in terms of financial resources, would be expected to do the worst job, was in fact one of the better performers. Often the only explanation for this variation between performances was the individual initiative of the management of particular authorities. Typically, in housing, while the larger authorities would have the most professional staff or trained managers, it was the smaller authorities which had the best record of client contact or personal service. In its conclusion the study group summed up the conflicting data by saying that 'Perhaps the greatest value of this material is its demonstration that no easy generalisations are possible about local authorities.' (REDCLIFFE-MAUD COMMISSION REPORT, study 1, p. 11)

The Government Social Survey reached a similar conclusion, stating that population size on its own accounted for only a small proportion of the differences between the local authorities' provision of services. While they did show a correlation between the social make-up of the area and the performance of services (for example better education in high social-class areas) there was little to show that a grouping of social strata over a large area was feasible or that it would appreciably improve the service delivery of the lower class sub-areas. (REDCLIFFE-MAUD COMMISSION REPORT, study 5)

3 *The Possible Models*

The two-tier approach. One method of dealing with the problems would be to keep the existing basic system but redraw the boundaries so as to eliminate the smallest counties and unify the hodge podge of local districts into a small number of larger second tiers. While this would not make a more responsive structure, since it would in fact eliminate a great many political 'communities', and although it is doubtful whether it would be more efficient in terms of administration, it would certainly be easier to administer from central government.

The single-tier approach. This plan would be to have a basic optimum population size-unit (250,000 to 1,000,000) and to have one administrative unit for the delivery of all local services in that area. While exceptions would have to be made for some five urban areas which would have a two-tier metropolitan approach, the great bulk of the country outside the huge cities would have a centralised unitary local government. This system would have the advantage of allowing the citizens at least to know where to focus their attention and it would allow for easier comparison between areas as to performance. This would also allow an easy evaluation of various programmes from the centre.

The city region approach. The idea here would be to have one unitary government structure for the entire area, which focuses on the central city. The advantage of this idea would be that all interrelated services of a population, its work, transport and education, could be co-ordinated through one local government. This would allow for a sub-regional type of approach and would facilitate long-range strategic planning. It would have the disadvantage, however, of being even further removed from the notion of a local political community and, furthermore, many parts of rural England simply do not focus on any one city for all their services.

It should be noted here that the Royal Commission's terms of reference specifically precluded what would normally be option four, which would be a region-wide, or provincial, type of local government. The Commission was bound to investigate structures within the existing functions of local government, and it could not consider the possibilities of divesting the central government of some of its principal powers affecting local areas, such as transport or economic development. This problem was left to another Royal Commission, the Royal Commission on the Constitution, known as the Kilbrandon Commission, which was convened in the same year the Redcliffe-Maud Commission reported.

Devolution

The Kilbrandon Commission was established in direct response to the serious political challenge that the Welsh and Scottish Nationalists posed to the Labour Government in 1966 and 1967. In one very candid review John Mackintosh, a Labour M.P., described the process of establishing the Commission:

> Within the Labour cabinet, there was a division over the policy that should be pursued. . . . The outcome was a victory for those who wanted to do nothing but to resist the pressure, arguing that by the next General Election the Nationalist threat would have dwindled. . . . [They] felt they had to have some answer to those who pointed to the rise of the Nationalists. . . . To meet this, it was decided to appoint a Royal Commission. (MACKINTOSH, p. 115)

The Kilbrandon Report showed a remarkable lack of consensus on the issues of the need for, or mechanism of, devolution of powers to some regional-level government. The Commission found that there was a general feeling of dissatisfaction with the existing framework and that some 10 to 20 per cent of the population in the areas of Wales and Scotland favoured more regional autonomy (KILBRANDON, Research Paper no. 7). What could not be agreed upon between the majority and the dissenting members of the Commission was the level of dissatisfaction over the country as a whole, or the possible solutions to that dissatisfaction. The majority finally looked to the pressures exerted by the Scottish and Welsh Nationalists, and decided that the best way of meeting that pressure was to establish popularly elected assemblies which would have legislative power over most local services, such as local-government planning, transport, education and health.

33

For the remainder of the country the majority recommended a series of regional councils composed of non-elected members chosen from the local authorities and central government. Even on the majority side there were four different possible methods of devolution of powers, ranging from assemblies with merely advisory capacity, to uniform treatment of all areas. Adding to the confusion, two members of the Commission (Lord Crowther-Hunt and Professor Peacock) wrote a memorandum of dissent calling for seven democratically elected assemblies.

It was generally assumed that the Kilbrandon Report, which was published in October 1973, would be allowed to sit on government bookshelves unnoticed, for there seemed to be no clear reason why the Conservative Government should deliberately weaken their central-government control for the sake of some very ill-defined interest in regional government. However, with the formation of a minority Labour Government in early 1974, attention was again turned to these proposals. The new Government knew it would face another General Election within a short period of time and also knew that the power of the Welsh and Scottish Nationalists would have to be contended with. The Government mentioned the issue when it took office in March 1974, and issued a Devolution Green Paper in June. Finally, days before the calling of the General Election in the autumn of 1974, a White Paper was issued which contained a general commitment to regionally elected governments but described the idea only sketchily.

It is not entirely clear what such regional governments would do or what they would look like. There would be directly elected Assemblies for Scotland and Wales and further consideration would be given to similar assemblies for the English regions. The Scottish Assembly would have some executive and legislative powers within those fields where separate Scottish legislation already exists (housing, health, education, and so on). The Welsh Assembly would have mostly executive functions. The Westminster Parliament would remain as it is; and these new Assemblies would be established, based on single-member constituencies, and would receive block funding from the central government.

For our purposes, the most important aspect of these proposals is that they do not explicitly commit the government to a regional system for England and, even for the areas they do deal with, the proposals would seem to be a long way from implementation. According to the government spokesman, Mr Edward Short, a White Paper will be published in late 1975. Proposals will be presented to the House at the end of the year, but they will not affect England.* The most that could be hoped for within England itself would be some regionalisation of service delivery. It seems unlikely that there would be any major reorganisation of the units of land-use planning. The central government and the reorganised local authorities will most probably continue to be the major units in the land-use planning system.

THE REDCLIFFE-MAUD DECISION AND DISSENT

The majority report of the Royal Commission on Local Government recommended that, for the sake of efficiency of operation, contact with citizens and strengthening of local government *vis à vis* the central government, a unitary single-tier system of local government was in order. They drew up a 61-unit map of the country with three metropolitan areas, all the rest being single-tier all-purpose authorities. These authorities would have populations of between 250,000 to 1,000,000, which were considered to be administratively the most effective size for local-government functions such as schools, planning and housing.

Brief mention was made of a locally elected parish body which would serve the community contact function, but would have virtually no power either to spend or to tax. Similarly, the Commission said that there was a case to be made for an intermediate level of government between local and central government, and they recommended the establishment of a series of provincial councils. Again, since this was beyond their terms of reference, they left the issue in a rather confused state, recommending that the councils should have no taxation power or elected representatives, but should merely exist as appointed advisory bodies.

The aim of the unitary approach was to make more efficient operations, draw together the extremes of local tax bases, and make easier the comparison of performance between the local governments.

---

* *Hansard* (5 Aug. 1975) vol. 897, cols 243–4.

Dissent

Even on the Commission itself there was not unanimity in
favour of this unitary approach. Derick Senior, a journalist and
urban specialist, vigorously supported a city-region approach
and disagreed with the unitary concept entirely (REDCLIFFE-
MAUD COMMISSION REPORT, vol. II). He could find no functional
basis for the 250,000–1,000,000 size range and found the
divisions both artificial and illogical.

The dissent from the press, the existing governments and
various academics, was likewise vociferous (ROSE, SMITH). The
local governments, particularly the smaller ones that would be
eliminated, complained that a commission which was supposed
to increase the contact between the citizens and the local
governments had, in fact, cut the number of elected representatives from 35,000 to 5000. Traditionalists bemoaned the disappearance of ancient shire seats. More importantly, academics
pointed out that there was little in the Redcliffe-Maud Report
to support the contention that the increase in size would greatly
facilitate performance, or that efficient size of population for one
service was necessarily the same for another. As Dr G. W. Jones
of the London School of Economics expressed it in an article in
the *Local Government Chronicle*: 'was there really any interrelationship between different types of service at any level, and
do the 25,000–1,000,000 figures have any basis at all?' (in
SMITH, p. 34)

The general consensus among commentators seemed to be
that what was really needed was a regional approach, and since
that could not be accomplished, the Redcliffe-Maud approach
was not necessarily second best. Into this arena of debate came
one crucial change in decision-makers, due to the Conservative
General Election victory in 1970. The final reform which
emerged in the Bill passed in October 1972, put into effect in
April 1974, is very little like the Redcliffe-Maud recommendations. As might be imagined, rather than being a more radical
change it is modelled very closely on the old system of local
government.

THE ACTUAL REORGANISATION

When Peter Walker introduced the Reorganisation Bill he
stated that 'I came to the conclusion that a system of local

government where every function was centred in one authority
. . . which would be very remote from the people was not the
proper basis to reform local government.'* Basically the
Government, while paying lip service to the goals of the
Redcliffe-Maud Report, then proceeded to introduce a two-tier
structure, which except for the six metropolitan areas leaves the
upper tier much the same, with a consolidation at the district
level. The reformed lower districts will then have more power
in some fields (such as planning) than they do currently. The
drawing of the new boundary lines is *not* based on efficiency
alone, for as the government said in the White Paper describing
the new structure (REORGANISATION WHITE PAPER), the government obviously must seek efficiency but where the arguments
are equally balanced their judgement will be given in favour of
responsibility being exercised at the more local level.

There are a number of explanations for this rejection of the
Redcliffe-Maud unitary recommendation. First, the implementation of the Herbert Commission's proposals had caused a
great deal of political in-fighting in London, and the number of
problems that could be created by the existing local authorities
was well understood by the Conservative Government in 1971.
Second, the Conservative Government was concerned that
Parliamentary constituency boundaries might be redrawn in
such a way as to cost the party seats in later general elections.
Finally, the establishment of stronger, unified and urban-
oriented local governments could not but have detrimental
effects on the position of the Conservative Party at the local
level, for in 1971 the Conservatives held majorities in most of
the county councils throughout the country.

The Government's White Paper proposed a two-tiered
structure of local government, which was based on the existing
counties but which included some basic concessions to the idea
of unifying the urban and rural areas under one authority
(REORGANISATION WHITE PAPER). The county borough was
to be eliminated and six metropolitan counties were to be
established – Greater Manchester, Merseyside, South Yorkshire, Tyne and Wear, West Midlands, and West Yorkshire.
The rest of the country (excluding London) was to have the
familiar, county–district structure except that a great many

Hansard (16 Nov. 1971) vol. 826, p. 227.

Your at-a-glance guide to who looks after what	If you live in a metropolitan county Greater Manchester (1) Merseyside (2) South Yorkshire (3) Tyne and Wear (4) West Midlands (5) West Yorkshire (6)		If you live in a non-metropolitan county	
	DISTRICT COUNCIL	COUNTY COUNCIL	DISTRICT COUNCIL	COUNTY COUNCIL
Large-scale planning Roads and traffic Road safety Parking Highway lighting Police* Fire service		●		●
Education Personal social services Youth employment Libraries	●			●

Local plans
Planning applications
Housing
House improvement grants
Slum clearance
Environmental health
   e.g. *Dangerous structures*
    Rodent control
    Food safety and hygiene
    Street cleansing
    Shops
    Home safety
    Communicable diseases
Refuse collection
Rental rebates
Rates and rate rebates
	●		●	

Off-street parking Parks, playing fields and open spaces Museums and art galleries Swimming baths	These are facilities which may be provided by either county or district according to local decision			

*Controlled by a special authority of the County Council and the magistrates

FIGURE 2.1
SOURCE: Department of the Environment Advertisement (April 1974).

districts would be consolidated. Under the Government's proposals, as finally implemented in the 1972 Local Government Act, there are 6 metropolitan counties and 39 non-metropolitan counties. Within the metropolitan counties there will be some 36 metropolitan districts, and within the non-metropolitan counties there will be 296 local districts. The responsibilities of local authorities, with the major exception of land-use planning, will basically follow the previous scheme of things. Figure 2.1, a chart put out by the D.O.E. to explain the changes, will perhaps be useful.

The most crucial point to notice about the local-government reform as implemented is that it did not fundamentally alter the separation of government of urban and rural areas. The six metropolitan counties had their boundaries drawn in such a way as not to include the surrounding hinterland that would in the future be needed for expansion for housing or recreation. The counties, left in much the same form as before the re-organisation (although their member districts were amalgamated), were not at all willing to give either territory or political power to the metropolitan counties that bordered them. As John Silkin said during the debate in standing committee: 'Reform of Local Government is one of those ideas that everyone in theory supports provided that the lash falls on someone else's back.'* In the case of the counties they did not want their metropolitan neighbours taking any of their land. The initial Government proposals severely circumscribed the boundaries of the metropolitan counties, and, during the passage of the Bill, the size of some of the metropolitan counties was reduced still further. The representatives of the neighbouring counties were often in the Conservative Party, and their views turned out to be rather influential. As the Conservative M.P. for Worcester, Terry Davis, said during the Standing Committee debate: 'It is not that we do not want to provide land to help solve the housing problem of Birmingham; we do not want urban sprawl. . . . our objection is based on planning . . . the answer is not simply to build and build to extend and expand that swelling conurbation of the West Midlands.'† When finally passed the 1972 Act limited the metropolitan

---

* House of Commons Official Report, *Parliamentary Debates*, Standing Committee D, Local Government Bill, 2nd sitting (30 Nov. 1971) p. 56.
† Ibid. (25 Nov. 1971) p. 37.

counties to their built-up areas and, in the case of Merseyside and Greater Manchester, some of the large neighbouring communities were not included.

At the end of the day, then, the reform did not come to grips with the artificial separation of the town from the country. Further, the particulars of the reorganisation would lead one to believe that there will not be an integrated approach to the problems of the town and country. First of all an agency system was included whereby local districts containing major urban populations (often the areas that were, before reorganisation, county boroughs or urban districts) can deliver certain services as the agent of the county. Thus, there is again a two-level approach allowed in some areas for services which were to go all to the upper tier. This will naturally lead to disputes between the two levels of local government as to the correct policy to be taken on, for instance, minor road repairs or refuse disposal.

The two most important functions from our standpoint are the provision of housing services and planning responsibility. Here again there is not a unified approach but a separation of power and responsibility between the upper and lower tiers. In the planning area, which we will discuss later at some length, the plan-making function of drafting county-wide structure plans was hived off to the upper level, while the control of development, which is supposed to implement those area-wide policy documents, was given to the lower district level.

Similarly, while the counties were supposed to set area-wide goals and policies, some of the major powers to implement those policies were given exclusively to the districts. As Lady Sharp said during the House of Lords debate:

The powers that will be given to metropolitan authorities are not sufficiently comprehensive to enable the authorities to tackle effectively the root causes of their social ills [concerning housing]. I agree that the district councils should be the principal municipal builders and the managers of municipal housing. But the county councils – and this applies equally outside the metropolitan areas as inside them – ought to be made responsible for determining the strategy of housing throughout their areas. . . . They should be responsible for the overall planning of housing and for seeing that their plans are carried out.*

AN EXAMPLE OF THE DIVISION OF TOWN AND COUNTRY AFTER REFORM: THE WEST MIDLANDS

Under the reorganisation, then, some consolidation took place, but the basic problem of a division between the governments controlling urban and country land-use remained. If the major urban areas, such as the metropolitan counties, need to plan land for recreation, housing or industry at their periphery they will have to go to their neighbouring rural counties for permission to do so beyond their boundaries. As in the past, and perhaps intentionally, the disputes will most probably have to be settled by the central government. Perhaps the best example of this is in the West Midlands where the urban local governments of Birmingham and Coventry have been locked in combat with the suburban rural counties, particularly Warwickshire and Worcestershire, for a number of decades.

On the one hand the county seats of Warwick and Worcester have always been anxious to protect their landscape and, not incidentally, the interests of their landed, and more often (at least at the border with Birmingham) middle-class residents. Situated at their borders lie two of the most important industrial communities in England, Birmingham and Coventry, and these areas have the need for more land for industry, housing, and land to feed their economic growth. Since 1945 there has been a series of plans, beginning with the work of the West Midland Group on post-war reconstruction and planning (CONURBATION), a study prepared by the famous planners Patrick Abercrombie and Herbert Jackson, and, of course, the development plans of the various local governments.

As the West Midlands urban areas grew economically during the 1950s, there began to be more and more disputes between them and the neighbouring counties. Attempts were made under the 1952 Town Development Act to create new towns to accept this overspill, but the counties proved extremely reticent to accept large numbers of new inhabitants in a short period of time, and urban residents and employers proved equally unwilling to move great distances. These disputes culminated in a

---

* *Hansard* (1 Aug. 1971) vol. 822, cols 185–6.

series of public inquiries into planning-permission refusals on the part of the neighbouring counties for peripheral development, the most famous of these being the Wythall Inquiry (LONG). In each of these disputes the urban area sought to expand into the county and in each case the county protested that the area was to be green-belt agricultural land. In some cases, such as Wythall, the county won, but in other, later cases, such as the dispute over Chelmsley Wood, Birmingham gained planning permission. As might be imagined, this proved a very laborious method of plotting future growth patterns for the urban area. A number of scholars began to suggest that what was needed was an area-wide programme of new development which would not be subject to county veto. (See David Eversley's studies of the West Midlands, EVERSLEY, 1958, 1965.)

The central government was considering the various possibilities – peripheral expansion, overspill close to the urbanised area, or overspill well out into the counties (see WEST MIDLAND-REGIONAL STUDY) – during the time the Redcliffe-Maud Commission reported. Under Redcliffe-Maud the urban-metropolitan county would have had control over much of what had been Staffordshire, Warwickshire, and Worcestershire; all told, the land some twenty miles round central Birmingham would have been governed by one local authority. Under such a scheme the various possibilities for expansion would have been easy to co-ordinate, and overspill communities within the twenty-mile radius could have been established without any inter-local-government disputes. This would have meant that the metro county would have controlled the entire green-belt area up to and including such new towns as Redditch.

Under the actual reorganisation quite a different local authority was in fact created. The undeveloped peripheral areas, rather than being included within the metropolitan county, remained under the jurisdiction of the rural counties, which remained essentially the same as they had been before the reorganisation, that is when they had so vehemently resisted the expansion of Birmingham. Even some developed areas such as Bromsgrove were cut off from the metropolitan county. Thus, on most of the perimeter of the new metropolitan county, there will continue to be hostile rural counties.

There is, however, one very strange result of the drawing of the West Midlands metropolitan counties' boundaries, and that is the integration of Coventry and the connecting undeveloped area between Coventry and Birmingham. Under a unitary system Coventry would most probably have formed the focal point of a combined Coventry–Warwickshire county. When the Conservative Government first considered the area it was naturally assumed that it would be a county, with Coventry being the most influential member district. However, when the old county borough of Coventry heard of these plans, and particularly that, since it was a normal county not a metropolitan county, it would not be able to control its own educational establishment, it petitioned the central government to be included in the West Midlands metropolitan county with Birmingham. The government acquiesced and included both Coventry and the connecting green belt in the metropolitan county. In the words of Peter Hall: 'On every criterion of social geography, the resulting map made virtual nonsense.' (HALL, 1973, vol. 1, p. 543)

This is because on all the indices of shopping, commuting or industry, the community of Coventry has few ties with Birmingham and many ties with the surrounding Warwickshire countryside. On the other hand the connecting green belt which already houses Birmingham airport, a number of motorways, the National Exhibition Centre, and the overspill housing area of Chelmsley Woods, will allow the two communities some release from the strict containment of the surrounding rural counties. However, it can be argued that, of all the peripheral areas for expansion, this particular segment is perhaps the least desirable, although now the most likely to be developed.

REORGANISATION AS AN APPROACH TO REFORM

When Lord Redcliffe-Maud reviewed the results of the actual reorganisation, he was less than sanguine in his appraisal (REDCLIFFE-MAUD AND WOOD, pp. 52–7). He found that there were still local governments that were too small to function efficiently. He found that this was particularly true of some of the London and metropolitan districts in terms of education, and likewise that there are still some 14 of the 296 districts with populations below 40,000.

In terms of boundaries, he himself acknowledges that there has been a continuation of the separation of the urban areas from the surrounding countryside, and his book candidly states that 'it is less certain whether good relations between metropolitan counties and their neighbours can be maintained when the more controversial decisions arise over slum clearance and overspill housing' (REDCLIFFE-MAUD AND WOOD, p. 54). Similarly, the Maud appraisal found that there was a complexity of service delivery which might confuse the most conscientious local citizen. Because of the bifurcation of some services, such as planning and the agency agreements for the delivery of other services in the case of large districts, the affected citizen will often not know how he is being governed: '[the new system] remains difficult to describe largely because the actual operation of local government varies so much from place to place. Further, the widespread use by counties of devolution and of agency powers means that few members of the public can be expected to grasp where decisions are taken.' (REDCLIFFE-MAUD AND WOOD, p. 56)

It was not only the initial investigators who had doubts about the efficacy of the new system. Through the vicissitudes of politics, by the time the actual day of reorganisation came around the Labour Party was again in power, and the Secretary of State for the Environment, Anthony Crosland, himself was saying that: 'After a period of settling down, it will be more efficient, but it could easily become more remote.' Thus, while it may not make for more efficient local government, the new system may very well be less susceptible to the feelings of the people it services.

With the unsettling findings of the Redcliffe-Maud studies (REDCLIFFE-MAUD COMMISSION REPORT, vols II–IV), which showed little correlation between size and administrative efficiency, and the fears about political remoteness expressed by the chief politician in control of the change-over, it is perhaps necessary to consider whether a better purpose for a Royal Commission, or a reform-minded central government, might not perhaps be to investigate patterns of *ad hoc* provision of services rather than whole new systems and structures of government. Nothing in the Royal Commission pointed to specific sizes of authority which led to real economies of scale. In fact, the only conclusive evidence was that political involvement was only possible in a situation of a very small, almost neighbourhood setting. Since the goal is efficiency and the worry is remoteness from the citizen who is to receive the services provided, it seems that an investigation of the efficiency and responsiveness of particular service deliveries would be a better way to spend reformist zeal. This is not to say that there will not be some advantages to the reform in some areas, but simply that, certainly as far as planning is concerned, the reform represents an administrative digression and the energies of the Commission and central government could have been put to a better use.

There were, however, some real advances that came from the reform. The most obvious is perhaps that the reorganisation allowed for enough institutional flexibility to create a setting where internal management networks could be restructured. In a new authority, made up of new personnel, the various routines and personal loyalties had not yet been created. It is these ties which make the introduction of new priorities, chains of command or methods of dealing with problems hard to implement. Some of the recommendations of four different committees of inquiry on internal management arrangements (REDCLIFFE-MAUD COMMITTEE REPORT, MALLABY REPORT, SEEBOHM REPORT and DEVELOPMENT CONTROL STUDY) were implemented throughout this period. Often the recommendations of the committees made up of local government innovators as well as centrally appointed experts could not have come into being without the chance for change which the new reorganisation provided. For instance, the Bains Report recommendation of a strong local authority policy and resources committee to establish local priorities was implemented in a number of new authorities. Likewise, the reorganisation allowed enterprising local officials to implement the more recent organisational ideas in their authorities. While some observers might doubt the utility of the various techniques such as corporate planning and corporate management systems (formalised in the Bains Report as an official team to work with the Policy and Resources Committee), the reorganisation at least allowed the attempt to be made.

The most significant change was perhaps the introduction of the concept of a local government ombudsman. This change follows the pattern of the Parliamentary Commissioner: the office of ombudsman, styled on the New Zealand and Swedish model, was established to investigate and publicise (but not to remedy or adjudicate on) maladministration in the central-government administration. The idea is that there will be a new avenue through which to complain about local government administration. There will be a commissioner for local administration whose task it will be to take up the complaints of people in a local authority who have failed to receive redress through a complaint to the local authority or their elected councillor on that authority's council. There will probably be nine commissioners for England and one or two for Wales, and their major duty will be to protect individuals from injustice due to maladministration, such as incompetence, delay, prejudice, neglect, or conflict of interest. Like the Parliamentary Commissioner, these local government ombudsmen's major tool will be the publication of reports and the consequent publicity given to offending administrators. (Local Government Act 1974, CIRCULAR 124/74)

This, then, leads to a final area of local authority functioning which, while not yet reformed, is in the process of being reconsidered, and that is the question of the integrity of local government. With the notorious Poulson corruption affair, and the disclosures of shady dealings in local authorities, there was a call for new disclosure-of-interest laws for local officials. The *Sunday Times*, as early as 24 June 1973, pointed out that:

> The reconstruction of local government which is now going on has paid remarkably little attention to [the problem of integrity]. Municipal life is being radically shaken up . . . but the laws and traditions governing the work of council members, officers and committees remain virtually untouched. Since local authorities are becoming very much larger, with money and influence expanding in proportion, it is important that there should be some review of the present constraints on irregular practices.*

There are basically two major issues here, one the openness of the decision-making process, the other the disclosure of public officials' business interests.

Under the Public Bodies Act of 1960, the press was allowed access to the local authorities' council meetings. However, what happened was that the major issues were usually discussed either *in camera* in committee meetings or at the ruling political

---

* *Sunday Times* (24 June 1973) p. 16.

party's meetings before council meetings. To meet this the Local Government Act extended the right of the press (not the public) to attend local council committee meetings except in situations where the committee specifically voted to exclude them. Again what could happen is that the councillors could simply meet in sub-committees which are not open to the press, or the press could perhaps omit to mention various important facts. Coupled with this, even in situations where the public does have access, there is often not enough documentation of the issues being decided to make them intelligible.

The other issue is that of the disclosure of the financial interests of the local-authority councillors and personnel. While there is a long-standing rule that councillors must notify the town clerk what his and his wife's business interests are, and must not speak or vote on matters where his interests are at stake, the system has not been entirely successful in keeping officials from acting on their own behalf. For one thing, the system is not heavily policed and the councillor is left on his own to decide which of his interests may conflict with council business. Secondly, by disclosing matters to the town clerk early in the year, the councillor can often successfully hide an interest from view when the actual discussion comes before the council.

In October 1973 Edward Heath, then Prime Minister, established a committee on local-government rules of conduct, under the chairmanship of Lord Redcliffe-Maud, whose previous work on local-government management and re-organisation was greatly respected (if not followed). The committee reported in May 1974, and set out a draft Code of Conduct. They proposed that there should be a compulsory register of all pecuniary interests for all local councillors, as well as sanctions in the form of both fines and imprisonment for up to two years for failure to disclose pecuniary interests. Councillors should be required to mention the conflict of interest orally any time they were being discussed and to withdraw out of hearing range in the ensuing discussion. They should be prohibited from serving as committee chairmen in fields where they had a substantial pecuniary or even professional interest. These stringent rules should also apply to local-authority employees, who would have to disclose an interest in a contract, a proposed contract or other matter, and register their interest in the same way as the councillors. The

47

proposed Code of Conduct would place the onus on the local councillor to act as if all his actions were open to the public, and to treat even gifts and hospitality with extreme care. Taken in total the committee's proposals impose a much higher standard on the local councillor and his officer. (CONDUCT IN LOCAL GOVERNMENT)

This, however, is only the beginning, for with the continuing wave of scandals there have been more calls for stricter standards in government. In May 1974 Parliament passed a rule for the compulsory registration of M.P.s' interests. At the same time the new Prime Minister, Harold Wilson, established a Royal Commission on Standards of Conduct in Public Life, which will evaluate the entire range of government ethics at the central- and local-government level. Also various councils have already started voluntary public registers of councillors' interests.

Meanwhile various parties have called for more careful policing of local- and central-government affairs. For instance *The Times*, in an editorial,* called for the creation of a local-government inspectorate to which members of the public, council and professional staff could turn for an investigation of impropriety. All this has brought into sharp focus the lack of openness in local government and there will most probably be further changes in the rules appearing in the near future.

From this discussion of the attempt to reform the local government administrative units in mind we can now proceed to the financial resources of those local authorities.

---

* *The Times* (24 May 1974) p. 15.

3 Finance Reform: The Precondition to Viable Local Units

The following discussion should present the reader with a thumbnail sketch of how the local taxation system functions and how it is related to the local authorities' ability to plan land-use and future growth. If one is interested in the rate system for its own sake one of the excellent texts on the subject (such as HEPWORTH) would be useful, but for our purposes the following should be sufficient to bring out the problems of both the system's inability to actually equalise resources between authorities or, equally importantly, to allow the local authorities to have a firm commitment to levels of spending on municipal infrastructure.

THE RATE SYSTEM AS A SUPPLIER OF
LOCAL FINANCE

One of the most crucial problems facing the local governments, which must deliver not only the land-use planning service but also a great variety of related and unrelated social services such as education, sanitation, housing or local transport, is that of how to guarantee sufficient revenue. What is most important for both the quality of planning decisions and the equality of opportunity throughout the country is that there is not a great disparity of local-government resources where there is a great difference in tax base between local authorities. Britain has been attempting to solve this problem for over the last fifty years, and while these efforts have not been wildly successful they have to some extent guaranteed each local authority a minimum of spending resources.

Local government in the United Kingdom, by 1970, accounted for 14 per cent of the G.N.P., which amounted to one-third of all public expenditure. 27·5 per cent of this spending comes from local taxation and the other 72·5 per cent comes from the central government. This spending breaks down in millions of pounds sterling (1971–2) as shown in Table 3.1.

TABLE 3·1

	Capital	Revenue[1]
Education	295	2349
Housing	960	931
Police	25	406
Highways	232	388
Water and sewage[2]	234	321
Social services	36	298
Trading services (buses, ports, etc.)	85	245
Public health and refuse	25	172
Local health services[3]	12	133
Fire	8	85
Parks	21	84
Libraries, museums, and galleries	9	75
Planning	70	74
Other services	71	293
General administration	24	390
Totals	2107 m.	6244 m.

[1] Figures exclude expenditure from certain special funds (e.g. superannuation fund).
[2] From 1974 the responsibility of regional water authorities.
[3] From 1974 the responsibility of regional and area health authorities.
SOURCE: Department of the Environment, *Local Government Financial Statistics, 1971–2* (London: H.M.S.O., 1973). Compiled in MAUD AND WOOD, Appendix 2.

The local governments in the United Kingdom spend roughly two-thirds of their money on labour. Since wages are increasing at a faster rate than the rest of the inflation in the economy, this has made local expenditure the fastest growing part of the public sector. In the 1960s this meant that local government was growing at an average of 6 per cent a year (in fixed prices), which is about twice as fast as the economy as a whole has been growing (BLUE BOOK). Apart from labour costs, this can be accounted for by an increasing emphasis on services and perhaps a higher standard of these services. This is also coupled with often rapid population fluctuations which result in increased start-up costs in services.

Local governments have only one form of local tax and that is a property tax, known as the rates. Although there is occasional official discussion of other possible forms of revenue generation (such as a local income tax similar to Sweden's or the transfer of motor vehicle and petrol taxes to local governments, ideas which are currently being explored by the Layfield committee of inquiry into local government finance which is due to report in early 1976),* it seems to be the opinion of most experts and the opinion of the last Government as expressed in the 1971 Green Paper on the subject, *The Future Shape of Local Government Finance* (FINANCE GREEN PAPER), that the rates will remain the principal form of locally-raised funding. (For a theoretical discussion see PIGOU, 1962.)

The property tax, or rates, in the United Kingdom is based on the rental (not the capital) value of the property. Because of rent regulation and control, this base has risen more slowly than the economy. This value, called the rateable value, is then taxed at a specific rate determined by the authority. There are three ways that more money can be generated from the rateable base. One is to raise the percentage of tax on all rateable values, which is extremely unpopular with the electorate. The second is to revalue the property to reflect current rental values. The only other method of increasing revenue is for the base itself to grow through development.

The problems of local government finance should be fairly clear from the above. The growth of the base and the growth of the percentage of tax have not kept up with the growth of local-government expenditure (PREST, 1970). Up until the 1950s most of the difference between local taxes and expenditure was made up through specific grants for specific types of expenditure (similar in kind to the U.S. categorical programmes). This has generally changed over the recent decades to more discretionary types of grant with fewer strings attached, whose nomenclature has changed from block grants to general grants and finally to rate support grants (see BOYLE).

REBATES, VALUATION, AND CENTRAL CONTROL

One of the most controversial aspects of the rating system is its disproportionate impact on the poorer house-owning families, or, to use the economists' term, its 'regressivity'. In the early 1960s a revaluation led to the publication of a number of studies of situations of hardship for poor or retired families who owned their homes. A committee was established, headed by Professor Allen (ALLEN COMMITTEE), which investigated the problem, and concluded that a section of the population,

---

* *Hansard* (6 Nov. 1974) written answer 149.

C

principally the poor, retired or elderly, was suffering severely under the revaluations. In order to help this section and also to make it easier to raise the taxation levels on those families who could afford to pay (that is to add elasticity to the rate of tax), there was introduced in the Rating Act of 1966 (now consolidated in the General Rate Act of 1967) a system of tax-rate rebate and instalment-plan payments for families who, while owning property, have a very low income. (HEPWORTH, chaps 3 and 4)

These rebates account for some 18 per cent of the total property taxes, and serve an important function in allowing lower-income people to maintain private ownership of dwellings while still allowing a rising property-tax rate. The problem with the system, according to Molly Meacher's study for the Child Poverty Action Group, is that only some 12 per cent of those eligible do, in fact, apply in the lowest income areas of the country. While it is possible to raise this to as high as 25 per cent through an advertising campaign, the system tends to attract the pensioners who own their own homes, but does not, in fact, really serve those in the greatest need. 'Perhaps the single, most important finding of this study was that, amongst eligible households, those in greatest need tended to be non-claimers, while those with rather higher resources were more likely to claim rebates' (MEACHER, p. 43). Meacher goes on to recommend that the system's inherent weakness is the process of testing the means of the claimants, and suggests two possible alternatives. One is to abolish flat rates entirely for certain groups of people and introduce a 'greater degree of progressivity into the rating structure itself' (p. 46). This would entail a tax of a percentage of family income going directly to local government. A second option, according to Meacher, would be to weight the rate-support grant system (which will be dealt with below) more in favour of local authorities containing poor residential areas.

The administration of a general funding, non-specified system of grants was made extremely easy in the United Kingdom through a change in the method of computing the local property taxes effected in 1948. Until that time each local government had been in charge of the valuation of the properties in its district. Since the passage of the Local Government Act in 1948, the Inland Revenue Department of central government has the task of valuing all property in a uniform manner. This does not mean they set the rate but simply that they administer the property tax base in a uniform manner.

This system of central-government valuation does, however, contain some problems because of the essentially political nature of the timing of, and formulas used, to revalue property to take into account the change of prices. For instance, in the 1960s, due to a number of factors including a shortage of Inland Revenue staff, the Labour Government did not follow the usual time-table and omitted a five-year revaluation. This was, of course, popular with the rate-payers. However, the result was that the next revaluation, completed in 1972, had to take into account price changes for a 10-year period, and had the appearance of a rather major increase. To the home-owner this might mean a rather steep rise in local rates payments although since the rates were correlated to the new prices, there might not have been any rise in rate percentages. The newspapers were quick to point out some of the most egregious increases.*

The relationships in valuation between residential and industrial sites must follow valuation procedures which reflect the policy of government as to which sectors of the local economy should bear the burden for supplying local services. Under the Conservative Government evaluation there was a great deal of controversy to the effect that the home-owner was bearing the majority of the increase in prices whereas industrial property was not. In the words of Frank Roberts writing in the economics section of *The Times*: 'Insufficient account has been taken of the effect of inflation on property repair and insurance costs. This means that virtually all valuation on which rates will be based this year – [1973] especially for domestic property – have been set too high. Hardest hit will be occupiers of poorer property.'†

Returning to the non-specific rate-support system it should be made clear that, while each item of expenditure is no longer earmarked, central government is still very much involved in checking the local administration of services. For one thing these

---

* See the *Guardian* (1 Dec. 1972) p. 24; (3 Jan. 1973) p. 19.
† *The Times* (6 Feb. 1973) p. 19.

non-specific grants all contain a watchdog clause which allows central government to withhold funding if the local government 'failed to achieve or maintain a reasonable standard of efficiency' (Local Government Act 1966, chap. 42). Thus central government sets the national standards and goals which the local governments must live up to. In one interview with a local authority the treasurer put it this way: 'Before we had to get central government approval for almost everything we do, now its just for every important thing.'

There are a number of ways that central government exerts control over local government functioning. First, the District Auditor keeps a rather close watch on all expenditures in his area and compares these expenditures with the figures compiled for all of the authorities in the country. The office of District Auditor is very much a central-government institution; it is the stop-check on both efficiency and basic spending. When national programmes are changed it is the auditor who enforces compliance from the occasional maverick council (HELMORE). The auditor has the power to assess mis-allocations of funds, or non-collection of funds directly and personally against the non-complying elected or appointed officials. As one Housing Manager in Coventry put it: 'there is tight legislative control and it is the close interaction with the auditor which makes that control felt.'

The second major means of central-government control is the Capital Loan Sanction system. Under this procedure the local government must seek the consent of the central government before borrowing money for local capital expenditure (CIRCULAR 2/70). The purpose of this system is both to regulate total national capital expenditure and its impact in terms of the effect of local borrowing on the money market and to ensure that projects meet the central government's standards. In terms of national finance it is as important as the rate-support grant to the central government. Up until 1971 there was a fairly rigid set of approvals which required central intervention for even the smallest capital programme. However, under the new system, which went into effect in 1971, the central government has direct approval control over what are termed 'key sector' expenditures (RATE SUPPORT GRANT ORDER, 1972). These include the basic services of local government such as housing, education, roads, police and social services. However, the local governments have a somewhat freer rein over some expenditures such as land, and a free discretion for a certain annual percentage of total expenditure set by central government. This is basically a small sum which allows local governments to provide local amenities. Under this portion of discretionary capital investment the local authority can provide such amenities as parks, swimming pools or museums. According to officials in the Department of the Environment this has generally had the result that the more affluent districts have been erecting swimming pools instead of the programmes the central government used to be willing to approve, such as libraries and museums. A final factor to consider when evaluating local initiative and central control is that the basic outlines of settlements on wages are set at a national level between representatives of the major unions employed by local authorities and central- and local-government representatives.

THE RATE SUPPORT GRANT AS AN EQUALISATION MECHANISM

Perhaps the most interesting aspect of this non-specific funding of local governments by the central government is its method of equalisation (or, more properly, deficiency payments) between various districts. It should be clear from the following that the process guarantees that no authority will suffer unduly because of its tax base relative to its more affluent neighbours. As recent economic investigation has shown, however, it does not guarantee an eventual parity between authorities (GODLEY AND RHODES). Starting with the first block grants under the Local Government Act of 1929, central government has always differentiated between the richer and poorer local governments and attempted in its non-specific grants at least to bring the spending ability of the poorer authorities up to the national average. This equalisation principle has been carried through both the Local Government Act of 1948, which introduced the Exchequer Equalisation Grant, and its successors, the Rate Deficiency Grant and the present Rate Support Grant system. It seems apparent, however, that the creation of the present system is not based on some explicit set of norms or objectives but rather arose out of the bargaining process between the local authorities' associations and central government.

Under the present Rate Support Grant system the central

government and the local authorities have a series of negotiations to determine the total amount of central-government finance for local government for the next two years. Since this is one of the largest expenditures of central government, second only to defence spending, these negotiations take into account a great many factors, including not only local needs but also national economic policy and inflation. During these negotiations the relative priority of each type of service is established and general budgetary guidelines are drawn up for the individual authorities to follow. For instance the negotiations which established the total rate-support-grant expenditure for 1975 of some £4096 m. included funds not only to make up for the general increase of local authority costs but also for specific needs such as the funding of a rapid increase in teachers' pay. (RATE SUPPORT GRANT ORDER, 1975).

The Rate Support Grant takes into account two factors: (1) *resources* – basically the size of the rateable base, and (2) *need* – based on such factors as population density, numbers of old, young, handicapped citizens, distances, and so on.

The method of operation of this equalising grant is somewhat complex (PREST, 1970, p. 194). First as to resources: the average rate product (that is the amount of income the local government will derive from a 1 per cent tax on rateable value) per head in the population is computed for the entire country. Any local government which does not have resources sufficient to reach this national average receives a deficiency payment from the central government to bring it up to the average for the rest of the country. In other words, the central government theoretically acts like a property-owner who has just the amount of property to bring the authorities' tax-base value per head up to the national average. Richer local governments, that is those with a larger tax base, do not receive this part of the grant, but they do not have to pay the excess above the national average into the central government either.

The second half of the Rate Support Grant relates to needs. This is based on two factors: (1) the basic share is a sum given for each member of the served population with an additional allowance for each child aged under fifteen; (2) supplementary shares are given depending on the number of schoolchildren, the number of children under school age, the number of people over sixty-five, the population density, the population per mile of road, and special provisions for police funding.

There is also a third element in the computation, called the domestic element, which is essentially a subsidy to support a lower tax rate on domestic property. This figure is set by the central government (in 1971 it was 6p in the pound, meaning that taxes on domestic property will be reduced by 6 per cent of its rate).

One of the most important lessons to be learned from this equalisation programme can perhaps best be shown from an analysis of the very basic criticisms being levelled at it in conjunction with the debate on the reorganisation of local structures. The criticism is essentially that the system has no inherent object other than to quiet the most vociferous and thus often the most powerful local governments.

In the first place the system has not resulted in any uniformity of services between areas. An examination by Peter Hildrew in the *Guardian* of the most recent statistics put out by the Institute of Municipal Treasurers and Accountants shows great disparity in spending between authorities. For instance one authority (Doncaster) spent only 51p per 1000 in the population on family-planning services while another was spending £109. Similar discrepancies can be seen over the whole range of social-service spending, from education to the physically handicapped or the elderly. These fluctuations cannot merely be explained in terms of differences in social make-up, service preference, or inconsistency of data between reporting authorities. Similar large urban areas such as Birmingham, Manchester and Bristol have wide variations in spending on different services. In the words of Peter Hildrew, 'the figures show astonishing differences in the level of social services provided between one authority and another . . . for the elderly the variation in the service is positively alarming.'*

A recent study by the University of Cambridge Department of Applied Economics has brought to light some rather startling anomalies in the functioning of the present system (GODLEY AND RHODES). First as to the needs element the study group showed that differences of the age distribution in various local government areas resulted in varying levels of services in

---

* *Guardian* (14 Feb. 1973) p. 10.

those areas. In other words, the needs formula did not adequately reflect the real costs of servicing the elderly or schoolchildren. As the study group put it 'the present system . . . discriminates against areas with a relatively high proportion of children and in favour of those with a relatively high proportion of old people.' (GODLEY AND RHODES, p. 6)

Similarly, the evaluation of the resources element by the Cambridge group showed that while the system is touted as an equalisation measure, in reality it is only a system of deficiency payments, that is the poorer authorities are brought up to the average but the above-average authorities are not brought down to that average. While this might be justifiable in terms of policy, the method of equalisation acts as a disincentive to the development of an average tax base. Since any increase in property-tax base due to local development is matched by a pound-for-pound reduction in central-government contributions, there is virtually no incentive to seek such development. This is further compounded by the fact that while no new local income will be coming in from the new commercial development there will be additional expenditure in terms of servicing that development. In the words of the Cambridge group 'the existing resources element system produces a poverty trap in an acute form'. (GODLEY AND RHODES, p. 7)

The very political nature of the equalisation formula and central government's approach to it can best be seen in an article by the economics editor of *The Times* (27 November 1972, p. 21). Peter Jay took the information derived from the Cambridge report, that is the relationship between services and age structure, and correlated it with political party winners of the various authorities in the 1970 national election. The older and relatively more affluent districts under the rate-support-grant structure are those which tended to vote Conservative and those which are less affluent are those which voted Labour.

When reorganisation of local government was first considered, it was often mentioned in the same breath with the reform of local finance. One of the reasons, in fact, for the idea of redrawing local boundaries was to spread the tax base more evenly and establish units that might be more capable of administering new forms of taxation. In 1971 the Conservative Government issued a major Green Paper, *The Future Shape of*

Local Government Finance (FINANCE GREEN PAPER), which considered the various alternative taxation methods which might provide more revenue and financial independence to the local authorities. These included a local income tax, a local sales tax, and various types of motor vehicle tax. In the final outcome, however, the policy paper noted that in the past the

almost universal conclusion . . . has been that a property tax such as rates must remain the principal source of local revenue, though it may be possible to reduce the extent to which local expenditure is dependent on the rates by providing other sources of revenue to supplement them. (FINANCE GREEN PAPER, p. 4)

And when the 1972 Local Government Act appeared, it showed no new sources of finance, and little fundamental change in the rate system. With the change of government in 1974, the new Secretary of State for the Department of the Environment, Anthony Crosland, promised a re-examination of the rate-support-grant system, and established the Layfield Committee of inquiry into local-government finance to investigate the alternatives.

THE RATE SYSTEM AS AN ELEMENT IN LOCAL
LAND-USE PLANNING

The financing of local government is a major factor in determining how the local area will grow or develop, or use its land. At the general level, the disparity of resources will, of course, result in some areas with bigger and better schools, parks, or council houses. More importantly, the disparity between the rate of taxation in various local-authority jurisdictions will cause certain types of land uses to concentrate in lower-rate areas. As the Godley and Rhodes study showed, the structure of the equalisation formula would tend to cause some areas (with few resources in the tax base and a high rate of taxation) to fail in attracting new development, while other areas (already rich in resources and having a relatively low tax rate) would attract more and more development. For our purposes there are two further areas where the structure of local government finance is of special significance to the planning-law system. The first is the effect of the system's emphasis on taxing rental value on open-space planning and

59

urban plans, and the second is the effect of the central government's control over local expenditure upon the local government's ability to plan growth for any appreciable time in the future. The fact that rates are imposed on the rental value of property and not at all on agricultural property determines to a great extent how local-government officials can attempt to order future development.

On the one hand, since derelict property, under-utilised property, or even developed but unrented property (as in the case of the famous Centre Point Building, see ELKIN, chap. 4) may not cause the owners a taxation burden, the local officials have no clear idea as to when well-located but unused land will come into productive use. While the burden of property taxation may, in some foreign jurisdictions, ensure rapid development of prime locations, in England such areas may sit idle without any appreciable cash drain on the owners of the land or buildings. In central urban areas this has negative effects since there is no way to co-ordinate the various inter-related permissions, local government services, and related infrastructure.

Actually, it has taken the absurd example of the expensive skyscraper, Centre Point, constructed in 1967 in central London, which at the time of writing still sits idle, to accentuate some of the problems of the taxation system for local planners and to bring about some modest changes. The debate on that idle building has caused the various government spokesmen to devote considerable efforts to reconsidering the planning as well as the revenue effects of not imposing rates on empty buildings. The fruits of that review have now been finalised, and it is clear that there will be a good deal more discretion lodged with the local officials to tax developments selectively to enforce their use.

Under the 1966 Local Government Act a local authority may resolve to tax all empty property at half rates. However, under that legislation the local authority was forced to make a decision for all empty or unoccupied property and, once adopted, those provisions had to remain in force for at least seven years unless waived by the central government. This meant that the local authorities had no discretion to levy taxes selectively, or to attempt to enforce decisions relating to the use of land through taxes. In 1971 the Government Green Paper on local-government finance considered this problem and concluded that:

> It would be difficult to justify making the rating of empty property mandatory; but since empty property makes some call on rate-borne services, there are grounds for continuing the existing discretion to levy half rates on empty property. But there is a strong case for giving rating authorities power to specify classes of property on which the void rate either should or should not fall, and for reducing the seven year minimum period for operation of the rate to, say, three years in which event the provision for Ministerial waiver could probably be dropped. (FINANCE GREEN PAPER, para. 3.32)

By early 1974 the Local Government Act was passed and, amongst other things, it implemented the Green Paper's recommendations. First, the legislation abolished the requirement that resolutions on rating of unoccupied property may not be varied for seven years once they were established [sec.15(1)]. Second, the legislation allowed the local authority to limit its imposition of the rates to certain classes of property, that is the authority could impose a burden on some but not necessarily all unoccupied property [sec.15(3)]. Third, the new legislation eliminated the 50 per cent tax rate and allowed the rating authority to establish different proportions for various classes of properties [sec.15(4)], and to reduce or remit rates in cases of hardship. Finally, in a piece of drafting designed specifically to take care of Centre Point type situations, the 1974 Local Government Act allowed the local authorities to impose a rating surcharge on unused office property [sec.16]. After six months of disuse (where the building is capable of being rented) the authority can double the rates for the first year, triple them for the second year, and quadruple them for the third year, and go on progressively increasing them while the period of disuse continues. Thus the legislation seems to be designed to give the local authorities some powers to force the use of properties that they have already granted planning permissions for. Under the recent 'Land' White Paper the Government stated that it intended to allow compulsory purchase of empty office blocks at construction cost. The other side of the coin can be seen in the local government planners' relatively free hand in the area of open-space planning. Since there are no rates imposed on agricultural land or buildings (GENERAL RATE ACT, 1967, chap. 9), this allows the local officials to plan agricultural uses in close proximity to developed land without having to consider the possible taxation increase on the agricultural user. While the planner still has the unenviable task of selecting some parcels to be developed, and therefore making them worth a great deal more than those that are left in agricultural use, at least there is not the taxation consideration that is so important in some American jurisdictions. There the farmer who cannot get his land re-zoned must continue to pay property taxes to service the new residents who have bought his neighbouring land. In England the local planner may still be making some farmers who have turned developers quite wealthy compared to their neighbours, but at least such a choice is not going to increase the taxes of the farmer who stays on his land.

There is a second aspect of the local finance system which is quite important to the system's ability actually to control the use of land. As mentioned above the local authorities do not have spending authority in a great many areas (for example, hospitals, trunk roads, major transportation schemes and so on) where decisions will shape the growth and development of an area. But, as the paragraph on capital expenditure showed, they do not even have final authority on those programmes which are supposedly within their own competence. Since the great bulk of the capital programmes must be approved by central government and are subject to review, the local officials cannot count on expenditures for schools or infrastructure for a very long period in the future. As we deal with the new system of plan-making in the following chapters it should be kept in mind that the major variables of local-government capital expenditure are subject to change, often without notice, based on factors such as the balance of payments or the rate of inflation.

After looking at the structure of the units which deliver the planning system, the method by which those units are financed, and the effect of that finance on the planning task, we can now turn from the structure to the administration of the system itself and the attempts at reforming that system.

PART TWO

Reforming the Planning Approach:
Methods and Procedures

4 Problems in the Fabric of Planning

Major changes occur in administrative systems only when there are significant problems with their functioning. In the case of planning the process was one of slow deterioration of the public confidence in the institution, combined with a tremendous build up of workload in the administering of local- and central-government agencies. By the mid-1960s the English planning system that had been in force for nearly twenty years and had been hailed as one of the most advanced and comprehensive systems of physical planning in the world (HAAR, 1951), was beginning to show serious signs of strain. In order to evaluate those problems and the major reforms they necessitated, it is time to flesh out that brief skeleton of the planning system given in the first chapter and to add some definition to some of the inconsistent themes that run through the legislation.

As we approach this task it is important to keep in mind that there seems to be a confusion as to what the objective of the process is supposed to be. The reader should consider whether that objective is to produce plans for their own sake or to produce actions in the present which are best in the light of a desired future. Perhaps the factors which would lead to such action are so diverse and the decisions held in so many private and usually self-serving hands that such a notion of 'best decision' is unknowable. If that is the reality of the situation then a great deal more emphasis will have to be put on the procedures involved; not what the planners say they are doing but how they come to say it.

THE GOALS

First, the particular administrative process that we will concentrate on, namely the land-use planning-oriented process under the Town and Country Planning Acts, is simply one of a number of pieces of legislation spawned in the immediate post-war years. These laws all had a number of things in common, in that they were attempts to determine how and where physical development would occur. The various planning related Acts (the Distribution of Industry Acts, the National Parks and Access to the Countryside Act, the New Towns Act, and the Town Development Act) all had in common a united but very ill-defined set of goals about what was 'good' development. It is with these goals that one must start because it was the non-attainment of them that led to the major reforms on which we will concentrate.

The most basic piece of coherent policy for planning in general, and land-use planning in particular, is the Barlow Commission's Report on the distribution of the industrial population, issued in January 1940. As one of the more illustrious commentators pointed out (CULLINGWORTH, p. 25), it was this document which formed the basis for planning policy for all post-war governments. The terms of reference of the Commission were to

> inquire into the causes which have influenced the present geographical distribution of the industrial population of Great Britain and the probable direction of any change in that distribution in the future; to consider what social, economic or strategic disadvantages arise from the concentration of industries, or of the industrial population, in large towns or in particular areas of the country; and to report what remedial measures, if any, should be taken in the national interest.

Until the Barlow Report, the country had been dealing with planning on a very localised basis, and while there had been some sort of planning legislation in existence since 1909 (Housing and Town Planning Acts for example) the major thrust of that legislation was to concentrate on local planning schemes for small well-defined areas. What Barlow did was to emphasise that mere exercises in *civic design* (MCLOUGHLIN, 1973a, p. 115), while valuable, were not enough, and that what was needed was an administrative process to deal with planning from a national standpoint. What was needed was a national approach to planning that took in the various and closely interrelated economic, political and administrative problems of urban congestion and the despoliation of the countryside. This countryside aspect was taken further by the Scott Report, which pointed out the rapid loss of agricultural and rural land.

The Barlow Commission's idea was to spread the industrial population 'throughout the different areas or regions in Great Britain; [and] of appropriate diversification of industries in those areas or regions'. In order to accomplish this the Commission unanimously agreed that there was need of a centralised administration and a variety of mechanisms, such as New Towns and the transfer of industry. What was not agreed was what particular administrative approach to take and, particularly, what approach should be taken to land-use planning. With the coming of the war, however, a feeling grew up in the country that such schemes could be devised and would, in fact, result in a national and socially integrated approach to planning. In the words of Cullingworth: 'There was an enthusiasm and a determination to undertake social reconstruction on a scale hitherto considered utopian.' (p. 30)

In order to spread industry through the country and at the same time to save the countryside, administrative procedures were to be established which would allow for national supervision and co-ordination, as well as the particulars of local needs. As already mentioned, there were a number of approaches, such as the suggestions on New Towns and industrial location, but the central tool was the town- and country-planning legislation. The eventual mechanism was based on both positive interference with the value of land and a negative restriction in the form of a permission for all new development. The first part, namely the nationalisation of development value based on the recommendations of the Uthwatt Committee on Compensation and Betterment, was to prove the most contentious and short-lived. The second part, namely development control based on a development plan, was to form the cornerstone of environmental planning in the country and, while in need of reform, achieved almost total political acceptance.

While we will be concerned most with the administrative process of negative control, it is important to understand that the 1947 Act was really a two-pronged piece of legislation. In the framers' minds land values were indelibly bound up with the questions of planning. Land-use planning could only achieve its goals if the allocation of use was based on suitability 'irrespective of the existing values which may attach to the individual parcels of land' (UTHWATT). Since negative control gave some owners the right to develop, and thus a tremendously high market value, and others no rights and thus very little market value, the scheme as envisaged had, in some way, to balance the equities between them. While various approaches to this were considered (such as taking all land into public ownership) the final result was to nationalise only the development rights and its value. Under the 1947 legislation there was to be an initial payment to all owners of land that could be proved to have an existing development value, that is land which was worth in the market place more than similarly situated parcels used for the same purpose, because of its potential development for a higher or more productive use. This payment was not meant to meet current market prices realistically, but was simply to make some provision for payment for the transfer of development values to the Government. Once this initial payment had been made (through claims filed with a Central Land Board) the idea was that no owner who was denied development rights would receive any further compensation. Any owner who did receive those rights through the grant of development permission would be taxed or, in the local vernacular, be subject to a development charge or betterment levy on the full amount of that increase in value.

As it happened, this first prong of the legislation received such an immediate reform that we really do not need to dwell on it at this point, for land was sold at a price which simply added the development charge on top of the existing use and development-potential value. The administrative machinery reacted by selectively purchasing at the 'correct price' compulsorily, and thus hopefully damping the enthusiasm for would-be owners to pay more than the existing use plus development-charge price. What resulted was a haphazard approach, little property transfer and extreme dissatisfaction upon the part of the politically powerful landowners. The scheme thus died quickly at the hands of the Conservative Government (Town and Country Planning Act 1953), and the recouping of a portion of the development profit was left to the more normal means of general taxation. While strange anomalies existed for a number of years because of this half of the 1947 legislation (such as payment for compulsorily purchased land for public use being based on existing use value plus 'development value' and not upon current market price up until the Town and Country Planning Act of 1959) the basic idea of separating current use value from future planned use was finished off rather unceremoniously. (HAAR, 1964)

THE ORIGINAL APPROACH TO PLANNING AND CONTROL

The other and more enduring half of the legislation created in 1947 put most 'development' under a permission system of control. This regulation was to be based on an integrated 'development plan' for the area. The counties would be the local authorities in charge of the system and there was to be central-government review and co-ordination of these development plans. The plans themselves were to be based on a survey of the area and numerous interrelated social and economic factors. It is here then, in this system of planning and control, that we find the heart of the administrative process, and it is here that we will see the major changes being made to attempt to meet those goals of national co-ordination and content, based on more than the mere pleasantness of design.

The land-use planning-system administrative process that was created had two basic aims, and as it has turned out these two aims are separated not only in the legislation but also practically within the local governments administering the process. As we shall see, it is the functional separation of the plan-making and the plan-implementing which has caused the widest splits among the planners and government officials administering the system, the reformers attempting to change the system and, in fact, the public attempting to deal with the system.

Turning first to plan-making, the 1947 legislation envisaged that the counties would first undertake an elaborate social, economic and physical survey of the area. It was this survey which was to form the basis of an approach to planning wide enough to take into account national and multi-dimensional land use. In the words of Telling: 'By requiring that development plans should be based on the results of a physical, social and economic survey of the area, the Act moved away from planning primarily in terms of amenity and convenience to planning on the basis of securing proper control over the use of land' (p. 3). The hope of the survey was that it would provide enough information for a plan to provide clearly the basis of the particularised control procedure. Under the 1947 Act the development plan was not of itself to grant any permission, nor in fact to bind the authority in any definite way.

The survey which was to provide this data base was to encompass thirteen major areas of information – physical conditions, ancient and historic structures, rural-community structure, population, industry and employment, minerals, agriculture and forestry, communications, government developments, public utilities, social services, parks and conservation areas, and holiday development – and this was meant to entail highly detailed investigation of each topic. The counties received a mass of circulars setting out detailed guidance on how this material was to be assembled.

Armed with this survey the local authority was to prepare a development plan consisting of a report of the survey, a written statement and a series of maps. The purpose of the development plan was to show: 'The manner in which a local planning authority proposes that land in their area should be used, whether by the carrying out thereon of development or otherwise, and the stages by which any such development should be carried out' (TOWN AND COUNTRY PLANNING ACT 1947, now at 1971, schedule 5.2). It was hoped that by correlating the short formal statements of policy in the statement, the data in the survey, and the maps, that the planners doing the controlling, and the private owners being controlled, would have a clear idea of what type of development might be allowed.

In the local authorities it evolved that those administrators who dealt with the creation of these development plans generally were separated from those who actually gave the permission under the plans, once they were created. The plan-makers came to occupy the positions of most prestige, the least daily pressure (MCLOUGHLIN, 1973a, p. 74) and the most creativity. The major occupational themes (MARCUS) which came to dominate the profession were all best exemplified in the plan-making departments. It was there that the official could practise the 'craft of town planning', to design better cities and to shape people's lives through their physical surroundings. In general the youngest and brightest government workers were attracted to the plan-making, while the lesser professionally qualified, less well educated, and harder worked official ended up in control. It is important to bear in mind that the role of the two types of official rarely overlapped, and the plan-making staff did not work hand in glove with the plain implementers.

The plan-makers were to go through a very precise procedure in order to promulgate these development plans. First, all authorities had three years from the passage of the Act in 1947 to complete their development plans. Once the county had prepared a survey and a draft plan they then had to consult with all the districts which would be affected both before and after local-authority approval. Once they had done this and considered any objections, they then would formally adopt the proposed development plan and send it to the central-government Minister concerned (whose Ministry, as we saw in Chapter 2, changed its name a number of times over the years). Notices of the proposed development plans were posted in the press and the public was given six weeks to inspect copies of the plan. The public could then object or make representation on the plan to the Minister.

Under the 1947 Act the Minister was under a statutory obligation to provide either a public inquiry or a public hearing to all interested objectors (now T.C.P.A. 1971, sch. 5). It was this forum which was to provide the new inputs of information, public feeling, and give guidance to central government in a review of the development plan. Just as the survey and the statement were to provide the social and economic depth to the plan, it was the public inquiry which was to provide the Minister with access to the sentiments of both the affected neighbouring political units or sub-units and the affected public. These public inquiries were often lengthy, repetitious and, in the opinion of some, a source of tremendous delay. All objectors had a right to appear, and since the ordering of the issues tended to be defined by the participants the inquiries were often long, ill-defined discussions of the issues in the plans. Most importantly, because the maps that formed part of the development plans contained references to actual pieces of property and thus were intimately bound up with the value of the land, there was often very particularised discussion of specific parcels. A general right of cross-examination was allowed, and most owners came to rely on professional, especially legal, representation of their cases. While the system of inquiries was to create extreme loathing on the part of the central-government officials who had to undergo the ordeal of a series of lengthy

71

inquiries, it gained firm supporters among both the affected citizenry and the professionals involved in the process. In the words of one professional seeking to defend the system against the reforms of the late 1960s: 'Trouble or no trouble, delay or no delay, a citizen has a right . . . to know what effect official plans and official planning control are going to have on his property, and on the town to which they are applied and he has the right to have his objection, if he does object, heard by some authority other than that which has made the plan.' (T. SHARP, p. 214)

After this public inquiry the independent inspector would make a recommendation on the plan, and it then remained for the Ministry to approve the proposal with or without modifications. As the planning system took shape, central government did in fact modify some plans extensively, and this method provided the Ministry with a theoretical method of integrating the plans of neighbouring political units. As it turned out, it took the Ministry a great deal of time to go through this approval process. The more co-ordination there was between the two levels of government, the longer the process took.

The resulting approved plan was in theory to be built equally of the written and map sections. Even under the regulations, if there was a contradiction between the maps and written statement, the latter was to prevail (reg. 15). The difficulty was that in practice the maps took on paramount importance for the plan implementers and it was to the maps that the private landowner turned for guidance. The maps consisted of a county map (scale 1":1 mile) for the counties, a town map (scale 6":1 mile) for the county boroughs or large urban areas, each combined with a 'programme map' to show the time scale of development, and three different types of statutory planning schemes. These were the Comprehensive Development Area Map, the Street Authorisation Map and the Supplementary Town Map. In effect it was these three specific mechanisms which allowed the authority to guide the plan implementers or development control sections directly through very specific, block-by-block, guidelines to timing and intensity of use. Through residential-density and floor-space guidelines, combined with a programme map showing progress over five-year periods, the idea was to detail for the controllers what was to take place. In areas of comprehensive development the controllers were further helped by the power to take the land into public ownership through compulsory purchase. In the original legislation the written statement itself was to include the intentions of the authority as to which land it would compulsorily acquire so as to give the controllers and the public a firm idea as to which land would be taken over the next ten or twenty years.

Armed with this development plan the staff of the development-control section of the local authority were prepared to set about implementing it. Now, since the authority must 'have regard to the provision of the development plan' but need not necessarily follow it in any given instance, the officials, working on a case-by-case basis, have a wide degree of latitude. While their decision was subject to approval by the elected local council – their local authority in the great majority of cases – that approval was often not based on a thorough investigation by the elected officials. (CULLINGWORTH)

Very briefly, the person who wanted to develop land applied to the local authority for either outline or detailed permission. Virtually all development ('the carrying out of building, engineering, mining or other operations in, on, over or under the land, or the making of any material change in the use of any buildings or other land', to use the legal definition) requires prior approval by the local authority. There are limited classes of activity which are excluded from the permission requirement (basically changes of the use of a structure within the definitions of the 'use classes order') either because they are not defined as development or because they are allowed without *ad hoc* permissions (under the General Development Order). Apart from these, however, the control officials could refuse permission altogether, or give either a conditional or unconditional permission.

THE DEVELOPMENT OF THE PUBLIC INQUIRY

It is in this area of control that the particular landowner felt the actual pinch of the regulatory scheme, and a vast array of appellate law on the correct statutory interpretation of the various control procedures evolved around this case-by-case system. The individual aggrieved landowner had a right to appeal to the Minister if he was refused planning permission (although his neighbour did not if he received that permission) and the settling of disputes through a public inquiry became a major adjudicatory mechanism.

Because the controller's decisions clearly affected the rights of individual property-owners, those owners were quick to use legal, professional help to protect those rights. Since we will keep returning to the continuing argument about the validity of judicialising the planning-appeals procedure it is necessary here to describe the evolution of the system, for the forum of the local public inquiry has become the focus for not only the lawyer but the planner, developer and environmental pressure group.

Public inquiries as hearings into the use of administrative discretion came into their own as early as the mid-nineteenth century as a means to avoid having to use Parliamentary review of executive administrative action. Over time the system came to be used in a variety of situations, but the report of the inspector who chaired the inquiry was at first simply another 'piece of information, one further document which went into the file' (MCAUSLAN, 1975, chap. 5). Since the administrative decision on a local road or public-health measure was wholly within the discretion of the Minister, there was no duty to disclose the reasons for the decision and thus even to disclose the inspector's opinion. By the 1930s this was still the rule, although the courts came to require an open discussion of all sides of a dispute at the inquiry rather than individually behind closed doors.

With the introduction of the 1947 Planning Act there came to be a great volume of administrative decisions on planning-permission refusals which directly affected the economic position of the landowner. In the early 1950s the lack of procedural rules at the inquiries, combined with what seemed to be clandestine consultations between local officials and central-government officials, led to a great deal of dissatisfaction, and one *cause célèbre* led to the creation of the Franks Committee on Administrative Tribunals and Inquiries. This now-famous Committee recommended that a council on tribunals be established, a series of procedures for a fair hearing be published and, most importantly, that the public inquiry's inspector's decision be made public. With the implementation of the Franks' recommendations in 1958 (CIRCULAR 9/58), the public inquiry developed as a forum for decision-making in its own

74

right. It came to have its own procedures, promulgated by the Lord Chancellor's office, and to have various specialised formats to deal with various types of disputes. In the planning area there can be inquiries into refusal of planning permissions for private development, the issuance of an enforcement notice against a private owner, the calling in of a planning application before decision, the investigation of a projected development by a government department, and the inquiry into the making of a development plan. There are also a number of hybrids which have been developed, such as the planning inquiry commission (TOWN AND COUNTRY PLANNING ACT, 1971, sections 48–9), to deal with particularly large or important disputes. It is one novel offshoot of the inquiry model, the Public Examination, which will form the basis of our discussion of the new plan-making procedure and review in Chapter 8.

The lawyers, representing clients who were unable to develop their land because of a lack of planning permission, thrived on the procedures introduced because of Franks, and an entire section of their profession arose who were concerned with testing the factual validity of the local authority's employees' decisions. The lawyers did not seem, however, particularly inventive in applying those procedures to the benefit of other affected members of the community besides aggrieved landowners.

THE PROBLEMS: ACCESS AND PUBLIC DEBATE

It would seem that we now have a clear enough idea about the basis of the legislation and the actualities of it to look to what went wrong during the first twenty years of its operation. The problems can be broken down into two broad areas. On the one hand, the planning system did not seem to be meeting the criteria of administrative efficiency. It was neither taking into account matters of social and economic importance, nor co-ordinating the development of neighbouring local authorities, much less co-ordinating development over whole regions. Nor was it flexible or subtle enough in operation to keep up with rapid social or technological changes. On the other hand, those people directly affected or involved in it felt it neither allowed effective public access nor accommodated what democratic access it did allow in a sufficiently fast and efficient manner.

Turning first to efficiency, the 1947 machinery of plan-

making ran into immediate problems because the first development plans simply could not be completed within the three-year
deadline. By 1951 only twenty-two of the authorities had their
plans ready, and it was a number of years before all were
completed. When all these plans began to reach central
government for the review, inquiry and approval processes, it
proved impossible for central government to attend to them in
any quick or co-ordinated manner. By 1955 only one-half of the
development plans had been approved, and it was some fifteen
years after the passage of the Act that all of the plans finally
received approval.

From the outset, then, the development plans were not
current when they were put into force. These plans became
even more obsolete because of two major demographic changes
in Great Britain – a tremendous and unexpected rise in
population, and an enormous increase in the volume of automobile traffic. In the words of the group that was to introduce
the ideas for the major reforms:

> the development plans have tended to become out of date in
> terms of technique in that they deal inadequately with trans-
> port and the interrelationship of traffic and land-use; in
> factual terms in that they fail to take account quickly
> enough of changes in population forecasts, traffic growth
> and other economic and social trends; and in terms of policy
> in that they do not reflect more recent developments in the
> field of regional and urban planning. (P.A.G. Sec. 1, para. 23)

Under the 1947 Act it was hoped that the plans would be
kept up to date through a periodic review every five years,
but here again the slowness of local government, coupled with
the inadequacy of the central-government review procedure
with its public inquiries, tended to stop or delay these reviews.
By the mid-1960s most authorities were just starting on their
first reviews so that the operative document was dated, to say
the least. Some authorities did of course have the resources to
try to keep their development plans up to date by seeking
amendments to them, but the great majority simply operated
under plans which by the late 1960s had little to do with the
realities of existing land-use.

The local authorities of course had to keep dealing with the
problems of guiding the development-control officers in their

76

growing and redeveloping cities and towns, so they devised a number of internal sets of guidelines. These would either be informal policy criteria emanating from the plan-making staff, or the officials would make concrete, but non-statutory and thus unofficial, plans for specific areas. These informal plans or, as McLoughlin calls them, 'bottom-drawer' plans (MCLOUGHLIN, 1973a, p. 124), became the operable development plans. They may have been good plans or relevant plans, but there was no procedure established to assure that they had anything to do with the members of the public who would be affected.

From the standpoint of the plan-implementers, these guidelines were no doubt helpful in the continuing process of approving or rejecting the planning applications, but from the standpoint of the landowner planning began to seem like a very arbitrary process. The written statement, originally terribly terse, was so old and obsolete as to be nonsensical. The statutory maps were similarly outdated. To the landowner the discussion of a local authority's plans, or the review of an 'unofficial' plan for the area, often surreptitiously shown by the control section, was both high-handed and illogical. In the words of one major developer's spokesman, 'these local authority planners are working from maps that are years out of date. Even if you have a parcel of land in an obviously ripe area near a motorway or surrounded on three sides by development you often have to go to appeal to gain permission. There is no idea of a policy at all'.

It was exactly this reaction upon the part of landowners, namely to appeal because policy behind the *ad hoc* refusal was ill-defined in the first place, which led to the most obvious manifestation of the weakness of the administrative system. There was a tremendous rise in the number of appeals against planning-permission refusals, and likewise a corresponding delay in the ability of central government to handle those appeals. The mid-1960s saw the appeals number reach 13,620; this number dropped for a few years, but by 1972 there were some 615,000 applications with 14,408 appeals, and the appeals had increased to 17,000 by 1973. There was a shortage of qualified planning staff to handle the work and both the mid-1960s and early 1970s saw a rapid increase in the processing time for these applications and appeals. (DOBRY INTERIM REPORT, sec. 16)

This then leads into the second major category of problems about planning, which was a general feeling upon the part of the public that it somehow lacked legitimacy, that in terms of democratic access it was not meeting the demands of the people being affected by the plans. A planning process operating without any up-to-date or realistic statement of future policy, and applying personalised notions of design in a manner which has been described as a 'craft mystery outlook' (MCLOUGHLIN, 1973a, p. 135), was bound to bring about adverse public reaction. This came to be most pronounced in situations occurring in city centres, where the lack of foresight of population pressures or traffic demands caused great congestion. The new schemes devised to meet the problems created very great personal disruptions.

In the 1960s, the planned-for population in Great Britain came to many of the same conclusions as other similarly situated populations in democratic industrialised nations – that the formal representation allowed through the elected officials and the internal public inquiry method of review did not provide adequately for their views to be heard and acted upon. The planners could neither be made to start on new or needed projects, nor, once started on ill-conceived plans, could they be stopped.

As we saw in the first part of this book, this was partly blamed on the structure and size of the local authorities in charge of the decision-making. Few people actually used their representatives for help, and in general the elected members seemed unable, in many instances, to understand the technical, economic and sociological problems confronting local government, particularly in the planning area. As we saw, there were various institutional changes made in an attempt to provide a more rational local government structure, and a good deal of attention was focused upon internal management techniques to unify or integrate local government bureaucracies (see for instance FRIEND AND JESSOP's discussion of inter-departmental groups). The affected citizenry, however, began to complain rather vigorously that, irrespective of the size or management of local authorities, there simply was not any effective way of influencing the planners' decisions. To use the vernacular, there was no method by which the public could participate in the planning decisions affecting their lives.

For instance, in Norman Dennis's study of slum clearance in the last half of the 1960s, it was dramatically shown that the interest of the 'consumer' of the newly planned area played a 'minor part in the formulation of . . . the proposals' (DENNIS, 1970, p. 345). The planning decisions were based on policies of what the officials, not the affected public, thought that the public wanted. 'No attempt was made to ascertain what those interests were: the decision was reached by using an incorrect and outdated stereotype of the slum family, eager and impatient to be granted improved accommodation' (p. 345). Studies, such as those done by Dennis, showed that while the planners wielded tremendous power over the houses, property values and lives of individuals, they based those decisions on their own personal and often 'sociologically and politically naive' assumptions.

One of the major difficulties experienced by middle-class citizens, as well as the poorer groups investigated in Dennis's study, was that the decision-making process was hidden under a welter of very technical planning jargon. 'Rational' decision-making came, in the 1960s, to mean the use of techniques, often mathematical, that could confuse even the most educated of the public. Various studies began to show that the so-called facts which seemed to lead so determinably to the planners' decisions were actually based on their view of the end result (GREGORY). To meet this the planning system began to quantify even more of the items going into planning decisions. Thus, by the time of the famous Roskill Commission on the third London airport, even the most easily understood notions of peace and quiet had been reduced to numbers which could be added, subtracted and multiplied so as to produce an almost totally incomprehensible result (SELF, 1970). Not only was it difficult for members of the affected public to gain access to the planners, but once there it was becoming more and more difficult to understand what it was they were saying.

The attacks that were mounted on the planning machinery because of this lack of access and in some cases deliberate obfuscation (DENNIS, 1972) had two bases. First there was the general democratic or fairness argument, centred upon the usurpation of decision-making power by non-elected officials. This argument was much the same as that waged against other technocrats who, by assuming positions of responsibility while not being politically responsible themselves, were thought by some to be undermining the very basis of the British approach to local democracy. This argument was valuable as a tool, available to local conservation groups, for creating local opposition to particular projects. It did not seem, however, to influence central government as much as did the second basis of criticism, which was that it was simply a way to make very bad decisions.

One of the major reasons why local planning was making such obvious and, for central government, expensive mistakes was that they had little idea of the actual needs of those the planning was supposed to serve. This was particularly true in the lack of co-ordination between transport and housing. The siting of motorways next to council housing, or trunk roads next to schools, came to be an all too frequent news story. It became clear that the lack of an operational development plan and any clearly stated policy for planning which in reality integrated the served population's needs was causing a great deal of havoc in terms of actual spatial arrangement and land-use. In other words, the lack of an administrative vehicle to allow people access was making that process very inefficient.

This leads to the final controversy, which arose over the worth of the administrative review procedures. The value of public inquiries as the basic form of organised public participation in the planning process came into doubt. This was particularly true with reference to large open-ended 'planning' investigations, such as for development plans as opposed to specific plans for particular parcels. The specificity of an inquiry and the legal norms that came to be built into the process caused a great deal of comment upon the part of non-lawyers, who saw the 'judicialisation' of planning inquiries as a destruction of the right of 'ordinary' citizens to have access to the planners. In the words of one journalist, who also happened to serve on the Redcliffe-Maud Royal Commission on Local Government,

This has given the lawyers a chance to bend the public inquiry still further from its proper purpose. . . . this transforms the inquiry from a forum for the ascertainment of the public interest into a tribunal for the settlement of issues of right and justice between private property owners. . . .

80

Successive ministers have leaned over backwards to indulge this trend . . . ultimately to the point of abdicating their responsibility for making the final decision in respect of the small-scale developments which account for the great majority of planning appeals. Thereby the government itself has finally confirmed the popular misconception of the inspector as a judge and his recommendation as a verdict . . . and incidentally destroyed whatever value the appellate inquiry had as a means of public involvement in the planning process. (Derick Senior in COWAN AND DONNISON, p. 118)

Of course not all observers were as quick to indict the judicial character of public inquiries, nor as simplistic in their separation of private rights from the public interest, but there still was a large body of opinion to the effect that the public inquiry lent itself less well to certain types of decision-making. It was clear that legal representation was increasing, and in one study it was shown that some 75 per cent of all inquiries involved the use of lawyers (PAYNE). Even senior civil servants, such as Pamela Payne, began to worry publicly about both the intimidation involved in legal-style inquiry proceedings and the financial hardship of securing such representation.

In the most definitive study of the role of public inquiries in the planning process, the basic complaints against the forum were investigated to determine how sound they were (WRAITH AND LAMB). On the issue of over-judicialisation, after mentioning that some of the obvious trappings of a court proceeding are absent, the authors go on to say that as 'the matters in issue become weightier, the volume of paper increases, cross-examination becomes sharper, professional representation more expert. . . . Procedure inevitably becomes stricter and more formal and thus more intimidating to the ordinary person' (p. 318). Similarly, on the criticism of barristers' performances at inquiries, the study pointed out that the general feeling had come to be that the 'techniques of advocacy and the arts of legal combat, appropriate to the court . . . [are] . . . out of place at a public inquiry whose purpose is to determine how certain practical matters shall be arranged so as to bring the greatest good to the greatest number' (p. 318). While showing that barristers often gave an informed,

81

articulate and lucid presentation of the facts, it was also shown that 'they are prone to conduct attacks of a general nature [at the hearings] against [their clients'] alleged oppressors, rather than to isolate the particular issues that the inspector must primarily take into account' (p. 319).

The procedures of the public inquiry came to be viewed as a means for allowing deliberate delay upon the part of both planner and objector. The ordering and the cross-examination allowed for long, often tangential, discussions. Further, the mere volume and complexity of the supporting data came to present the outside citizen with a mass of paper work. Clearly, in the eyes of the critics, not only had the development plan not lived up to its promise to guide the control decisions, but the means of reviewing those plans were similarly inadequate. The public-inquiry procedure, while perhaps accepted for the appeal on a particular planning-permission refusal, was open to serious criticism as a tool for public involvement in the making of the plans themselves.

5 The Response: Reforming Plan-making

THE CONFUSION OF AIMS

It is evident from the preceding chapter that virtually everyone involved in the planning process came to see that there were certain problems in the fabric of planning. This was equally true of the bureaucrats who had to do the planning and the individuals who were being affected by those officials' decisions. However, just as we saw in Chapter 1 that there are major contradictions in the way in which the British perceive land and the reasons for the planning of its use, there are, similarly, contradictions in the reasons for, or aims of, reforming the planning system. In order to understand the changes introduced in the planning law and its procedures one has to start with those contradictions.

The most basic confusion has to do with where in fact planning intellectually and administratively takes place. As an administrative system, planning is divided between the forward-planning or future-planning process and the development-control, plan-implementing process. As we saw, this split is carried into the local authorities themselves and the staff and procedure divide the two functions, with different manpower, different career orientation and often different results. This is not because of inefficient management techniques, but it reflects an important division of opinion that can be seen throughout British planning. The split is between those who view the key to eventual outcomes as the process and procedure of articulating planning goals, and those who view the particularised *ad hoc* decision-making as at the heart of the process. It is the continuing tension between the concentration on matters of 'general strategy and policy' or the 'public interest' and the 'particularised rights', the 'individual' complainants and 'private interests', which explains a great deal about the reforms.

On the one hand, there is a strong body of opinion, particularly among the planning profession, that the course of future events is controlled or affected primarily by the policies of the government units. Thus, if the 'professional' could simply articulate these policies at a coherent and high enough level of abstraction, the development-control or implementation process could easily follow these 'policies' through. Systems and procedures are needed to allow for such high level abstraction upon the part of the planning official. Policy teams of officials should be engaged in continuous analysis of their policies, and planning theorists in developing models of planning operation to accommodate such a process (REDCLIFFE-MAUD COMMITTEE REPORT). It is this focus which brings forward the cybernetic models (MCLOUGHLIN, 1973a, chap. 8), the investigations of informational retrieval systems (CRIPPS AND HALL) and corporate planning. Inherent in this is a belief that the career government official can and does make policy and, because of his training and the information available, is capable of making statements that go beyond the particular choice of the day-to-day decision.

On the other hand there is a body of opinion to the effect that it is only the detailed decisions that are in fact in any way relevant. Some see the heart of the process as the application of very detailed decisions, either arrived at in a very specific plot-by-plot land map (KEEBLE) for a small circumscribed area or parcel by parcel. It is not only landowners and their lawyers who stress this importance and the uniqueness of each decision, but it is often also the view of the local-government officials in the development-control section. In interviews with local-government control officials the view is often put forward that 'we make our decisions on the merits of each case' and that the old-style development plans, or the new ones for that matter, will not be given excessive weight.

This ambivalence between the general and the specific, the abstract and the particular, guided the approaches to reforming the system. While it was an administrative overload which led to the actual reforms, they tended to follow this distinction, with the reform of the plan-making function virtually ignoring implementation or control and the more recent investigation of control reform ignoring the plan-making. This ambivalence was also involved in two further confusions which shed some light on the reforms, the first having to do with the correct role of central government.

We will consider at some length in the next chapter the particular procedures for allowing public access, but it should be noted from the start that there is no consensus of opinion as to what people should expect from the system. Should they be allowed to influence county-wide 'policy' or should that be left to the elected representatives? Was the purpose of the 'town and country planning legislation . . . to restrict development for the benefit of the public at large and not to confer new rights on any individual members of the public, whether they live close to, or far from the proposed development' (Salmon, J., in *Buxton* v. *Minister of Housing and Local Government* [1960] 3 All E.R. 408, at p. 411) or was it the legislative intention to give members of the public the right to influence a particular decision in their neighbourhood? This confusion is of particular importance when we try to discover how to have effective 'public participation' in a process whose end-product is to be abstract, 'policy' orientated, and thus extremely removed from any particular individual's remotest concern.

This ambivalence of the particular and general extends to a final area – the relationship between central government and the planning process. If the heart of planning is really in the creation of 'policy' documents, then the focus of central-government energy should be on systemising, co-ordinating and integrating the future plans of the local authorities. If, however, it is in reality with the day-to-day decisions, then central government should be concerned not so much with the broad sweep of the brush but the particular appeals on particular applications. Its energies, rather than being devoted to how to limit the number of appeals, should be applied to ensuring the appeals represent a cross-section of current plans and that their particular decisions guide similar decisions elsewhere.

With this in mind we can now proceed to the reaction of the government to the problems in the planning system. Throughout the 1950s there were continuous minor changes in the workings of the system through the ministerial circulars. These documents were meant to serve as guidelines to the local authority in carrying out the 1947 legislation. The case law developed by the courts around the meaning of the statute and particularly the workings of the control system similarly served as a guideline for the development of the legislation. There was also the occasional governmental investigation or reappraisal which directly affected the workings of the system, and in particular the working of the plan-implementing, or development-control process. The most noteworthy of these was perhaps the already mentioned Franks Report of 1957. Franks firmly supported the idea of enlarging the review role of the inquiry and fundamentally altering its workings by requiring the publication of inspectors' decisions (FRANKS, p. 98). The Committee also suggested the creation of a supervisory body to scrutinise the workings of all the administrative agencies (FRANKS, p. 130). The resulting Council on Tribunals serves as a forum for complaints and a watchdog on arbitrary or unfair procedures in the public inquiry process.

Various statutory changes were also introduced in the first fifteen years of the system's operation, which are important to note. As we saw in Chapter 4 the financial provisions of the 1947 Act were eliminated by the Conservative Government under the 1953 and 1954 Acts but, apart from these, fundamental changes were not made in the early years. The T.C.P.A. of 1959 concentrated on the implementation side of the system, with some strengthening of the enforcement system, and such particular changes as the extension of reverse compulsory purchase or the purchase-notice system to land which had been planned (blighted) for future public development. Also on the plan-making side of the equation an attempt was made to bring forward informal plans for specific sub-areas. The most important of these was the introduction of the Town Centre Maps in 1962 which was an attempt to formalise renewal schemes for urban areas. (TOWN CENTRES BULLETIN)

No concentrated reappraisal or rethinking of the operation of the system was made until the mid-1960s. This was not really contemplated until the public inquiry review structure in central government was deluged under some 13,620 appeals in 1964. The spur to reform came, not from the general disquiet about the system, but from a particular administrative overload. And the approach to that reform concentrated on the general, the policy-making side of the system. Without giving away the plot the administration is, some ten years later, still heavily 'overloaded'.

THE PLANNING ADVISORY GROUP

In 1964 the Government appointed a group to review the planning system and suggest ways to deal with the delay and poor-quality results. This group, the Planning Advisory Group, was made up of twenty-one members, who were conspicuous for both their experience in the local and central administration and for their identification with it. Eleven were local officials, eight were in the central government and two were planning consultants. There were no academics, no representatives of tenants or amenity groups, nor, more importantly, any local councillors. In the words of one very vehement critic: 'There was absolutely no representative of the outside public interest. Undoubtedly it was a most curiously constituted group' (T. SHARP, p. 209). But it was the P.A.G. which created an entirely new approach, which has been accepted by both the major political parties and all governments since they wrote their report.

The P.A.G. was faced with a number of possible options. They had to decide first where the trouble lay, in the general or the specific. If they took the specific they would have had to deal with the day-to-day functioning of the system. The *ad hoc* case-by-case permission system could not be tampered with to any great extent without throwing a great deal of the system away. There was the option of attempting to change the system to allow for a great deal of development, within specified areas, as of right. In much the same way that American cities follow zones for permitted development, Britain could have eliminated a good deal of the work load on a case-by-case basis by relying on a 'plan' that would in fact control development, rather than relying on a 'plan' which, while interesting, depended on case-by-case decision for actual control. In one paper presented recently by an American Professor of Law the option was put in the following terms: 'Control is too detailed in England and . . . more control should be exercised by general rule rather than by permissions . . . the £5 million annual cost [of development control] is substantial . . . can England afford the cost?' (HAGMAN, 1973, p. 1165)

The P.A.G. did not, however, chose the specific, but rather focused on the process of plan-making. They wanted to institute a change 'which would distinguish between the policy or strategic decision on the one hand and the detailed or tactical decisions on the other' (P.A.G., p. iii). Even in their concentration upon this abstract level they were faced with a number of choices; they could either have gone for long-range physical planning, or again concentrated on local sub-area plans. They eventually decided to concentrate on a fairly traditional approach to long-range physical plans, but to present them in non-categorical physical terms. In other words they chose to state the policy in words, without having to state it in an on-the-ground map. Their most significant contribution was to attempt to wed the long-range plans to the major communicational lines, those important determinants of urban form; of these the most important was transport.

The P.A.G. statement of objectives in fact pointed to their results. Once they decided that what was wanted ᵗwas to 'strengthen the policy content' of development plans and 'to get the level of responsibility right, so that only matters of general policy and major objectives are submitted for ministerial approval' (P.A.G., p. 1), they had already gone a long way towards suggesting reforms. In Thomas Sharp's words:

> P.A.G. wanted to reduce physical plans as far as may be to mere policy documents. That, and to keep the public as much in the dark as possible, so far as the practical details of the application of the policy are concerned. In spite of their declared hopes in other directions [their main] concern [is] . . . to get rid of the tiresome objections and the public obsession with detail which they believe have been impediments to planning and the prime cause of delay in the planning process . . . these proposals could achieve what the Group mainly seem to want to achieve – to make planning easier for the planners. (T. SHARP, p. 209)

The scheme was fairly straightforward. Development control was to remain as it was: 'we recommend no change . . . the present system of development control is basically sound and can work efficiently' (P.A.G., sec. 1, para. 11). 'The plan-making system however does not serve their various purposes satisfactorily and the delays they incur aggravate their defects. . . . The present development plan system is too detailed for some purposes and not detailed enough for others' (P.A.G., sec. 1, para. 30, sec. 1, para. 31). So the plan-making system should be replaced with a new one. The idea was to bifurcate the process; on the top level, for the counties and urban areas, would be a structure plan. This would deal in 'policies, objectives and standards rather than in the detailed and static land-use allocation' (P.A.G., sec. 2, para. 5). These policy documents would 'establish the land-use transport relationship in an integrated way' (P.A.G., sec. 1, para. 35). They would also pinpoint those 'action areas' for concentrated development. On the second level there would be a local plan which would translate these policies into a local and more important map form.

There are two important points to note about these proposals for reform. The first is the relationship between central government and the local units. Since the P.A.G. went on the assumption that what was important was plan-making, by dividing that process into a policy and local map-making exercise, central government could concern itself only with 'those matters in which the Minister has an interest'. The original Barlow idea of national co-ordination and national policy-making can thus be seen to resurface here. Since planning was viewed as a process which can be guided or steered from the top, then by separating off the steering the full energies of central government could be focused here, and it is here that a system of review was needed. Similarly since these articulated policies would control local plan-making (basically a map based on the policies) then there is no need for central government to review these local plans.

The second important point is that the hope of the high-level (some might say rarefied) investigation was to return planning to a consideration of factors other than specific land-uses. The idea was to accent a process of policy-making, and to integrate into that process a consideration of the social and economic factors which should go into a final development permission. The attempt to follow up the Buchanan Report, which emphasised the administrative separations between those planning roads and those planning everything else by integrating transport planning into what had before been land-use planning, was a significant change. Similarly, the emphasis in the P.A.G. was on the close relationship between the economic implications of local decisions to regional development (P.A.G., sec. 1, para. 44) and a much more sophisticated plan-maker was called for than had heretofore existed.

What is important here is that the procedure was evidently viewed as a method of taking the 'regional context' down to the local level. This is likely to be primarily concerned with creating the conditions for economic growth in some regions and controlling the pace of growth in others, within the framework of national economic planning. 'As a part of this process they will have to be concerned with physical planning issues which are of regional significance, with the over-all distribution of population and employment, green-belt policy and any other limitations on growth in the conurbations' (P.A.G., sec. 1, para. 44). Thus the original idea of having national planning and national co-ordination, which had been so easily lost sight of amongst the welter of obsolete, much delayed, development plans, was resurrected at this new structure-plan level.

THE 1967 WHITE PAPER AND THE INTRODUCTION OF THE 1968 LEGISLATION

The central government followed up the P.A.G. proposals in spite of the fact that there was a drop in housing demand, their administrative overload had disappeared and that the total appeal level had dropped to a mere 8000 appeals by 1969. It was generally accepted that reform of the procedure at the generalised level would greatly improve the speed and results. In order to implement the P.A.G. proposals there was to be:

(1) A structure plan submitted for ministerial approval: this would be primarily a written statement of policy accompanied by a diagrammatic structure map for counties and major towns only, designed to expose clearly the broad basic pattern of development and the transport system. These structure plans would form the main link between policies on a national and regional level and local planning. . . .
(2) Action area plans . . . to be adopted locally: and . . . other local plans, to meet local needs, again to be adopted locally. (1967 WHITE PAPER)

The White Paper emphasised 'consultation', but did not specify what that meant.

Based on these proposals the Government introduced the 1968 Town and Country Planning Act. It was an attempt that, at least in the eyes of its proponents, was to provide a very great improvement. As Anthony Greenwood, the Government Minister on planning matters, said, the new two-part process would 'complete integration into the planning process of land use, transport and investment programmes, and for the integrated approach to the examination and approval of plans'.* There emerged from the debate a general consensus that the correct focus for reform was at the level of policy-making and that the new procedures for that process would eliminate delay and 'rationalise' planning. It seems that politicians accepted the premise of the government officials making up the P.A.G. that the concern with 'policy' and the elimination of 'detail' was important. For example Mr Greenwood went on to state that:

> This hiving off of local detail is the only workable way of unclogging the machine and doing away with the intolerable delays, often a matter of years, . . . which will be with us permanently if central government is going to have to continue to deal with the objections that may be made on any line drawn on any map for any part of the country.†

Even the Opposition joined in this hearty endorsement. Geoffrey Rippon, later to be Minister in the Conservative Government, said: 'This represents a major devolution of power from central government to local governments, the first such change since the Barlow report in 1940 advocated stronger central direction and the most significant change in planning in nearly a quarter of a century.'‡

While there were not any criticisms to the effect that the entire premise of the reform was wrong, there were some notes of caution to the effect that the programme presupposed two very basic conditions. The first was that the new planning needed a system of local government which ensured that the plan-making authority had jurisdiction over enough of the social, economic, and land-use factors to be able to logically make 'policy' strategy over those areas. In the words of Graham Page, M.P., unless the local authorities 'were right this bill will not work'.§ There was a consensus that the reforms presupposed new local authorities based on the then as yet unpublished Redcliffe-Maud recommendations. This was why the re-shaping of the planning approach should precede or, in the words of the Minister, 'move progressively along with and in

---

* *Hansard, 1967–8*, vol. 757 (31 Jan. 1968) p. 1363.
† Ibid. p. 1366.
‡ Ibid. p. 1377.
§ Ibid. p. 1461.

advance of local government reorganisation'. Little did they then suspect how unregional or unsuitable the actual reorganisation might in fact turn out to be.

The second note of caution was that an adequate procedure for public objections was not allowed for in the new system. Since the structure plan would not be related to specific parcels of land it was realised, even as the Bill was introduced, that there would be little incentive for local property-owners to bother with the plans. However, since the action area and local plans must conform to the structure plans it might be too late to complain at the later point when the landowner actually was affected. As Derek Walker-Smith said, rather than being a devolution of power of decision-making from central bureaucrats to local citizens it was a devolution of power to lower bureaucrats with less, not more local citizens' interaction and no central-government review.*

THE 1968 ACT

The legislation calls initially for a survey:

> It shall be the duty of the local planning authority to institute a survey of their area . . . examining the matters which may be expected to affect the development of that area or the planning of its development and in any event to keep all such matters under review . . . [they] shall include the following. . . .
> (a)   The principal physical and economic characteristics of the area of the authority (including the principal purpose for which land is used) . . .
> (b)   The size composition and distribution of the population of that area . . .
> (c)   . . . the communications, transport system and traffic . . .

and then for the preparation of the structure plan, a written statement:

> (a)   Formulating the local planning authority's policy and general proposals in respect of the development and other use of land in that area (including measures for the improvement of the physical environment and the management of traffic);

---

* Ibid. p. 1397.

(b)   stating the relationship of those proposals to general proposals for the development and other use of land in neighbouring areas which may be expected to affect that area

having regard to
current policies with respect to the economic planning and development of the region as a whole the resources likely to be available for the carrying out of the proposal for the structure plan [and indicating]: land . . . (an 'action area') which they have selected for the commencement during a prescribed period of comprehensive treatment. (T.C.P.A., 1971, part II, sections 6, 7).

It is thus an attempt to put in a statute a process of tremendous complexity. We will look carefully at how this procedure is supposed to work and in fact does work (particularly the publicity and review by central government) in the next three chapters. Under the Act, once the procedure of preparation, publicity and approval has been dealt with, then the local authorities (at the time of the 1968 Act it was assumed that the policy plan-makers would also be the local plan-makers and controlling or plan-implementing agency) can prepare local plans which would consist of:

A map and a written statement [which] formulate[s] in such detail as the authority think appropriate the authorities' proposals for the development and other use of land. . . . In formulating their proposals in a local plan the local planning authority shall secure that the proposals conform generally to the structure plan as it stands for the time being (T.C.P.A., 1971, sec. 11).

THE DUTIES OF THE NEW LOCAL GOVERNMENTS UNDER THE 1968 ACT

When the then Ministry of Housing and Local Government made its submission to the Redcliffe-Maud Royal Commission on Local Government they stated that in order to implement the 'more relevant and more technically sophisticated' structure plans, they 'should be submitted for ministerial approval, but that there should be a much greater devolution of responsibilities to local government for the preparation of a wide range of local plans. Such a system could not be put into full effect until the local government is reorganised by the creation of much larger planning units' (REDCLIFFE-MAUD COMMISSION REPORT, vol. 1, p. 31). As we saw, a unified single tier or even the new city-region types of authority were not in fact the end-product of the reorganisation attempt. In fact, what occurred was a reimposition of a two-tier system with the only major changes in physical jurisdiction taking place at the second or district level. What is important to understand is that the new planning reforms had to be adapted to this two-tier local-authority system.

The method of fitting the planning reforms to the local-government reforms again followed this split between the general and the specific, but carried it to a degree which even the members of the P.A.G. might feel a bit excessive. The counties or upper tier will do the structure plans, and the policy formulation will thus be established for areas of some size. However, the local plans, which are meant actually to relate the 'policy' to a map and thus to people's property, will be done by a different level of government, namely the local districts, who will carry the plans out through the imposition of the day-to-day permission or control work. While the upper tier will have the powers to establish (through a 'development-plan scheme') which districts will draft local plans, and will determine when and where local plans should be made, it will in most instances be the lower-level districts who make these plans.

The 1971 Town and Country Planning Act (incorporating the 1968 legislation) simply says that 'the local planning authority' shall submit a structure plan (T.C.P.A., 1971, sec. 7). The 1972 Local Government Act delegates the survey and structure-plan functions to the county planning authority, and requires the county to make a development-plan scheme which will designate which level of government shall prepare local plans for each area, establish the programme for such preparation, and indicate the relationship between the structure and local plans (1972 Local Government Act, sec. 183, amending sections 6–10 of the 1971 T.C.P.A.). The county planning authority must certify whether the district's local plan is in conformance generally with the county structure plan. If the county and district disagree as to this general conformance, the central government can review the matter and, where necessary, direct the county to issue such a certificate of conformance (section 182, schedule 16[3]). As the Secretary of State for the Environment said during the debate on the Bill in the House of Commons 'If a local plan, prepared by a district, and the structure plan do not agree, it will be a matter of arbitration by the Minister'*

The most important aspect of this 1972 change was not only that it separated the structure and local plans between the county and district, but that it also laid the groundwork for endless inter-authority disputes by reversing some of the district authorities' powers as the development-control authority for the county in situations where there is a 'county matter' involved. Generally the district authority, not the county, is to decide on applications for planning permission, a determination on the need for permission under Section 53 of the Planning Act, or on applications for an established use certificate under Section 94 (Local Government Act, 1972, section 182, schedule 16[15]). However, in determining any such application 'which appears to the district planning authority to relate to a county matter [it] shall be exercised by the county planning authority' (schedule 16[15] para. 2), except in cases where the district was going to refuse such planning permission anyway. Thus, under the legislative scheme, the district must send a copy of all applications to the county and then argue about whether the matter is, or is not, a county matter. The 1972 legislation was not particularly helpful in defining this term (schedule 16[32]). It categorised a number of types of application which would fall under the heading, such as mineral workings, tips, matters relating to national parks, or prescribed uses. It then went on to include any application for the use of land which 'would conflict with, or prejudice the implementation of, fundamental provisions of the structure plan for the area in question'. (Local Government Act 1972, section 182, schedule 16[32a])

The statute was, however, rather silent as to how the district or county were to determine when any individual application was of such importance that it was in conflict with what was fundamental to a structure plan. Presumably various local authorities will disagree on what matters are, or are not, county

---

* *Hansard* (16 Nov. 1971) vol. 826, col. 283.

matters under such a definition, and such disagreements will occur regularly.

What happened then was that the 1972 Local Government Bill instead of leaving the county-level planning authorities in charge of plan-making and plan-implementing, actually created a second tier of 370 plan-implementing districts. The reaction to this from the professional planning spokesman was, as might be expected, vehement:

Technically and professionally the planning process embracing development plans (structure and local plans) and the control of development, are indivisible. The [Royal Town Planning] Institute therefore favoured the unitary authority . . . because it foresaw that the quality of the planning services would be impaired by a division of the planning function and because such arrangement would inevitably be artificial and complex. (R.T.P.I. MEMORANDUM)

There was similar outspoken comment on the Local Government Bill by M.P.s. John Roper said:

On planning we must remember that one of the strongest arguments for reorganisation of local governments was to have large organisations that could plan a whole area at one time. . . . I am sceptical whether the concept enshrined in the 1968 and 1971 Town and Country Planning Acts, of the local planmaking authority being the judge and jury in its own case [by not having central-government review of local plans] would have been accepted by the house at the time if we had imagined that there would be 350 local planning authorities responsible for this important quasi-judicial function.*

The most important criticism brought forward by the groups representing the planning officials and the M.P.s in the debate was that there simply were not enough people trained in the area of planning to man 400 planning departments throughout the country. We will follow this argument through in Chapter 10 when we look at the control at local level, but for the moment it is enough to note that even at the time the government system was being fitted with its new structure-plan dress there were those who agreed with John Silkin when he said that in

* *Hansard* (July 1972) vol. 835, col. 312.

terms of experienced manpower the 'new authorities would be strained'!

We shall proceed now to see how the upper-tier county level is actually supposed to go about the procedure of creating that abstract document known as a structure plan. We will concentrate on the procedures for public access and the very different system of central government administrative review. From this we can see how local governments are actually going about the process and speculate on the usefulness of the end-product. This in turn will allow us to return from the, at times, high altitudes of policy to the more recent discussions of, and attempts at, reforming the plan-implementation or development-control process.

6 The Reformed Plan-making Procedure

The title of this chapter might have been: how to plan the future taking into account the views of the planned in a short enough time not to have the final product appear in the past. What we shall be concerned with is both the techniques for local-government officials to articulate policy, and the procedures for allowing changes in these statements of policy either through the influence of certain of the affected public or through central government.

TECHNIQUE

In order to go about the task of creating this strange new animal called a structure plan, the local authorities were given guidance through a series of central government publications: the *Regulations* (REGULATIONS, 1972), a *Development-Plans Manual* (MANUAL, 1970), a *Management-Networks Study* (NETWORKS, 1971), and various circulars. Starting from a very elementary level the structure plan is defined as a 'plan for a county, county borough or large or important area which formulates policy and general proposals, and which is subject to the Minister's approval', with the key word 'structure' meaning: 'aspects of the social economic and physical systems of an area that are subject to planning control or influence.' (MANUAL, p. 98)

The idea is that 'the plan should be designed to satisfy social and economic aspirations as far as possible, through the creation of an efficient physical structure, and a good environment: the policies should be set out to provide a framework for the continuous process of making planning decisions, and the proposals should be expressed as firm statements of intended action' (MANUAL 2.2). Thus the concept is very close to that of the American master plan, a document which in Charles Haar's words is 'a source of information, a programme for correction, an estimate of the future, an indicator of goals, a technique for coordination and a device for stimulating public interest and responsibility' (HAAR, 1959). The problem in the

United States has been that since the master plan is a statement of 'policy' and again 'by theory and by law, mere indications of future policy' it is virtually ignored by all decision-makers at the federal, state, and local zoning-board levels. In the United States it is worth noting that, in many academics' eyes, the more abstract and 'policy' orientated the document becomes the more 'this master plan plaything of the planning department is routinely ignored by departments that have operational responsibility not only for building things but for planning them . . . [In the United States] . . . governmental bodies, particularly executive and legislative bodies, only make plans for the ritual of it' (HAGMAN, 1973, p. 164). Such being the case in the United States, perhaps we should look carefully at the central government's instructions to see how, in their own words, the intentions of the local authority will 'not be submerged in technical data, nor confused with general expressions of good intent' (MANUAL, 12.9) without relying on 'two-dimensional land allocations in . . . maps'. (MANUAL 1.8)

Under the *Regulations* the written statement is supposed to look some twenty years into the future; in the *Manual* it is referred to as – 'look forward over twenty or thirty years'. What is required evidently is some type of growth projection for the basics of population, employment and housing. In fact the twelve areas which must be dealt with cover most of the breadth of human existence: population, employment, housing, industry and commerce, transportation, shopping, education, social and community service, recreation and leisure, conservation, townscape and landscape, and utility services.

The process is to begin with a survey of the existing situation in each of these areas and then to attempt a forecast of each of the areas in which growth will take place and thus determine the physical land resources which will be necessary. The initial stages of the endeavour are occupied with trying to define the main parameters within which growth might take place. The *Manual* includes an elaborate list of headings that should be covered in the survey and the follow-up circulars and advice from central government on possible statistical ways to measure or forecast growth. What was not laid down, however, was a specific method that had to be followed, and since the method of counting or forecasting to a great extent determines the results, it was here that there was to be a good deal of

99

intergovernmental dispute depending on what forecast was desired.

Once the basic information is gathered the authority is to then select out the various land-use policies, in particular to decide how much growth is envisaged in each urbanised area, in order to meet the problems presented by the survey forecasts. This gives the local authority a variety of possible strategies (less growth in the north of the county, more in the south, more high-rise flats, fewer parking facilities, and so on). Since the possible factors even in a fairly small area give rise to infinite permutations and combinations the local authority is expected to select a few main policy choices or alternative strategies, and then seek to have some 'feedback' or comment on them from the citizens of the neighbouring localities.

Based on this survey data, possible strategies, and comment, the local officials are then to arrive at a draft proposal. Like the final structure plan, this proposal is a written document with an attached diagramatic map. Diagramatic is supposed to mean 'generalised illustration in a plan, usually to an approximate scale and not on a topographical base' (MANUAL). However, as might be expected, this means in fact that people cannot really tell what land-use is projected, although perhaps Sharp rather exaggerates when he says that 'the public will be treated as a collection of children to be fobbed off with pictures reduced to a level of elementary simplicity' (T. SHARP, p. 209). It is this draft plan which is then presented for public review, and public 'representations' or objections are then taken, usually through a series of meetings. The authority adjusts the plan to meet the representations, and the final draft is then ready for submission to the central government and for a formal administrative review.

The way in which a group of local government employees is supposed to go about this task brings into focus two central issues: the way local officials can attempt to co-ordinate the different tasks and services they provide; and the difficulties of planning future land-use across inter-authority lines without mentioning which land.

First, one of the major interests of the late 1960s and early 1970s among local government officials was 'corporate planning', which means a management structure in a local authority which correlates the direction of the various separate services delivered by local government and attempts to save money and bureaucratic energy by eliminating duplication. Since corporate planning is to be concerned with the 'social, economic and physical systems of an area so far as they are affected or can be affected by the activities of the authority' (STEWART AND EDDISON, p. 367) it fits in very nicely with the all-encompassing approach envisaged in structure planning. The corporate-planning idea is one of an on-going and self-correcting process.

The introduction of the structure-planning idea provided a means for a somewhat specific plan dealing with land that could be seen as a model for various concerns of the local authority. The central government used the structure-planning process as a model for how to create an internal group which can be self-correcting. The management-network scheme created had a dual purpose, and thus the flow chart shown in Figure 6.1 is interesting not only because it shows us how the authorities were to go about structure plan-making but also a possible approach to many of their activities.

The difficulty was that, while structure planning might point to a way to make policy in one field, it was nevertheless a single document requiring specific approval and merely hoping for 'continuous monitoring' to keep it current (see EDDISON). Thus it could not serve as a Bible for all of local-authority decision-making.

A second important point was brought out by the instructions which central government gave to the local authorities, and that was a basic internal inconsistency of approach. The *Manual* was muddled about how the local authorities were to go about planning all the inter-related factors when in fact they basically had decision-making power in one area only, namely the permission system under development control, and did not have any decision-making power in a myriad of other related areas (for example, most transport decisions, trunk roads, and so on). While the plans were to consider over-all investment in an area, they could not control future budgets in any meaningful way, or in fact do anything but guide the physical land-use. The central government thus did not come to terms with the 'land-use' dominance of these documents, which were supposedly going beyond that stage. Similarly, the *Manual* recognised that the interlocked spheres of influence of educa-

101

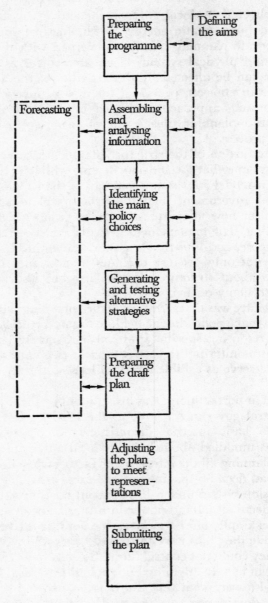

FIGURE 6.1
SOURCE: *Management Networks – a Study for Structure Plans*
(Department of the Environment, 1971).

tion, employment and recreation, will seldom fit nicely into the physical boundaries of the local authorities but could do no more than recommend that local authorities co-operate in this planning. The 1972 legislation even allowed for joint structure-planning efforts by neighbouring authorities, but this hardly creates a 'structurally plannable area which internalises the major problems with which a structure plan has to deal, and so make them solvable at local government level' (SENIOR, p. 3). It is this type of inconsistency which will help explain some of the gaps in the first actual documents prepared under the reformed procedures.

ACCESS

With this skeleton of the procedure in mind we can continue to the development of the procedures for allowing those people who will have to live with the controls based on the local and structure plan to have some part in their formulation. The draft structure and draft local plans, after having been prepared by the planners, had to be approved by the local councils, which allows for an input from the planned through the rather normal means of representative democracy. What we will deal with here are the methods adopted to make up for the shortcomings, supposed or otherwise, of the elected-representative system. This question of access, of public involvement, in the creation of plans really has two different focuses. First, there is the question of public participation in the creation and preparation of the development plans, and second, there is a formal central-government review, which attempts to co-ordinate the views not only of the affected local populace but also of the central government and neighbouring authorities.

The question of what 'public participation' means is certainly not one that there is any consensus about among those being affected by planning decisions and those making the planning decisions. As we saw, the complaints from one side of the counter seem to be based on a lack of fairness, a lack of real democracy or 'the ability to control one's life', and from the other on a lack of efficiency in correctly forecasting the public's needs. Just as it was an overloading of the administrative appeal system which spurred the central government into devising the new approach to planning, it was a concentration of this second view, on the need for plan-making to keep track of

103

the effects of planning decisions on its affected public, which spurred an investigation of possible techniques of public participation. With the passage of the 1968 Town and Country Planning Act, the Government of the day appointed a committee on public participation in planning, chaired by A. M. Skeffington, M.P., and it is this Committee's Report which serves as the guide for the inclusion of the public in the making of structure and local plans.

PUBLIC PARTICIPATION IN THE UNITED STATES

Before examining these recommendations, and the statutory provisions (few as they are) implementing them, we must consider the setting in 1968. While the problems with public participation in the United Kingdom were only beginning to surface in that year, the United States was already deeply involved in a set of programmes that attempted to share decision-making power among both traditional local-government units and the residents who were to be served by the programmes. These programmes had various aims and a wide variety of approaches. Some, such as most of the housing programmes, were based primarily on the existing local governmental approval and delivery system. Others, such as the demonstration or model cities programme, or some of the educational programmes, sought to establish either parallel local-delivery systems or entirely new, area-wide or municipality-wide government structures. While this is not the place to delve deeply into the great arguments concerning 'maximum feasible participation of the residents' in plans affecting them, a brief note on the American experience and particularly on the one American programme mentioned by the Skeffington Committee is in order.

The setting for the public-participation wars in the United States was the attempted administration of a number of federal programmes designed both to rebuild and restructure urban areas, and under the Economic Opportunity Act of 1964 to wage a much publicised war on poverty. The early legislation in the 1950s for federal programmes carried a requirement that to qualify for urban renewal funds, for instance, there should be a 'citizens advisory committee to examine constructively the workable program goals' (HAGMAN, 1971, p. 178). But by the mid-1960s an attempt was made to establish local programmes which would not only be consultative with existing local governments but would be manned and administered by the affected populace. According to Professor Moynihan it was supported by the Federal Government Bureau of the Budget, the chief funder of such programmes, as a way to make the most efficient project in terms of local people making local plans for local needs. Its results however were quite disappointing:

> First a period of organizing, with much publicity and great expectations everywhere. Second, the beginning of operations, with the onset of conflict between the [local public participation] agency and local government institutions, with even greater publicity. Third, a period of counter-attack from local government, not infrequently accompanied by conflict and difficulties including accounting troubles, within the agency itself. Fourth, victory for the established institution, or at best, stalemate, accompanied by bitterness and charges of betrayal. Whatever else had occurred, the quest for community had failed. (MOYNIHAN, p. 78)

This same formula, of allowing the affected people to form a mini-government for the particular programme or plan-making, was varied to allow for the sharing of local power for the programmes between the elected existing representatives of local government and representative groups of local citizens. But here again it was not particularly successful. The citizens' groups did not really believe that the federal and local governments actually wanted to share power. The model cities programmes ended in most instances in stalemates between the three centres of power, often without the funds ever actually being spent. To the local citizens' groups, seeking to 'participate' but actually being denied the decision-making power, this was often a very frustrating and rarely productive activity. In one article, called ironically 'Maximum Feasible Manipulation', one spokesman put it thus:

> No matter what H.U.D. says, model cities is first and foremost a politician's game. Although the mountains of H.U.D. guidelines and technical bulletins insist that model cities is a technical planning process, everyone but community people seems to know by now that it's really a political process. (NORTH CITY AREA WIDE COUNCIL INC., p. 37)

105

Since these political disputes led to frequent court cases, the occasional violent confrontation at public meetings and very little real planning being done *by* the people whom the programmes were supposed to serve, it was not this aspect of American public participation which was particularly attractive to the English advisers. In Britain in the late 1960s the hope of public participation was to make planning in particular easier, not harder – to eliminate the unnecessary development that would not be used or that would cost a great deal. There was, however, a second type of 'public participation' being attempted in the United States, which was not attached to federally funded national-spending programmes. This was a method of planning *with* people, at the local level. The idea was that while schemes to give the planned-for populace actual decision-making power did not seem to work, there could be methods devised to include the people and their views in the preparation stages of planning schemes.

The archetypal model was that used in Los Angeles to consult the city's people in the preparation of a comprehensive general plan. During the five years of consultation and preparation the professional staff had made up a series of four different possible plans for the city. These alternatives were, low density, dispersion or medium density, growth along corridors based on radial mass transit, and metropolitan concentration around centres. The idea was that the best possible model could only be selected based on the views of the people living in the city, so a series of committees were devised to find out what the people felt on the four choices. By using a series of town meetings throughout the urban area, which described the alternatives through the use of films and displays, the planners hoped to be able to receive back enough of the views of the people to select the 'correct' alternative.

The Los Angeles programme was felt to be very successful by those involved in the process. Some 10,000 people came to the meetings held at over sixty centres. There was a series of questionnaires sent to various samples of people which resulted in over 50,000 replies. The people on the committees then used this material to write a report setting up recommendations on the area's general plan. This report contained some interesting but obvious data on the feelings of the people in the area (such as they like the weather and single-family homes)

106

and some very sound goals about what the good life should be.

The difficulty with the Los Angeles approach, however, was that no real planning decisions (who gets what where) were really made or even recommended. In the words of an English observer: 'the report reads like the liberal Bible, applied to the problems of Los Angeles . . . [they] produced worthy goals, very often in general and undefined terms.' Maurice Ash goes on to say that the only part of the report which would have any real impact was the specific recommendations on design concepts, but that the committee declined to make specific recommendations, stating that it doubted 'whether the alternative concepts are a subject which can be meaningfully evaluated by the public at large through questionnaires or superficial exposure.' (ASH, p. 1069)

As it happened, the Los Angeles general plan was not enacted in the 1960s and to this day there is still no such plan. In retrospect those who looked at the public-participation attempt in Los Angeles in the light of the rapid decline in metropolitan growth and the current problems with fuel for automobile transport have found the proposed plans virtually useless. There are even those who ask whether there was any point at all in going through the expensive and time-consuming process. (HAGMAN, 1973, p. 213)

THE SKEFFINGTON REPORT

It was against this backcloth that the Skeffington Report was written. As Damer and Hague have said, this American experience was just one of a number of factors influencing the growth of the idea of public participation. Mixed in with this were a number of trains of thought: the evolution of planning since Ebenezer Howard's day as a social ideology, a growth in the idea of participation as a substitute for electoral democracy, the continuing unrest with the slowness and inefficiency of the administrative process, and of course the then-blossoming political interest in the environment (DAMER AND HAGUE). One of the difficulties this wide base of interest presented was that the term came to mean a variety of things to a variety of people.

The meaning of the term 'public participation' has been discussed extensively, but perhaps Arnstein's ladder of citizen participation, Figure 6.2, is the most useful tool for under-standing the importance of the various shades of meaning. In England, with the American experience in mind, there was not a great deal of official sentiment for the creation of community groups with political power separate from the elected poli-ticians, that is for any programme that went beyond rung 5. There was, however, interest in preventing possible obstruction (some would say for the purpose of diffusing the community's spirit), educating the public, and supplementing the workforce of the local government officials, that is, in Arnstein's vocabulary, rungs 1 to 4.

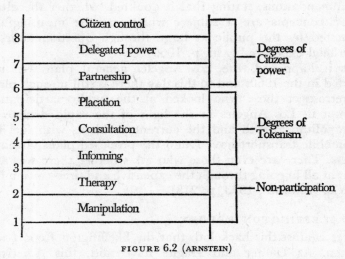

FIGURE 6.2 (ARNSTEIN)

The Skeffington Committee definitely chose a mode of public participation which means, at the most, public consul-tation in the Los Angeles style at rung 4, rather than a meaning which would involve the sharing of actual policy determination. The problem with the report, however, was that it did not really come to terms with this choice, and, as we shall see, the debate between those in local government who view the process as consultative and those outside who view it as a partnership or vehicle for citizens' control has caused no little trouble.

The Report of the Committee was basically a 'how to do it' document for plan-making authorities with nine basic recom-mendations listed below with my comments. (SKEFFINGTON REPORT, p. 47)

(1) People should be kept informed throughout the preparation of a structure or local plan for their area. A variety of methods should be used, and special efforts made to secure the co-operation of the local press and broadcasting. [Good public relations.]

(2) An initial statement should be published when the decision is made that a plan should be prepared. It should state how the authority proposes to inform the public and should contain a time scale showing the main opportunities for participation and pauses for their consideration. Although there should be full opportunity for public debate it should not run on endlessly. [A plan for consultation should be made.]

(3) Representations should be considered continuously as they are made while plans are being prepared; but, in addition, there should be set pauses to give a positive opportunity for public reaction and participation. [The views expressed will be 'considered' but they will not necessarily determine the decision.]

(4) Local planning authorities should consider convening meetings in their area for the purpose of setting up community forums. These forums would provide local organisations with the opportunity to discuss planning collectively . . . and might also have administrative functions. [Here we have the Los Angeles style meeting to consult with the affected citizenry; educational. Also a means of supplementing the local planning workforce through volunteer labour.]

(5) Local planning authorities should seek to publicise proposals in a way that informs people living in the area to which the plan relates. These efforts should be directed to organisations and individuals. Publicity should be sufficient to enable those wishing to participate in depth to do so. [Good public relations means the prevention of possible obstructions later – tokenism.]

(6) Community-development officers should be appointed to secure the involvement of those people who do not join organisations. Their job would be to work with people, to stimulate discussion, to inform people and give their views to the authority. [Definitely a potential here for organising groups to try to share decision-making power with the local authority. This idea was rejected by the central government.]

(7) The public should be told what their representations

109

have achieved or why they have not been accepted. [Again a device for preventing possible future obstructions.]

(8) People should be encouraged to participate in the preparation of plans by helping with surveys and other activities as well as by making comments. [Supplementing the local planning workforce through volunteer labour.]

(9) Better knowledge of planning is necessary. Greater efforts should be made to provide more information and better education about planning generally, both through educational establishments and for the public at large. Only if there is a better public understanding of the purpose of planning and the procedures involved will a local planning authority's efforts be fully rewarded when they seek public participation in their own development plans. [The prevention of future possible obstructions depends on the acceptance of the validity of the process by the planned-for populace.]

So the Skeffington recommendations, apart from the call for a community-relations officer, seem really to point towards participation in the sense of consultation, education and the prevention of obstruction. They do not call for the sharing of decision-making power with any members of the affected citizenry. The community relations officer concept was rejected and the required criteria was for adequate 'publicity' in connection with the preparation of plans. The provisions are much the same for local and structure plans so a look at the structure-plan section (T.C.P.A., 1971, Section 8) will suffice:

When preparing a structure plan for their area and before finally determining its content for submission to the Secretary of State, the local planning authority shall take such steps as will in their opinion secure –

(a)   that adequate publicity is given in their area to the report of the survey . . . and to the matters which they propose to include in the plan;

(b)   that persons who may be expected to desire an opportunity of making representations to the authority with respect to those matters are made aware that they are entitled to an opportunity of doing so; and

(c)   that such persons are given an adequate opportunity of making such representations;

and the authority shall consider any representations made to them within the prescribed period.

110

Since the local authority was left to meet a standard based on their own opinion of the adequacy of publicity (called participation?) they were required to furnish central government with a statement of the particulars of this exercise including 'the authority's consultations with, and consideration of the view of, other persons with respect to those matters'. The central government was allowed to return the plan if it was inadequate and could direct further action to make it meet the intent of the statute.

The reaction to the Skeffington proposals and their reception by central government caused no little controversy. The dispute was simple: on the one hand the professional government officials who were increasingly finding their pet projects subject to disruption from civic amenity and conservation groups were happy enough with the idea as long as it meant 'consultation' and provided some possibility of warding off future obstruction to those plans. They were not particularly pleased with the possibility that the publicity exercise might actually allow the affected populace, or segments of it, to make decisions. In the words of one official:

> it is exceedingly difficult to see how as a matter of general practice the public can be directly involved . . . is public participation in the policy-making process even desirable? . . . the role of the individual councillor as a representative . . . may be undermined. . . . The burden of responsibility . . . requires the decisions to be taken by those people who have been entrusted with this responsibility, and who have to take the consequences. . . . Public participation as a particular facet of local government is unexceptionable; as a predominating policy it may very well be a synonym for abdication from responsibility! (MITCHINSON, p. 63).

On the other hand the students of the planning process were quick to point out that it was the government officials, not the elected representatives, who made the basic decisions and backed those decisions up with often irrefutable 'expertise'. The critics of Skeffington viewed the proposals as centred towards only one goal, namely ensuring that planners can get on more quickly with their daily jobs: 'They [the Committee] point to one criterion only: success in reducing the number of public objections and in shortening the process of decision

111

taking for the planning authority' (DENNIS, 1972, p. 224).
There was little in the *Report* or its implementation to lead
people to believe that the citizen's voice had been strengthened
or that the officials were under any obligation to listen more
carefully to specific proposals. As Norman Dennis put it,
'What if Skeffington's continuous assumption, that the local
planning authority has nothing to present but a case that any
reasonable man of goodwill can accept once he is clearly aware
of its contents, did not apply in every case of public participation?' (DENNIS, 1972, p. 225). There were no means to diminish
conflict between groups, no means to establish that perhaps
local officialdom had initiated a particular project to the detriment of a small and non-organised segment of the community.
The emphasis on co-operation and voluntary labour for the
local authority and the lack of emphasis on what is meant by
'public discussion' and comment, in terms of the decisions
made, all point to a process designed to help the planners rather
than the inarticulate members of the public who might be
affected by them.

One final point should be noted in this criticism of the
approach, namely the conspicuous absence of adverse comment
from lawyers. As Professor McAuslan so succinctly pointed out:

Sir Desmond Heap, a solicitor, President of both the Royal
Town Planning Institute and the Law Society, a unique
honour, set the tone of opposition to wider public participation at the Town and Country Planning Association's Annual
Conference in 1969 and has since repeated his criticisms of
the Skeffington Report 'People and Planning' [for including
too much 'participation']. Mr N. MacDermot Q.C., now
Secretary-General of the International Commission of
Jurists, led for the Government in the Committee debates on
the Town and Country Planning Bill in 1968, and, in many
respects aided by Mr Graham Page, solicitor . . . a minister
at the Department of the Environment and then leading for
the opposition, fended off demands for greater participation
to be written into the Bill from members on both sides of the
Committee. More public participation would lead to more
delay; delay would hinder the developer and might blight
property; this was the analysis that led to the form of words
on participation . . . which ensure that the style, amount and

112

adequacy of participation is decided exclusively by those who have to provide it in the first place. (MCAUSLAN, 1974, p. 136)

ACCESS THROUGH CENTRAL-GOVERNMENT REVIEW

The disquieting thing about the Skeffington Report and the reliance on public participation, defined as consultation, was that the reform was viewed as an adequate substitute for other existing types of access and review mechanisms which it certainly did not match in terms of the effectiveness of the vehicle for the individual member of the public. While consultation was probably better than no consultation (although those that view it as a means to co-opt the more vocal parts of the community might not agree), it was not the same as a public or a judicial inquiry, for example, or even as the representative democracy it was supposedly bolstering at the local level.

We saw how the local plans will not be subject to central-government review. This is due not only to the fact that the local plans will have to 'conform' to the centrally approved structure plans but also because the process of public participation will hopefully ensure that individual views are listened to. Similarly, the basic mechanism for central-government review of structure plans could be tampered with to the detriment of particular persons' interests, since they had already had their chance to 'participate' in the formulation of the plan. It is not an idle coincidence that, while the original 1968 legislation included central-government review through a judicial-style public inquiry, the post-Skeffington changes in the legislation introduced a new animal called a Public Examination for the review of structure plans. While we will explore at some length the undoubted value of this new administrative device, it is important to note that one of the reasons for its imposition was a trust in 'public participation' which was not necessarily well-founded.

THE PUBLIC EXAMINATION

In order to understand this new *un*-judicialised form of inquiry or examination we must start with the official reaction to the problems with public inquiries, and also deal with the clear repudiation of an American notion called 'advocacy planning'. As already mentioned, there was no little disquiet upon the part of local-government officials over the fact that their plans

113

and proposals were being reviewed by lawyers in what seemed to them to be longer and longer, and more legal, public inquiries. In the late 1960s there were two mammoth inquiries which seemed to confirm these doubts about public inquiries. The investigation into the third London Airport and the Layfield Commission's review of the Greater London Development Plan both took years and involved the talents of some of the best-known members of the local-government Bar. The very size of these inquiries and the hundreds of participants who appeared as of right led the Government to suppose that if the first goal of speedy and up-to-date structure plans was to be met then the administrative review must not be open-ended or even necessarily allow all objectors to have their say.

What happened was a clear acceptance of the idea that 'policy' matters could be separated from private or individual rights, and that the review of the structure plan should be a time for discussion of policy not of personal rights. Perhaps the most coherent proponent of the idea, Professor Peter Self, in his article on planning by judicial inquiry, stated the difficulties of the inquiry thus:

> The public inquiry is a reasonable way of listening to specific objections, it is in principle a poor and inefficient tool for making policies . . . [it] creates an atmosphere of conflict: the planning authority is put on the offensive, and the experts appearing before the inquiry are thrown into opposing camps . . . the whole emphasis is on gladiatorial contest, conducted to a considerable extent by counsel according to judicial or quasi-judicial rules. . . . [it] is very expensive and laborious . . . and wasteful of the skill of [its members]. The judicialisation of inquiries is bad. . . . It breaks the link which ought to exist between the expert members of the commission and witnesses and persons appearing before it. . . . the procedures necessarily favour the big battalions (SELF, 1970, p. 303).

What Professor Self advocates, then, is a return to 'consensus politics'.

What was clearly being rejected was the idea that the best way to discuss policy might be mechanisms to allow for more advocacy, more representation of the particularised view and the clear articulation of the specific, often very private, interests of particular groups. In the United States just such an idea, called 'advocacy planning' and spawned by a lawyer–planner, Paul Davidoff, had received widespread support. In the United States at least the lack of clear political-party identification and fractured decision-making responsibility had made the idea of policy formulation through the pursuit of particularised goals very attractive. In a pluralistic society with a current distribution of resources favouring certain groups over others it seems only logical to allow private interests to be heard in the decision-making process. 'The planning advocate functions in much the same context [as the lawyer]. His role is to defend or prosecute the interest of his clients. The planning advocate links resources and strategy alternatives to objectives and joins issues at the request of his client when other interpretation of facts overlooks, minimises or negatively affects his client's interests' (KAPLAN, p. 97)

In Britain, with a unified party-political structure and a great deal of confidence in government officials, this notion was rejected and the public inquiry was replaced by a scheme which depends on consensus building, government orchestration and to no little degree on the elimination of particularised, specific detail in favour of the consideration of more general policy.

It should be mentioned that there were, and are, numerous people who felt that what was needed was a greater, not a lesser, pursuit of particularised interests, and that the advocacy-planning idea had much to commend it. One plan put forward by various groups, in particular the Royal Town Planning Institute's Planning Aid Working Party, was that individuals would receive money and/or professional help in the preparation of their views for public inquiries both at the plan-review stage and at the particular appeal of a control-decision stage. As the environmental reporter for *The Times* expressed it in his book on the *Battle for the Environment*: 'To equalise the contest, and to answer the lack of cash and expertise available to objectors is to provide a Sir Galahad organisation which will come to their rescue in cases where their cause is most worthy and their resources most hard pressed. . . . [What is needed is] some effective means of providing planning aid' (ALDOUS, p. 282). However, this radical and expensive suggestion was not implemented although an equally radical plan for the examination of structure plans was prepared.

115

When the 1968 Town and Country Planning Act was first introduced there was, in Lord Kennet's words in the House of Lords, 'no intention of departing from the [public inquiry] procedure . . . which has long prevailed in this field'.* The Layfield Panel's recommendations on the Greater London development plan published in 1972, cast substantial doubt on the matter however. The Layfield Panel, which was perhaps the most extensive public inquiry of all, had some very uncomplimentary things to say about the process. According to the Panel the procedure took up inordinate amounts of time because all individuals had to be heard and the judicial system of cross-examination and reply caused the local authority to take a 'defensive attitude' and therefore be unwilling to seek constructive compromises (LAYFIELD, sec. 1, para. 6; sec. 2, para. 15). While some diehards were insisting that perhaps local authorities were not particularly prone to adopt constructive alternatives irrespective of the mode of questioning on review, the Government accepted the basic premise and introduced an administrative review modelled on the ideas of Professor Self and others for a 'non-combative' hearing.

The basic idea is that before the central government either approves (in whole or in part and with or without modifications or reservations) or rejects the structure plan there should be a consideration of the plan which takes into account any objections made to it. To do this the Secretary of State can: 'Cause a person or persons appointed by him for the purpose to hold an examination in public of such matters affecting his consideration of the plan as he considers ought to be examined.' (T.C.P.A., 1971, section 9)

This examination panel, in consultation with the Department of the Environment, is to decide what is to be considered and what is not, and in what order the consideration will take place. Further, the examination can consider joint plans for neighbouring areas.

While the central government still has to consider every objection, it does not have to allow every objector to be heard at the examination:

[They] shall not be required to secure to any local planning authority or other person a right to be heard at any examina-

---

* *Hansard* (1967–8) vol. 293, col. 617.

tion . . . and the bodies and persons who may take part therein shall be such only as [the Secretary of State] may, whether before or during the course of the examination, in his discretion invite to do so.

This deprivation of the right to be heard caused no little concern in some areas since it smacked of a deprivation of natural rights. However, the Government and various supporters of the idea could point to not only the Layfield Panel's recommendations but also the existence of public participation 'requirements'. In an article written for a law review by Layfield and Whybrow it could be rather blandly stated that one of the basic justifications for the new scheme was: 'a growing realisation of the scope and value of the publicity and public participation required by the 1968 Act. In particular these requirements, if properly implemented, enable the promoting authority to take account of potential objections before the form of the plan is finally settled' (LAYFIELD AND WHYBROW, p. 520).

At the time of the debate in Parliament on the new provisions there was some concern that while the plan would meet the Ministry's objectives of reducing delay and would allow for the investigation of key policy issues, it might have deleterious effects in other ways. The restrictions on the right to be heard might result in more objections to the local plans. It might mean that only the well-represented and articulate interests would be heard, whereas the aggregate of individual views might not be listened to. There were fears that the process would prove to be impractical because the large issues would necessarily swallow up the smaller ones. The most basic fear expressed during the debate was that the process would mean that a person's views could be easily overlooked in such a way that they could never be brought forward. If the issue is not heard at the structure-plan public examination, it still may be that a policy would be established to determine that issue at the local level. Thus, when the person went to the local plan examination he would be precluded from bringing the subject up again. (LAYFIELD AND WHYBROW, p. 521)

The Minister's replies during the debate were basically centred on the values of the programme and the methods that would be used for its implementation to meet some of these

117

objections. The idea was that the speedy process would allow the overseeing administration to focus the public discussion and make up for defects in the local authorities' public-participation scheme or analysis. By selecting participants on a representative basis and encouraging them to present a common viewpoint the hope was that the distilled policy could be 'probed' and evaluated by the panel. By having an independent chairman on the panel and by allowing for public comment on both the selection of participants and issues and upon the published report of the panel it was felt there would be adequate checks on any oversights.

The justification for this new device depends then on its implementation for its openness and accessibility to members of the public. While the procedure allows for the rapid review of local structure plans and national co-ordination on some policies, whether it will serve the goal of keeping the affected populace actually involved in the planning process is open to doubt. The particulars of the code of procedures and the actual selection of issues and participants could go a long way towards meeting the criticism that too much is being lost in terms of the individual's right to appear, to order his presentation, and to cross-examine the witnesses. By looking at the process of making structure plans and then at the process of reviewing them we can see the fruits of the reformed approach.

7 The New Plan-making: London

Some nine years after the P.A.G. was formed and six years after the Act was first introduced, the first structure plans are seeing the light of day and ground-work is being laid for the first local plans. While the process is still in its infancy, there is enough information available, both through personal interviews and the occasional article, to give us a clear idea how the process works. The starting point should be London for, as in local-government reorganisation, it was London's experience with a strategy plan (but not its method of public review) which served as the prototype for the structure plans which are now being drafted in the provinces.

THE GREATER LONDON DEVELOPMENT PLAN (G.L.D.P.)

When the London Government Act was introduced in 1963 it was generally felt that the existing development plans were inadequate to guide the development of the city. To meet this need an over-all strategy plan-making exercise was embarked upon, the first such all-encompassing review since the Abercrombie Plan in the early 1940s.

Until the creation of the Greater London Development Plan (G.L.D.P.) most of the development-control decision-making had been based on a view of London that was spawned in the mid-1930s. London at that time had nearly 8·6 million people, and the poverty and overcrowding were linked to the size of the population. The method devised to help the overloaded housing and transport facilities was to contain the city, stop its spread and growth, and thus hopefully increase the level of social services and amenities. The Barlow ideas of New Towns and spreading the industrial population throughout the country fitted in well with Abercrombie's ideas of green belts and spilling the population out of the congested urban area into separated and self-contained communities. Most of the plans

119

and policies of the 1950s and the 1960s were designed to further these notions; green belts checked urban spread, industrial- and office-development certificates restricted the number of jobs, and a great deal of money was channelled into the development of New Towns.

By the mid-1960s a number of things had changed, but the problems of slums, lack of housing and an overloaded transport system still remained. The G.L.D.P. was designed to come up with a fresh approach to these problems. In form it consisted of a slim volume of written strategy supported by a massive volume of studies. These studies sought to compile and correlate four extensive surveys on land-use, housing, employment and transport. The studies consist of a great deal of diverse (but perhaps interesting) facts such as journey-to-work time, rail passengers, pipeline capacity, wholesale markets, ownership in housing estates, job types, unemployment by area and the tenure of households.

The important question is what effect can a system, which is concerned mainly with the types of use that land can be put to, have upon these disparate factors encompassing virtually the entire fabric of city life: how can policy in fact be articulated to guide the development? When the document first appeared there were severe doubts expressed as to whether the plan had accomplished its aim. Professor Peter Hall wrote: 'Totally lacking in the Greater London Development Plan is any sense of a grand design. . . . In trying to keep his options open to suit changing circumstances in a dynamic city, the planner may . . . [fail] to provide any proposals the people can grasp at all' (in HILLMAN, p. 136). The written statement is an interesting piece of work, for it manages to say a great many fine-sounding things, but does not back them up by describing the ways they are to be accomplished. It is often only in areas of direct public spending (which has to be approved elsewhere anyway) that there are any concrete proposals.

Looking at the document, it begins with a statement that 'it states a set of principles for the future development of Greater London which will have to undergo a process of validation extending perhaps over several years' (G.L.D.P., 1.4). The problem is that looking at those principles, validated or not, one is struck by a certain sense of self-delusion concerning the planners' own powers to shape events:

120

It is the council's intention to do everything within its power to maintain London's position as the capital of the nation and one of the world's great cities (2.1).

Improvement of London's housing conditions must rank high in the council's priorities (2.8).

The council's overriding aim . . . will be to secure a progressive improvement of the environment so that London as a whole becomes a much more attractive place to live in than it is at present (2.8).

The council proposes, through the medium of the plan, to initiate a more vigorous and comprehensive policy for the conservation of the features that give London its distinctive character (2.12).

Finally the articulated premises upon which the city is to develop have a certain familiar ring to them. These aims are, for instance: 'To liberate and develop, so far as planning can, the enterprise and activity of London, promoting efficiency in economic life and vitality in its society and culture. . . . To treasure and develop London's character, capital of the nation, home and workplace of millions, focus of the British tradition . . . (2.16).

Beneath these glorious sentiments, the written statements contain a general commitment to stop the outflow of population that has been going on since the Second World War (now reduced to approximately 7·6 million) and to begin an extensive road-building programme. As laid out in the plan, the ring-way system of motorways would certainly have been one of the most expensive public-works projects of this century in Britain. This commitment was followed by proposals for redevelopment projects in some areas, the creation of new market facilities and the improvement of certain other public facilities such as docks and public utilities.

THE LAYFIELD INQUIRY AND CRITIQUE

When the *Greater London Development Plan* was formally submitted in August 1969 it caused no little furore, principally of course from the people who read the transport section carefully and discovered that one of the major ringways or radial-feeder networks to it happened to go through their homes. By

121

December of that year some 20,000 objections to the plan had been received by the Ministry. To handle the inquiry into the plan the Government proposed to establish a large panel of inquiry. The Panel, chaired by Mr F. H. B. Layfield, Q.C., was composed of a transportation expert, an independent planner and a number of well-respected Ministry inspectors. This group was instructed not only to hear the objections but to 'probe and evaluate, fully and searchingly, the policies embodied in the plan, the objections made to them and possible alternative strategies' (LAYFIELD, introduction). Clearly Anthony Crosland, the then Minister of Local Government, realised that the political repercussions of the parts of the written statement which were not so amorphous as to be unintelligible needed to be met.

The Layfield Panel sat for almost two years with some 237 days of hearings, considering 28,207 objections to the plan, and over 300 oral presentations concerning the various proposals. Although the reason for the interest in the plan centred on the motorway scheme and some 80 per cent of all objections were related to it, the most interesting aspect of the inquiry, from the standpoint of one interested in the establishment of the approaches to planning and the mechanisms for access to that process, was the wide-ranging investigation of the notion of what a plan could do, how it should be presented and how central-government review should be structured in the future.

The Layfield Commission's Report on the G.L.D.P. statement had a good deal to say about the content of this plan *vis-à-vis* all other structure plans in preparation. First Layfield, by implication, states that the ministerial directions concerning how to make one of these documents were obtuse to say the least. The discretionary list of possible topics and the 'large measure of freedom' given to local planning agencies seem to guarantee that the resulting documents will vary greatly in content and approach. Second, the panel was so impressed with the complexity and difficulty of making a plan, and so little impressed with the fruits of the Greater London plan-making body that it seriously questioned the ability of the less-well staffed counties to create any sort of valid document:

We were also impressed by the very high calibre of the staff needed to do some of the work. Whether authorities themselves will have staff of the requisite calibre to prepare plans of a suitable quality is a matter which gives rise to great concern. . . . If the G.L.C. could only, with the greatest difficulty, and after extensions of time, produce a plan containing relatively limited information, diffuse aims and vague policies, the chances of success for those structure plans presented by local authorities lacking the resources and skilled manpower of the G.L.C. must be open to doubt. (LAYFIELD, 2.13)

The basic criticisms that the Layfield Panel had for the whole notion of strategy planning were (2.17):

(1) *Over-ambition.* The report states that the G.L.D.P. tries to do far more than it can do and that many matters, such as employment or population trends, are beyond their power. The planners seem to have run a bit amok trying to make decisions about which 'there is no information at present upon which to base them and no indication that they could lead to any useful or ascertainable result . . .'.

(2) *Inconsistent treatment of the substance.* The authority dealt with areas over which it had spending control in much greater detail than over areas outside its domain. For instance the treatment of roads and the creation of them is 'planned' far more thoroughly than other types of transport simply because it is an area in which the local government can spend.

(3) *Failure to relate information to policies.* Here the panel found a great disparity or, in their words, 'independence' between the data accumulated in the survey and the final policy-decisions made. The panel went on to state that the plan makers here 'when faced with a variety of solutions to a problem, chose one on political grounds and then presented it as inevitable'.

(4) *Failure to relate policies chosen to aims.* The G.L.D.P. makes a number of policy choices without articulating how these plans will go about meeting needs. Without aims, the central government can neither verify the correctness of the goals of the policy nor check to see if the policy is the best method to reach those ends.

(5) *Failure to present aims in meaningful terms.* Here, quoting passages such as those above, the panel found much of the

123

'strategy plan' to be mere gibberish. 'The statements of aims . . . do not mean anything because they can mean anything to anyone. It is not perhaps being too cynical to believe indeed that such aims were inserted because they could mean anything to anyone.'

(6) *Failure to distinguish between what is strategic and should appear in structure plans and what is merely of a local nature.*

Once having stated these very broad criticisms of the approach the Panel goes on methodically to dismember most of the major propositions laid out in the document. Clearly what is not pious verbiage is rather lacking in supporting documentation. For instance the first notion, that the population decrease in the city should be stemmed, was thrown out half-way through the hearings by the plan-makers themselves, and changed to a policy of stemming the rate of decline, rather than decline itself. However, the Panel found that the entire notion of using land-use control strategy to change over-all demographic movement was an exercise in attempting to control the uncontrollable. Since there were so many correlative factors in individual choices of where to live, such as jobs, housing, leisure, the general economic picture, and so on, and since the G.L.C. plan-makers could not even substantiate the feared grievous effects of such depopulation the Panel recommended that the local government should leave matters well alone. (LAYFIELD, chap. IV)

The Panel proceeded on this general theme through a number of the various 'strategies' with a marked disdain for the often unsubstantiated, if lengthy, general policies. For instance, while acknowledging that an authority could deal with the planning of a specific employer's premises, or perhaps even marginally attract employers for a short time, they took 'the view that the local planning authority can, within its area, over the long term, influence only marginally the tendency of employment to contract or alter or retain its nature'. (5.6)

There is a second area of criticism concerning plans for public works of one sort or another, and that is the fact that there is a serious dearth of information upon which to base public-spending decisions. For instance, in the area of providing public housing the Panel stated categorically that while quantitative assessments might be valuable for spurring the bodies to action to build units they would almost certainly be wrong in terms of actual numbers and need (chap. VI).

The lack of real data to support public-expenditure policy can best be exemplified by the motorway controversy, for that is what caused the extensive review in the first place. In areas where the planning government unit did not have either the spending power or the ownership of the land their policy statements were found to be vague, meaningless, and often deliberately abstruse. The policy decision which did express real choices was based on political not 'planning' criteria, and the most political of all strategies had to do with areas where the local government, rather than planning land-use, could in fact build projects.

The Ringway Plan has been one of the most important political issues in London since its inception in engineers' minds in the late 1950s, and as part of the then Conservative opposition group platform during the Greater London Council elections in 1967. The Conservatives won both the 1967 and 1970 elections, and translated what had initially been a general commitment to do something about the fact that the use of automobiles for transport in the city was an extremely slow and frustrating process into the three motorway rings and twelve radial routes. This plan was couched in an enormous complex series of traffic surveys, ride-to-work data, goods vehicle journeys, increase in vehicle-registration statistics and so on. The final decision, as presented in the development plan statement, was one of technological necessity rather than political choice. 'The situation can only be met by a major programme for improvement for the road system, and by complementary policies in parking and public transport' (G.L.D.P., 5.10). There were cost–benefit studies, yields of return, and a great many studies to show that the motorway system would reduce traffic, help amenity, and benefit the city.

However, with the Layfield inquiry providing a public forum, a great many of these 'technological' truths were shown to be fallacious at best, or deliberately manipulated at worst. The fact that in a growing economy traffic might easily grow to fit any given roadway capacity could easily be proved by the planners' figures. To quote Layfield:

125

It seemed that the council's original claim that the primary road system would produce lower traffic levels on secondary roads than are experienced today, might have been abandoned for the more modest claim that conditions in the future would be better with the primary network than without it. The evidence is neither clear nor conclusive (chap. VIII).

The entire development strategy is biased inordinately towards road rather than other forms of transport. While there are a variety of factors which led to this circumstance, such as the central government form of grant finance for capital outlay *vis-à-vis* a lack of finance for maintenance of public transport, the basic one is that it is one area in which the plan-maker is in fact a developer. That is, it is one area where, rather than trying to control other development or allocate land to certain types of uses, the plan-maker can actually go out and do the development. Again, to quote Layfield, 'It is one of the few areas in the entire plan in which the G.L.C. actually has full responsibility for planning and execution, in short, for getting on with the job' (8.51). This did not seem to ensure that the plans would be thoroughly researched, however. The hope that the motorway scheme would relieve secondary roads and improve the environment, and that the construction itself would be subject to great caution in terms of its environmental impact, were 'all stated in the plan as expressions of faith . . . [but they are not] stated in the plan in a sufficiently clear and practical form to give any confidence that they can or will be carried into effect' (8.52).

THE RESULTS: ABANDONING MOTORWAYS AND PROCEDURES

The Layfield inquiry finally recommended a much abridged form of the ringway system, and the vicissitudes of politics eventually brought about its entire demise when the recently elected Labour Greater London Council cancelled the project in 1973. The importance of the public inquiry, in what was eventually a political decision, should be stressed. It was in many ways the character of the planning document, and more particularly the review by the Layfield Panel, which allowed the public-spending programme to be vigorously discussed, the premises sorted out, and the eventual political decision to have a factual basis.

It is also important to stress that, while the G.L.D.P. could easily be faulted, the Layfield Report itself fell victim to a good deal of criticism. Foster and Whitehead showed fairly convincingly, in a recent article in *Economica*, that the Report itself failed to relate the suggestions it makes in the various areas of housing or employment or jobs to the responsibilities of the various tiers of government. In their words:

> The Layfield Report itself perpetuates many of the errors which it claims were contained in the original plan and the resulting policy is almost as unsatisfactory. In particular it sets up specific requirements (e.g. the size of the overspill policy) without giving reasons and in no sense attempts to set up a decision-making framework to aid in determining strategy when the values of major variables change. (FOSTER AND WHITEHEAD, p. 450)

It seems, then, that even the planners' planners cannot draft a document that logically states policy which will lead to present action and result in the desired future use of land.

What is most peculiar about the review by the public inquiry is that, although the inquiry into the G.L.D.P. led to a re-evaluation and cancellation of one of the nation's largest public-works plans, the processes of that inquiry were subject to extensive and damning criticisms, even by the inquiry itself. To quote for instance one political commentator, Simon Jenkins: 'Despite the hopelessly cumbersome nature of this enquiry, saddled as it was with the whole paraphernalia of legal representation, it did [demonstrate] . . . the value of outside criticism in inducing a political institution to look again at its own assumptions and evidence' (JENKINS, p. 260). This same type of criticism of the 'legal' aspects of the inquiries, with the idea of cross-examination, notice, and statement and counter-statement, was almost universal, while the fruits of the approach, such as new directions being taken by the frequently embarrassed officials, were given wide acclaim. The inquiry itself pointed out how the planning authority was frequently forced to change its premises, and the fact that the policies were put to rigorous testing resulted in extensive clarification and alteration during the course of the inquiry.

The same inquiry panel, however, also had to deal with all objections and to hear everyone who wanted to be heard, even if they were making similar, or in the view of the panel, irrelevant points. The panel decided that the value of the process as an institution for evaluation and outside criticism could be maintained while limiting the amount of access to the reviewing body. The panel did not realise that perhaps the efficacy of the inquiry procedure might depend on just those rights of unlimited access and quasi-judicial proceedings. In the end, the same panel that had done such a thorough job of evaluating the G.L.D.P. through the technique of a public inquiry suggested changes in the format of the procedure which resulted in the 1972 legislation.

The panel's changes led to the Public Examination, where all objectors do *not* have a right to be heard, and where the forms of cross-examination and counter-objection can be eliminated, or certainly orchestrated to a significant degree.

From this look at the prototype of structure plans there are a number of discernible trends which should begin to become apparent. First, the most valuable aspect of the plan-making was the process rather than its final fruits. The assembly of the survey information and the data was the only matter which was criticised in terms implying that there should have been more of it, rather than it was either wrong, meaningless, or unintelligible. Turning to the 'plan' itself, we can begin to see that there were in fact two aspects to it. Firstly, there are the parts of a plan perhaps best dubbed 'controlling the uncontrollable', which have to do with the over-all development of policy. The important factors for this aspect of the plan are the statement of fairly small decisions related to very specific and well-articulated policies. One accomplishes virtually nothing by stating, for instance, that the planning authority gives 'first priority to the eradication of slums, overcrowding and lamentable domestic environments' (G.L.D.P., 3.2). But one may help to guide the approval of specific developments if one states that the general density range of 70–100 rooms per acre will be the norm and that exceptions will only be allowed in specifically delineated circumstances (for example, lower density to preserve woodlands, higher for upper-income families without children).

The second aspect of the plan, which is clear from the London

128

programme, is that it can serve to amalgamate a list of public spending and development programmes and put them through a process of public scrutiny. The public agency, in the London situation at least, really only seemed capable of 'planning' with any specificity that which it could, in effect, develop itself. Thus a strategy plan or structure plan provides a very good vehicle for reviewing the public development which it is seeking to impose, whether it be roadways, as in the case of London, or tower blocks, schools, parks, or whatever. While such a 'structure' plan may not add much to the control of local private development, it does perhaps serve to provide a forum for discussion of the programmes of the biggest developer of them all, namely the government.

In the case of Greater London, the Strategic Planning Committee had to recant and issue a statement of revision saying that many of the factors it sought to control were outside its control. Whole sections of the document had to be rewritten. It might be hoped that the counties learned from the experience in London and heeded the advice given on the preparation of structure plans by the Layfield Panel. To see how the creation of structure plans is progressing in the provinces we will now turn to the West Midlands.

8 Plan-making in the Provinces

A CASE STUDY OF THE WEST MIDLANDS

The following information is derived from a series of interviews with D.O.E. officials, local-government officials, local citizens, and various spokesmen for amenity groups in the West Midlands, held during 1973 and 1974. The author attended the initial series of public examinations, reviewed the various planning documents, and discussed his conclusions with the major participants in the process such as planning officers, local councillors, members of the public examination panel and D.O.E. support staff.

In order to avoid yet another administrative overload, the D.O.E.'s planning section was very careful to give out the commencement orders (under T.C.P.A., 1971, section 21) to start the plan-making process at a very measured pace. The area selected for the first plans was that of the West Midlands, an area of economic productivity centred on the industrial cities of Birmingham and Coventry and surrounded by Warwickshire, Worcestershire, Shropshire and Staffordshire. Behind London, this area has provided the climate for the most growth, development and population increase in the country. There were a number of reasons beyond mere size and economic importance which contributed to this selection. The most important was the local authorities' own interest in seeking to have an operative structure plan before local-government reorganisation. Also there was in existence, albeit in its formative stages, a regional strategy for the area. This document set out a basic figure for growth for the area (1·5 million) and made a very rough estimate of where that growth would occur (in selected towns or New Towns, north-east and south-east of the Birmingham urban area). The regional strategy was in fact not approved by the Secretary of State until 11 January 1974 after the structure plans were well under way. What was important was that the process of working out the compromises for establishing the plan had created some means of communicating between the various local authorities.

The reason why this area had developed these regional strategies was that there had been a long history of antagonism between the urban city governments and the chiefly rural county councils. The area had been plagued by disputes centring on the cities' attempts to take land from the counties for expansion. The regional strategies set some agreed limits on the amount and location of this type of growth. With reorganisation due to come into effect in April 1974, the old local authorities were more than happy to establish structure plans that kept to the agreed arrangement and would guarantee, to some extent, that the new authorities would not have to battle it out again as to how much city growth there would be and where it would go.

It must be remembered here that, under the 1972 Local Government Act, the counties and not the districts were to make the structure plans and, under the provisions concerning 'county matters', have the final say on local district-planning applications. Old county boroughs, such as Coventry or Birmingham, which were being subsumed into the new West Midlands metropolitan county as member districts, were eager to establish a structure plan before the metropolitan county came into existence. By having the old county borough draft the structure plan for the new metropolitan county district, those planners were able to assure themselves of the right to make their own local plans later (with maps) the way they wanted to.

To start with we should look to the officials who undertook the task. One problem that the West Midlands suffered from was that the simultaneous structure planning and reorganisation process resulted in a good deal of staff changeover. This meant that there was not a consistent approach in any of the areas. In one county the chief planning official left for a better job a few weeks before the public examination was to take place. In another there was a virtual desertion upon the part of the younger staff for jobs with the new (and higher-paying) local district-planning offices.

Turning to the question of the sophistication and training of the local planning staff, it is difficult, before looking at the final plan, to make any categorical statements as to whether the

131

Layfield Panel's doubts concerning the lack of staff of the requisite calibre were well-founded. McLoughlin's study showed that, of all plan-making personnel, some 31 per cent have either no degree or a degree in surveying or engineering, 20 per cent have architectural degrees, 23 per cent have geography degrees, and 23 per cent have degree or diploma qualifications in planning (MCLOUGHLIN, 1973a, p. 154). The interviews conducted with West Midlands planning personnel showed much the same sort of breakdown, but it seemed that there was a higher representation of engineers among senior planners.

What this does not tell us is how sophisticated the planners trained in 'spatial and locational skills' are at integrating the important new factors of social networks, cultural needs, and economics. One indication is that the local council officials interviewed mentioned that frequently they had to seek advice and help from the professional staff in the regional office of the D.O.E. in order to make use of new techniques. Also, at the public examinations, it seemed that a not infrequent source of conflict was the dubious nature of the methods used by the local authorities to support policy. (This was also the case with the 'skilled manpower' in London so perhaps it is not altogether informative.) The only other indication would be a very conjectural and very personal feeling based on the interviews, and attendance at the public examinations – a feeling that, on the whole, the officials had only a dim idea of what the purpose of the structure plan was. Further, they had very little confidence in the usefulness of the final product they had created. Whether this is a function of the type of exercise they were engaged in or whether they simply did not understand the skills involved is, of course, another matter.

Because of the local authorities' desire to complete the structure plans prior to reorganisation in the Spring of 1974, the process was, to say the least, hurried. The Regional Office of the D.O.E. was acquiescent in this and there seemed to be a general commitment not to let reorganisation hold up the process of developing and approving structure plans. The result has been that the draft structure plans submitted for the West Midlands have varied greatly in their quality and have not exactly lived up to the idea of example plans to be followed by the rest of the country. Further, because all the plans were being prepared by 'lame-duck' planning departments, there is no little confusion about how much of the plans will actually be followed by the new political organisations once they take over upon reorganisation.

In the author's opinion the structure-planning work product has not been notably successful. Most of the West Midland region structure plans have been rushed, and the brevity of one plan, that of Warwickshire, even leaves it open to question whether it meets the bare statutory requirements of a plan. Several other structure plans would appear to provide only the barest of frameworks for the development of local plans.

The problems facing the D.O.E. are further compounded by the fact that some major planning decisions upon which the structure plans hinge are simultaneously being discussed in alternative forums. There are currently three major motorway inquiries, one new village scheme and two out-of-town shopping centres under review by the Department. The hope of coming up with anything definitive, then, is subject to doubt, but it is useful here to look at the initial documents.

THE SURVEYS

There was a great disparity in the quality of the collection of data. Some areas, such as Warwickshire, relied heavily upon the regional and sub-regional strategies and did not institute major investigations of their own. Others, such as Staffordshire or Worcestershire, carried out extensive investigations, the results of which took the form of massive, often multi-volume, reports. Since the *Manual* only laid down the list of topics to be covered and not the extent to which those topics could, with benefit, be investigated, the counties were left a good measure of freedom as to what they chose to pursue.

The basic idea of the survey is to provide the officials with a core of data on the various topics of employment, population, housing, transport, conservation, and so on, upon which to base their plans for development. The Staffordshire survey, for example, is a 250-page book of material, with a mass of information under each of the topics. Population growth is detailed, forecast, split into age groups, related to educational facilities, correlated to household formation and tied to employment forecasts. Similarly, employment figures are broken down by occupational type of worker, length of

133

journey to work, and forecasted for future labour demand (not surprisingly, at a very high figure when compared with the previous rate of growth of employment demand). When one turns to the transport section there are figures on car-ownership (by area), accidents per mile, public-transport usage, freight traffic and, again, projections on future growth. Again, concerning housing, the figures for existing dwellings are provided, as are the age of the stock, the numbers of houses being built in both the public and private sectors, and the number of derelict or unfit houses.

The surveys go on and on, detailing a mass of information on drainage, agriculture, educational facilities, health services, social services for the mentally ill, shopping, trees, sand-pits and football pitches. Reading through them one is struck by two thoughts, the first being that a great many of the things surveyed are in areas of planning and expenditure over which the authority has virtually no control, and over which the structure plan itself certainly will not be able to determine future events. Since the plan, irrespective of its appellation, will still statutorily be a land-use plan, with power to determine physical development, it is certainly open to question why it should seem to be guiding, for instance, the growth of employment, the expenditure on public transport or the extent of local expenditure on education. Secondly, even if the structure plan were to be given the power to set both national (that is, transport or grant level) priorities, as applied to the local area, and to guide the local area's expenditure over a wide variety of areas (for example, health, social services, or education), which will certainly never be the case, the very size and complexity of the survey show that establishing such a plan would be extremely difficult. If the surveys are, in fact, representative of the factors which must go into making a land-use decision, then it would seem that there is a tremendous variety and complexity of possibilities in a mixed economy during a time of rapid technological development. It may be beyond the capabilities of the most experienced planner with the most sophisticated computer models, to say nothing of the capabilities of the provincial county-planning office in the Midlands.

Be that as it may, the counties decided to assemble this data and then proceed to select where, in terms of land use, the projected growth should occur. To do this the counties had to give some order of priority to the various ingredients, and also had to allow for public participation.

PUBLIC PARTICIPATION

The experience with public participation in the first structure plans cast significant doubts on its value as a substitute for other forms of access, but it does show that as a consultative tool it can be very useful to an authority's officials if, and only if, they are amenable to outside suggestions. The statute, as we saw, gave considerable leeway to the authorities as to what was an acceptable standard to meet the public-participation requirement.

The circular (52/72) on publicity and public participation stressed how important central government thought 'participation' was, but merely made suggestions about possible methods, and did not set minimum standards:

> Publicity and public participation are essential factors in the new development plan system and the [Government] fully support them. They take this opportunity to stress how important it is, in embarking on that new system involving new concepts, to seek the views of the ordinary citizen and to listen to them. . . . Giving the public the opportunity to participate in the formative stage will, when handled with skill and understanding, not only make the plan a better plan, but also do much to improve relationships between the planning authorities and the public. (CIRCULAR, 52/72)

Since the statutory requirements of public participation are of such a general nature, the counties are given a relatively free hand with the only check being the possible D.O.E. sanction of non-acceptance of the entire plan. The D.O.E. has, on occasion, written to local authorities before the submission of their plans to point out that what they had proposed did not meet the statutory requirements, but so far they have not refused a plan on public-participation grounds. In the author's opinion the D.O.E. has taken a very limited view of its role in ensuring such participation. It is evidently not felt by the D.O.E. officials that it is their function to censure local authorities publicly for relatively lacklustre programmes of public involvement. The difficulty is that, while it may not be to the D.O.E.'s advantage to bring up such matters publicly during the public examina-

135

tion, there is virtually no other way to ensure compliance with the spirit of the Skeffington proposals. While it may be too early in the process to know the extent of involvement of the D.O.E. in ensuring public participation, at least some of the local authorities who are to follow in the footsteps of the West Midlands have already concluded that they will not be held to a particularly high standard. As one fellow spectator, a local planning official, at a session of the public examination, put it: 'If they will take some of these as adequate, I can go back and tell my authority that we have already done too much by simply having a public meeting and handing out some pretty pamphlets.'

The least effort was probably that put in by Warwickshire. It consisted of some questionnaire work at the survey stage and a series of meetings around the county after, not before, the draft structure plan was prepared. In interviews county officials stated that one of the major reasons for the lack of public involvement during the formulation stage was that they had to meet a deadline from central government. However, this did not seem to be the case, for interviews with D.O.E. officials revealed that, if anything, the pressure for speed came from the counties. What was more likely was that the county-council planners and elected officials wanted to finish in time to set the plan for the new county that would be taking over after reorganisation. The written statement only mentioned the subject of participation once, saying that 'exhibitions and public meetings were held throughout the county' in the three months following the preparation of the draft plan.

The Warwickshire 'public participation' meeting, referred to so sketchily, did not exactly meet the hopes of the Skeffington Panel, that it would 'facilitate the giving of information when issues are reasonably clear but before decisions are made' (SKEFFINGTON REPORT, p. 157). At the meeting which the author attended, two officials simply arrived and described the already printed document. The attendance was in the neighbourhood of thirty-five people out of a town of 50,000, and the discussion between the people and the officials consisted of a justification of the plan and a meeting of various arguments put forward by the local footpath or amenity group. As a member of the audience one was led to believe that the decisions on growth were based on a 'professional' judgement and, at least at the meetings attended, there was no discussion whatever of reconsideration of certain points in the light of the 'participation'.

One participant, who was fairly representative, stated at the public examination that he had met with the Warwickshire planners and:

> at the time of that meeting it was not made clear by the . . . officials that that was the moment [the public meeting] for testing the survey material, the options or the alternatives, nor for deriving information as to how the conclusions were likely to be reached when the public participation stage was concluded. . . . Mr. Shelley [a senior Warwickshire planner] quite clearly had no idea of the D.O.E. view . . . that public participation was the time when survey material should be tested. It was news to him; he thought it was going to be tested . . . at [the public] examination. (TRANSCRIPT, 27 Nov 1973, p. 2)

What seemed evident from the Warwickshire case was that if the authority chose not to involve people significantly it was sufficient statutorily simply to run some advertisements, do a survey, and have a meeting or two.

This is not to say that the scheme could not be made to yield some dividends, because the situation in, for instance, Coventry or Worcestershire was appreciably different. In Coventry there was a phased programme of participation by which even the Los Angeles prototype dimmed in comparison. The description of the participation process took up almost 100 pages of typescript, and the expense itself was considerable.

In Coventry there were, firstly, two months of publicity about the impending structure-planning process. Reports were issued to groups and over 500 letters sent to bodies, stating the hopes for public involvement, the location of meetings and the details of the survey. Coventry even introduced a *Planning Survey Report*, which encapsulated the survey material for a series of sub-areas within the borough. The second stage of participation saw the distribution of these reports and a series of twelve public meetings, chaired by elected members as well as officials, with an average attendance of fifty to sixty people. There was also an exhibition bus, which visited various schools and shopping centres and had over 4000 adult visitors. Staff from the local newspaper were hired to write a series of ten half-page articles which appeared in the newspaper, which has a circulation of over 100,000. The authority then published a special edition of its own handout, in newspaper format, which was distributed to 100,000 households in the city. All these efforts were augmented with a series of posters, press statements and radio coverage.

During the third stage of participation the officials publicised those issues that were to be included in the structure plan and held another series of meetings – first, a major meeting which the spokesmen for the various groups in the city were invited to attend, and then a series of local meetings run by the interested organisations. The draft proposals were again prepared in newspaper form, and again distributed to 100,000 households, and various media coverage was obtained for the proposals. Added to this effort a series of questionnaires were drawn up, which were distributed through the meetings, the exhibition bus and a random sample of postal addresses. Based on all this a draft structure plan was prepared. A general public meeting was again held and again the officials considered the various representations.

What this elaborate scheme does not tell us is how much attention the local officials in fact paid to these ideas, or the actual depth and quality of their effect. It does tell us that they made an effort to solicit those views, and if one starts from the position that participation means consultation, the bus and the newspaper are certainly innovative approaches. From an article by the Assistant Principal Planner for Coventry, Peter Masters, one would think that the programme was significant:

> It must be accepted that policy planning is a highly political process. Public involvement in the processes of policy formulation within a local-authority framework must, therefore, be highly political. Policies are influenced by the complex interaction between various groups in society, and a lot depends on how effectively various groups can articulate and make their views felt to the policy makers . . . the only effective way for the 'public' to influence policy plans is to become much more politically active. (MASTERS, p. 462)

Peter Masters goes on to state that the most the local authority can do is to try to disseminate the information and perhaps augment the disadvantaged's ability to represent themselves through some sort of planning aid. In spite of all this he still comes back to the proposition that the role of 'participation' is information and consultation, not the actual decision-making itself: 'No matter how much the public are involved in the planning process it will always be the elected members who make the final policy decisions' (p. 462). Others in the community had, however, a slightly different picture of the Coventry attempt at 'participation'. As a spokesman for the government-funded, but independent, Community Development Project put it:

> When we first experienced Coventry Corporation's programme of participation [it] . . . concerned us a great deal in that we felt that it was only a half-hearted effort at trying to find the felt needs of the people of Coventry. As a result of our discussions . . . we had several public meetings with people and talked, and the general feeling from those public meetings was that the opportunity to partake in the structure plan in Coventry was very inadequate. (TRANSCRIPT, Mr Hallett, 12 Dec 1973, p. 17)

Between the non-existent approach of Warwickshire and the elaborate attempt at Coventry, there were various intermediate approaches by the local authorities. For instance, Solihull discussed its participation for eleven pages in the written statement, but, in the words of one observer, 'it appears that the council went through the motions of inviting public comment, but without departing too much from the conventional pattern' (HANSON, p. 984). They invited comment, but without meetings, before the publication of the draft, circulated a questionnaire and had two public meetings. In the case of Solihull the view expressed at public meetings and on questionnaires seemed to be set fairly against any growth or development in the area. The borough, however, declined to follow these sentiments and decided on some slight growth in any event.

In the case of Worcestershire, the County published an entire volume on 'consulting the people', and devoted an amount of effort to consultation on the scale, if not the intensity, of Coventry. They circulated a leaflet to 20,000 people and used a series of questionnaires to determine which factors from the survey should be given the highest priority. A series of exhibitions were mounted, which over 7000 people turned up to view, and a public-relations firm was called in to give advice on publicity. Some 2600 people completed the questionnaires, which gave them a choice on the strategy of growth, shopping, green belts and public transport. Not surprisingly, 80 per cent were in favour of a better system of public transport, for instance, 90 per cent were in favour of traffic-free shopping and over 80 per cent were in favour of extending the green belt.

In interviews in Worcestershire it became clear that the public-participation exercise did provide some guidance to policy decision-making, because, although it was frequently repeated that the elected councillors had to make the final choice, there was a wide variety of factors which the officials said they simply did not have any opinion on. Perhaps a rural upper-class county area has a natural inclination towards certain types of policy, but the consultation exercise allowed the officials to point to 'issues raised by the general public' (5.1.5 WORCESTERSHIRE STRUCTURE PLAN, vol. 2), such as the fact that population growth should be reduced to a 'more acceptable level' or that growth should be concentrated in certain areas, or that commuters would like a better public system of commuting to the Birmingham urban area.

Worcestershire was not unique in having this type of self-evident message as a result of a questionnaire. In Leamington a survey reported in a local paper* showed that, of the 3000 people asked about where they would like new housing growth to go, there was virtual unanimity that it should go to areas other than where they happened to live.

What should be remembered about these various attempts at consultation or participation is that the authority has the final say as to whether to take or ignore the advice of any member or group of members of the public. The system of public participation resulted in widely differing approaches to the same end-product and presumably widely different amounts of attentiveness to various representations. While the interested private person in Warwickshire might not even have heard about the structure plan, and stood no chance at all of changing the already drafted document, the concerned citizen in Coventry or

---

* *Leamington Spa Courier* (7 Sep. 1973).

Worcestershire might have heard of the plan and been able to make representations before decisions were made. However, he still would have had those representations judged by the very officials who made up the plan. This then leaves only the public examination as a possible independent forum for the presentation of their views. Before turning to that, however, we should see what the plan itself was actually like.

THE WRITTEN STATEMENT

The written statement with its 'diagrammatic' maps is the heart of the plan, and it is that which will hopefully guide development. The first statements, like the surveys and the participation attempts, seemed to vary dramatically in their particulars. On a superficial level, however, they were very similar, since they all followed the basic *Manual* format. As Professor Peter Hall described them:

> The written statement . . . is divided into chapters, and is liberally illustrated by maps and charts. It usually starts by outlining the background, including the regional and the sub-regional strategy recommendations. It then sets a detailed list of objectives and sub-objectives. Usually, it makes fairly elaborate alternative projections of the main components of population and employment, and discusses their merits or shortcomings in detail before picking one of them. It then describes and evaluates alternative broad physical strategies for the area, before picking a preferred strategy, which is sometimes described in great detail. . . . Lastly it . . . considers the financial implications of the strategy in terms of likely available resources over the next 15 or 20 years. . . . (HALL, 1974, p. 702)

When one looks at the particulars, there is not quite the same uniformity. While the small county borough of Solihull' written statement is 122 pages in length, the county o^s Warwickshire's is only thirty-five pages. Whereas Coventry deals extensively with the whole range of social services and education, and tries to fit physical planning into a large number of other policy decisions, other authorities deal mainly with physical land-use.

There are a number of problems with the documents. First, they all tend to overestimate wildly those factors (stated as

141

projections based on facts) which support particular policies which the authority is seeking to foster. For instance, the growth of both population and employment seems to be uniformly overestimated. Staffordshire proposes an increase of population of 325,000 for the period 1971–91, which is nearly one-and-a-half times the growth of the previous twenty-year period, in spite of a regional projection of a marked slowing of population growth. Similarly, during the Worcestershire public examination, it was shown that:

> Whilst Worcestershire had only accounted for just over one sixth of the total regional increase in the period 1951–1971, the structure plan forecast would achieve about one half of the total forecast regional increase over the period 1971–1991. . . . Whilst the structure plan was bidding for an annual average increase from migration of 8000 per annum, the actual increase achieved per annum over the period 1966–1972 was 4400 per annum. (DAILY NOTES, Day 5)

The total provision in structure plans for the West Midlands provides roughly twice the estimated regional growth, since each area tends to guess, through figures, that it will be the most popular and productive area, bringing in employment and population increase.

This puffing of statistics and projections, which, it should be remembered, was one of the Layfield criticisms of the G.L.D.P., can also be seen in the analysis of particular sub-problems that the plans are supposed to deal with. For instance, Coventry's programme for housing renewal in its action areas received severe criticism at the public examination, due, in part, to the manipulation of the statistical data. As the spokesman for a community group said:

> the estimates of the size, scale and nature of the (housing) problem appear understated and in places unsound . . . it is not clear how and where the council's estimates come from and how they are derived . . . to an outside person looking at the published report it is not possible to see where these figures are estimated from. (TRANSCRIPT, 12 Dec 1973, p. 14)

A second major problem with the documents is that, in trying to blend social and economic factors with physical land-use, there is a great deal of both well-meaning but hollow

142

statements, and internal inconsistency. Some of the statements are so flimsy that even the planners who drafted them cannot explain their meaning, for example: 'it is the council's policy to rationalise the existing footpaths and bridleways systems' (WARWICKSHIRE STRUCTURE PLAN, section 4, para. 4.19). And

> I think all this sentence means is that whatever is appropriate to be done to footpaths and bridleways it is the council's policy to do it, but there is a procedure for doing all this and chances for objections to be made, etc. so it is a long drawn out business. (TRANSCRIPT, Mr Norris [Chief Planner, Warwickshire] 5 Dec. 1973, p. 23)

There are a great many of this type of rather obvious statement thrown into most of the plans:

> It is the council's policy to ensure that sufficient land is made available in and adjoining urban areas to allow proper living, social and recreation standards to be achieved, consistent with the conservation of farmland and good landscape, and the efficient use of urban land. The council will review land requirements in the light of economic and social trends. (WARWICKSHIRE STRUCTURE PLAN, section 4, para. 2(2))

> It is the planning authority's intention that there should be a plentiful supply of land for house building in the county, both immediately and in the future. The structure plan will provide, in its existing commitments and new proposals, sufficient land for housing for at least twenty years. (STAFFORD-SHIRE STRUCTURE PLAN, section 5, para. 2)

> The council will continue to lay down standards to ensure that new housing development is suitably located, conforms to appropriate standards, and provides a range of dwelling types appropriate to the anticipated needs of the community. (SOLIHULL STRUCTURE PLAN, section 5, para. 2(1))

In those subject areas where the plans are not actually locating growth the policies tend to be obscure. For instance, when Staffordshire discusses social services:

> To encourage the provision of social and health facilities in such a manner as to afford the greatest opportunity for cooperation between allied services and the joint planning

143

of certain types of facilities where appropriate. (STAFFORDSHIRE STRUCTURE PLAN, section 6, para. 32)

Or when Warwickshire discusses its policies on public transport:

> It is the council's policy to regard the railway system as a potential asset to be safeguarded, particularly the lines from Nuneaton to Coventry, Coventry to Leamington Spa, and Birmingham to Stratford-upon-Avon via Henley in Arden. (WARWICKSHIRE STRUCTURE PLAN, section 4, para. 4(49))

While Warwickshire could subsidise the railway, it has little to do with the running of the railways, but such a statement is somehow felt to be necessary.

A second difficulty is that, even if these broad social pronouncements do have meaning, they tend, by their nature, to be inconsistent with each other. An interesting discussion by a representative of a group seeking to have a shopping centre located out of urban areas stated it this way:

> It appears that some of these objectives are very widely drawn and could easily lead to conflict between one objective and another. Take for example, objective no. 22, to provide a choice between the private car and public transport and to create optimum conditions for the operation of efficient and convenient bus and rail services. That, as an expression of an objective, might be regarded as quite unexceptional, but then one turns to objective 25, to meet car-parking demand. If, in fact, one studies, for example, in the Coventry plan, any attempt to meet the car-parking demand necessarily means that it would not be possible to have efficient and convenient bus services because of the congestion that would undoubtedly arise on the access road to the centre . . . let us look at objective no. 5, to locate new housing where good living conditions can be ensured. A wide and general statement with which no-one could disagree, but compare that with no. 7, to provide the widest choice of housing location, which presumably means that instead of being selective as to where the new housing is to go, that new houses should go, in terms of location, to the widest number of places. (TRANSCRIPT, Mr Nardecchia, 27 Nov 1973, p. 25)

The major area where the plans do become specific is, as one would expect in a land-use exercise, that of the geographical

144

location of new growth. Worcestershire's strategy is to keep the growth in the New Town or 'expanded' town areas near the urban area of Birmingham (principally Redditch and Droitwich). Warwickshire puts its growth near the edges of both the Coventry and Birmingham urban areas. Solihull will keep to a phased expansion in line with the sub-regional strategy worked out with its neighbours, and Staffordshire will open up housing land throughout the county. The only authorities to complain are the urban ones, and Birmingham is not of the opinion that the rural counties to the south have provided enough peripheral growth to accommodate the cities' hoped-for economic expansion.

Each of these authorities' land allocations are detailed in a map which shows the area but not the specific parcel. The final product then has certainly met the criteria of being 'flexible' and not overly map-based and rigid. The question is, however, if the final product is actually worth the effort. As an eminent counsel for a participant said at the examination:

> When you look to the document, do you not expect to find the means for resolving . . . [conflicts]? Not merely a set of utterances which could have been put down by anyone. . . . But in the end have some clear guidance as to the way in which irreconcilable or conflicting or even inconsistent views are to be viewed in the future by the public authority . . . unless that is done the structure plan may be a very nicely printed document and have everybody's signature on it in the end, but it will be found in practice, as we know so many plans have in the past, to be of remarkably little value. (TRANSCRIPT, Mr Layfield, 27 Nov 1973, p. 28)

In interviews held with planners in each of the areas, the question was put as to what was the usefulness of the content of the written statement in subject areas which did not bear directly on land allocation. The consensus of opinion seemed to be that it was 'good to have thought through some of the matters which, while not under our control, do directly affect our plans'. It was often stated that it was a good 'thinking' exercise, a way to make them (meaning the chief planners and politicians) reconsider some of the excuses given when planning decisions were made.

There seemed to be a basic contradiction present in the views

145

expressed by the local officials. On the one hand, they expressed appreciation of the Coventry type of 'corporate' framework that attempted to pour virtually all of the city's functioning into some type of relationship with the land-use allocation. They agreed with Professor Hall that this was 'the model of the future' (HALL, 1974, p. 703) and they liked to talk about how 'wide', 'diverse' and 'integrated' their approach had been. They all agreed that the organisation of the survey data and the testing of various possible alternatives for the location of growth had been extremely beneficial to their understanding of the area.

On the other hand, there was also virtual unanimity that the 'real' decision would come when the policies and the general ideas of each part of the county were actually translated into the local plans. It was often said that the 'actual' or important decisions would only be made when the local plans were drawn up and the actual land-use map for the sub-areas drafted. It was as though the learning process was all very well, but that it would not settle disputes when it came to a housing development appearing at a particular place on the edge of a particular urban area. Again it was here that the planners felt that they would run into strong local opposition from the affected neighbours, and few were very hopeful that the participation exercises would prevent that opposition.

One observer, commenting upon a professional conference on structure planning, put the contradiction this way:

It proved impossible to reconcile these qualities [variety innovation, diversity where planning is a learning process] with the more conventional outlook and organisation of planning. It proved impossible because the fundamental characteristic of 'learning processes' . . . the process itself seemed unacceptable. At one extreme, the preconception of traditional departmental executive activity and financial expenditure [and the immediate direct products of houses, schools, roads, etc.] was adamantly maintained. Similarly, the pre-occupation with the fixed point of a statutory structure plan was irreconcilable with the other extreme . . . the [learning process] in which planning becomes part of a more subtle, but essentially continuous, process of policy formulation and implementation. (ZETTER, p. 373)

146

When one looks at the structure plans this contradiction is evident. The written statements end up being a mixture of two things. Partly they consist of interesting, commendable statements on a wide variety of social topics, which are so commendable that they seem self-evident: 'It is the council's policy, because of the danger of noise nuisance and the need to ensure freedom of operation, to limit development in the vicinity of airports, and under approach and take off flight paths' (WARWICKSHIRE STRUCTURE PLAN, section 4, para. 4 (13)), and partly they are simply the first stage in the drawing of a land-use map of a very traditional type, with only minor modifications such as pinpointing problem areas through the use of action areas.

> The statement is remarkable for what it does *not* say. . . . But so many of these [policy statements] relate to matters over which a county council has little or no control . . . and what is the usefulness or relevance of a policy document like this, which includes statements about broad policy making and employment change on the one hand and aerial masts and bridleways on the other? That, of course, is not for the county council to answer, but for the central government who conceived the structure plan idea and enshrined it in statute. (MCLOUGHLIN, 1973*b*, p. 184)

What this look at the first structure-plan written documents does then, is call into question the very idea of a high-level strategic plan, and thus far it has not been seen to be particularly successful. Some view it as helpful but innocuous, while others see the process itself as wasting valuable government resources on a basically useless exercise. Another spokesman for the community-development project in Coventry questioned the very concept of structure plans, saying that:

> It appears to us that . . . beginning with abstract long-term objectives for housing has prevented the city from really grappling with the strategic implications of a very concrete problem like homelessness. It is almost as if the process beginning as a 'top down' process has strangled the planners from recognising what ordinary laymen are recognising . . . we would argue that, if the planning process had begun from

147

the concrete social problems that the residents of the city, and politicians, have identified, one would have in fact reached the strategic issues. (TRANSCRIPT, Mr Benington, 13 Dec 1973, p. 8)

It is interesting to note that in a recent circular concerning structure plans (CIRCULAR 98/74), the Department has had to remind the local authorities in bold type that they should stick to relevant matters and that: 'In preparing their structure plans, **authorities should therefore concentrate on those issues which are of key structural importance to the area concerned, and their inter-relationships**. . . . Issues which are not of structural importance should **not normally be dealt with**' (para. 5). It seems as though it is not only the outside observers who are worried about the meaning and content of the structure plans.

The *Circular* cautions the local authorities to stick to the basics of employment, housing, transport and major local issues such as shopping centres. Further, the Department again tells the authorities to make more explicit the assumptions upon which the structure plan is based, and it is perhaps significant that the *Circular* suggests a time-orientation of not twenty or thirty years but a mere fifteen years (para. 32).

Returning briefly to the ideas discussed in Chapter 3, it is useful here to include a note on finance. In one instance, a local authority had based its entire planning exercise and public participation over a number of years on the central government's avowed intentions to build a certain number of motorways and trunk roads in the county and to allow a number of major capital investments in schools and new streets. By mid-1974 the structure plan was ready for the public examination. However, due to the increase in the cost of petrol, the roads and road-building section of the D.O.E. had to inform them some weeks before the examination that the transport routes were being largely curtailed. Similarly, within a short time, they also received notice from the D.O.E. that, due to the rate of national inflation, all government capital expenditure was to be reduced and their major projects would have to be eliminated. As might be expected the structure plan tended to lose its relevance since it was no longer based on realistic data.

Since the local governments do not have actual control over their own budgets, it is worth considering whether the making of the plan and the great expense in time and money that it entailed were in fact worth the effort. Again the question that we have asked before seems pertinent: are plans for their own sake a worthwhile endeavour, and might the local officials' administrative energies be put to a better purpose? As suggested in Chapter 3, the local-government finance system may not be particularly well-suited to the purposes of the local planning system. Some observers, such as Hepworth, suggest that an attempt should be made to make local government more financially independent from central government. However, it seems equally plausible that an attempt should be made to make the decisions of both central and local government on finance more accessible and visible through a procedure of open budgetary review. The solution may lie not in a new system or institutional arrangement but simply in better access to the arrangement that currently exists.

To end this discussion we should remember that the process of structure planning may be a valuable one for its own sake, not for the sake of the documents it actually produces. It may lead a local authority to assemble data and consider aspects of its programmes which might not have ever been thought about in an ordered manner. Similarly, the method of public-examination review may well present a pleasant middle ground between no review at all and a review so thorough that the plans or documents are hopelessly out of date. These are the positive arguments for the structure-planning process. On the other hand, there is this rather disquieting note. At least one newly reorganised county – East Sussex – is, in spite of the old county's efforts on a structure plan, contemplating the submission of an 'instant plan'. This document would be prepared every ten to twelve months and contain programmes and strategies not for the next twenty years but for the next twelve months. Some counties, then, are already discarding the long-range or strategic for the more relevant and concrete day-to-day decision guide.

LOCAL PLANS

Irrespective of one's view of structure plans, great reliance will have to be put upon the local plans. It is the local plans that will

149

contain the actual land-use maps and, if the local control official is guided at all by local policy rather than his own wisdom, it will be by these local plans. The fundamental thing to keep in mind about local plans is that, although the local districts will have the responsibility for drafting local plans, the county will, through its Development Plans Scheme (Local Government Act 1972, part I, section 183), set the timetable for the production of the local plans and, most importantly, determine which areas are of such 'strategic' importance that they are county matters and that the county will draft local plans for them. There will also be a non-statutory 'Development Control Scheme', which will delineate which categories of strategic developments will require county permission and which will be left entirely with the districts. Any disputes between county and district can be referred to the D.O.E. for settlement. Also, the county must issue a certificate of acceptability of local plans before they become operative (Local Government Act 1972, schedule XVI, paras 2, 3, amending T.C.P.A. 1971 section 14 as from 1 April 1974).

Thus far, few of these local plans have been drafted and some observers (such as Mr Stoddard, the County Planning Officer of Berkshire, speaking at a conference of the Regional Studies Association on the topic of 'Structure Planning in Perspective', 22 April 1972) feel that the first set of local plans might take some fifteen years to prepare. Nevertheless, even in these early stages, comments in the press and interviews with local officials show that there will be no little amount of friction between the counties and districts.

This rivalry between the smaller districts and the counties could have a number of results besides mutual administrative ill will. Local districts will most probably follow local sentiment in their plans, even if this risks conflict with the generalisations in the county plan. They will be more likely to protect the local interests, whether they be development-prone or exclusionary. The devolution of power to the most local level may reinforce the differences between the types of communities represented, the wealthy area being less likely to have poorer neighbours, the poorer area taking on more industry to supply jobs for its population. Just as in the United States where 'local democracy' has created insulated, 'lily-white' suburban enclaves, the vesting of local decisions, under the local plans, in the smallest government unit may intensify the differences between those units.

Another possibility is that the central government, under its power to decide what is a county matter, will be involved, particularly in the early stages, in a great many disputes. Just when the D.O.E. thought itself free from the responsibility of approving local plans through lengthy public inquiries, it may be involved in settling all the major disputes involved in those local plans. The local matter which the district decides on and the county matter which the county decides on is nowhere clearly delineated, and the conflict arising from establishing those boundaries may very well prove to be a burden to the central government. For instance, one of the ideas of the P.A.G. was for the structure plan to delineate 'action areas' for intensive co-ordination of local-authority servicing and planning. Once it is established in the structure plan by the county the local district has a fixed time (ten years) to prepare a detailed local plan for that area. In districts that do not want to prepare the plan or spend their resources in supplying the servicing, the resulting district–county disputes will certainly draw upon the administrative energy of the D.O.E.

The problems resulting from the government reorganisation and the allocation of structure and local plans are beginning to come home to roost. In one article by Arthur Osman* a dispute between a Labour-dominated county council in Nottingham-shire and its Conservative local districts was described. It seemed that the area's draft structure plan contained a series of proposals to retain corner shops, discourage the use of private cars, and set up pedestrian precincts. The district councils were rather upset with these proposals which they felt were steam-rolling them and, most importantly for us, they felt that the county was reserving too much control for itself. The Broxtowe District Council made a statement that: 'If operated as drafted, the statement could result in a considerable increase of applications becoming county matters.' There were complaints in the press that the county was attempting to control district political decisions, which is not surprising since this is exactly what it might be supposed a 'policy' document is intended to do.

Undoubtedly difficulties will be experienced by the districts

---

* *The Times* (2 Mar. 1974).

when they attempt to draft the local plans, irrespective of the matters reserved as county matters and the degree of success of the development-plan schemes. Professor Graham Ashworth, President of the Royal Town Planning Institute, said in a speech that: 'District Councils, inadequately staffed, are insisting on their right to make local plans when and for where they like irrespective of county based priorities' and he went on to say that this is leading to 'chaos'. (Unpublished statement of the R.T.P.I. to the D.O.E., 15 March 1974)

The new districts, created in April 1974, without any previous planning departments, will not, however, be starting completely afresh. First, they must, as stated earlier, obtain a certificate from the county of the acceptability of their local plans, so there will be some county guidance. The actual staff of the districts will often have been drafted from the pre-reorganisation county planning staff. Secondly, as we saw earlier, there are already in existence not only the statutory types of old-style local plans, but there also are a great variety of informal plans for specific problem areas. Thirdly, since the districts will be just starting up an administrative structure, there will undoubtedly have to be a good deal of county–district co-ordination, at least in the early stages. Fourthly, of course, the development-plan scheme, stating who draws what where, will have been drafted by the county and will reserve some strategic county areas for local plans.

What will most probably happen is that, rather than follow the *Manual*'s suggestions for an elaborate design framework modelled upon the structure plan, the local districts will draft partial *ad hoc* plans for the immediate and urgent problems that are facing them. In an article by MacMurray it is suggested that the new district officials will probably define a limited annual programme of the most pressing local problems, concentrating upon immediate ways of meeting those problems, and simply look to the structure plans as a background or encyclopaedia of information. (MACMURRAY)

In one of the areas outside the Midlands, Hampshire (which has already drafted a structure plan, although it has not yet been examined or approved), the Deputy County Planning Officer has described how the local plans are being made ready to fit with the structure plans. In Hampshire there were a number of trouble spots, areas where growth was imminent but where no provision had been made for the water and street infrastructure, so the county began major local plans for these areas, at the same time as they were readjusting their structure plan. The county intends both to pass on partially formulated local plans to the new districts and, in the case of the growth-area plans, to retain the power, under the development-plan scheme, to draft the local plans for these areas. In the Hampshire case there are already some seventy-two plans or policies for various problems or problem areas, and this amalgam of town maps, village plans, and policies, not only helped to formulate the structure plan, but will serve as the core of the district's local plans, since in many cases they deal with the same town or village or action area. The Hampshire planner stressed that in his area

> complex webs of relationships will emerge to steer the many plans involved. These arrangements will be part of the corporate management process of the authorities and may need to be much more flexible than at present. This process of cooperation will, of course, be necessary in many other fields of planning, but it seems likely to be at its most critical if the requirements and guidance given in the structure plan are to be met in local plans. (BROWN, p. 508)

The fact that, in Hampshire, the structure plan and the beginnings of the local plans were drawn up simultaneously is not likely to be unique since, due to the staggering of structure-plan submission, there will be a great many district-planning staffs busily engaged in local-plan preparation before the counties submit their structure plans. What will be different is that the simultaneous process will take place in two different administrative structures. Since the process of participation and examination will take a number of years, the operative local plans will be virtually the only guide given to development control in some areas for years.

What this all brings into question is the original Planning Advisory Group's presupposition that strategy formulation is in fact at the heart of the planning process. Taking the views of a commentator introducing a symposium issue on local planning in *The Planner*, perhaps we should

> question the value of the time-consuming procedures now being adopted in producing very long-term strategies. In

153

time it may become necessary to go further still, and actively redeploy strategic planners at the local level. Local government reorganisation is certain to reveal that a good deal of local planning has simply not been done, partly because of the creaming-off of planning staff into structure planning, which may never succeed in getting to grips with the major strategic issues that it was intended to concentrate upon. (PERRY, p. 492)

Perhaps one has to go down to the specific, not the general, the particular parcel or block level, to reform the process successfully. This will be considered in Chapter 10, but first the central-government review of the structure-planning process needs investigating.

9 The Administrative Process of Reviewing Structure Plans

An exploration of the new model of administrative review being developed to deal with the structure-planning process is extremely important for a number of reasons. First, it is the whole central-government involvement with the process of making plans affecting local land-use decisions, so it is crucial to an understanding of the reform of the planning process. Secondly, it shows an administrative approach which is rather novel, and may serve as a prototype of the administrative review of various other official decisions or of long-range forward planning in various areas. Thirdly, the material may give the student of public administration some insights into the process of decision-making within a large central-government department.

The following description represents the author's own personal conclusions after a series of interviews with local planning-authority and D.O.E. officials. Besides the interview data, reliance was of course placed upon the various publications and the Public Examination *Code of Practice* of the D.O.E. We will start with the preparation stage within the D.O.E. and work through the examination to the final decision on the structure plan.

THE INTERNAL D.O.E. PREPARATION

While the structure-plan public examination is the principal public forum for considering the policy plan, and the report of the three members of the panel is of great importance in determining what action the central government finally takes on the plan, it is still only the tip of an administrative iceberg of negotiation and consultation. This process, and particularly the subtlety of it, must be understood in order to see how neighbouring authorities' land-use policies are co-ordinated.

The Department of the Environment is the central-government Ministry which must oversee the development-plans process. It should be kept in mind that, although the D.O.E. can in special circumstances call in the second-stage local plans, the basic idea of the two-tiered system is to let central government review only the basic policy questions in the structure-plan statement and leave the actual map-making of the local plans to the districts. Although the central government may have to step in from time to time when the local plans do not conform to the structure plans, the idea of the system is that the approval of the structure plans will be the only focus of central-government intervention.

At the national level the D.O.E. is composed of three ministerial wings under the Secretary of State for the Environment – Local Government and Planning, Housing and Construction, and Transport Industries. The regional offices of the D.O.E. are split along similar lines but, depending on the region, some of the subject matters are grouped together. In many of the regional offices there is a Regional Controller for both the Housing and Planning activities. In some of the larger regional offices, such as in the West Midlands Regional Office, there are three different wings (Plans and Planning, Housing and Environment, Roads and Transportation) which mirror the central-government configuration. In each department there are both the technical staff and the administrative (1st division) staff. The fact that both housing and transport are under the same administrative umbrella with planning is a great boon, for it ensures that adequate technical expertise is available in these two important areas to deal with projections and predictions.

The process leading up to the public examination takes a number of years and, while we have some idea of the various stages already in mind, it is the central orchestration by the D.O.E. which it is hoped will avoid delay in review and institute co-ordination between neighbouring planning areas' policies. Under the legislation, the D.O.E. selects the areas and the order in which the areas will start the structure-plan process. They began with the Midlands and are moving into the South-East, both areas of economic and population growth. Their plans have been delayed by the slowness of some local authorities, but generally the D.O.E. attempts to set the time-table for review.

The actual liaison with the local planners who are in charge of making the plans is done by the technical staff of the Planning Branch at the regional level. In the first stages the major contact between the D.O.E. and the local authority is a member of the technical staff, usually in the middle rank of the civil service, who has access to a variety of relevant skills such as statistics, planning methodology, demography and economics. He begins by having a series of very informal talks with the planning officers of the areas. In authorities without sophisticated manpower, planning officers are often not planners but have come to the field via engineering or municipal road construction. They rely on the D.O.E. liaison man a great deal for the methodology to deal with population projections, housing needs, employment availability, and so on. As this liaison progresses and the local units go through the various stages of survey and alternative strategy design, the technical man keeps his superior on the administrative side of the D.O.E. informed of his view of the various problems as they come up, and also of possible problems which will have to be dealt with between neighbouring units, or as issues at the public examination.

Within each regional office an appraisal team will be established during this early liaison stage. This team will consist of both professional and administrative planning staff, representatives from the transport wing of the regional office, and representatives from other departments of central government such as Agriculture, Trade and Industry, or the Countryside Commission. As the liaison progresses there are frequent meetings between the technical person and the local authority on methods or policies and, in the case of particular problems, there can even be an exchange of working papers and comments from various central-government departments. In the early structure plans this liaison was conducted on an informal and, because of the pressure of time, rapid basis. Elsewhere, when more time is available, this appraisal team within the D.O.E. will probably form a Consultative Committee which could meet on a regular basis with the local authority to discuss its proposals.

As this liaison progresses the local authority prepares a draft structure plan. Ideally this should be done after significant public participation has taken place but before the authority has finalised all its plans. When this draft plan is produced it is

157

presented to the regional office of the D.O.E. at a 'presentation meeting'. This meeting, while not a statutory requirement, in actuality represents the time when both the reason for the major policies and, more important, the major disagreements with the D.O.E. over the plan, will be presented by the authorities.

Throughout the consultation process the technical officers develop a knowledge of the techniques used by the authority, the main content of the plan, and the reactions of other government departments. By the time of this presentation meeting they can prepare a brief of the major difficulties that they foresee could arise and those matters that will have to be discussed at the public examination and perhaps modified by the Department. The idea of the presentation meeting is to alert the local authority to matters which must be reconsidered and possibly changed. The brief, then, includes a list of the contentious issues as well as the D.O.E.'s policy with regard to those issues. For instance, in Chapter 8, the public-examination discussion of overestimation of the scale of growth was mentioned This issue was mentioned continually to the authorities during consultation, was discussed with the D.O.E., and the authorities were notified at the presentation meeting that it would be an issue at the examination.

These presentation meetings between the D.O.E. and the local authority are not public and are in fact not even open to elected or political representatives of either central government or local councils. The meetings are essentially a local-authority show for the central government. In urban areas there has even been a coach trip to problem areas to allow the local authorities to point out the most severe problems to the appraisal team. The presentation meetings are attended by not only the technical personnel involved in the appraisal but also interested representatives from the Departments of Trade and Industry, Employment, and occasionally from the Ministries of Agriculture, or Health and Social Services. The central government hears this presentation and then replies with a series of statements of the problems it sees in the plan. Typically in one of the early presentation meetings one of the rural counties had a very optimistic view of employment growth, and both the Department of Trade and Industry and the D.O.E. representatives stated their concept of what comparable but more realistic figures would be.

An interesting factor to note about these presentation meetings is that, while the D.O.E. is obviously under some obligation to present all the factors that may be subject to criticism at the later public meeting, there is still no little disagreement about how definitive these comments should be. In the early meetings, while the high-ranking administrative officers would be very subtle in their criticisms, the technical staff who spoke the same language as the local planning officers would follow the meeting up with a letter detailing the possible areas of conflict.

The idea of the presentation meeting is to allow the local authority to rethink its draft plan with a clear idea of those factors which the central government will dispute. Also, since there is supposed to be a major public-participation exercise during this time between draft and final plan stage, it is hoped that the local authority might compare the ideas of the central-government departments with those of the local authority's affected public. Finally, after considering these two sets of ideas, the local authority then finalises its structure plan and formally submits it. It is this final plan which is publicly considered at the public examination. It is important to note that it is at this stage of final submission that the appraisal team has to decide whether the document submitted is, in fact, a 'structure plan' and statutorily acceptable. Considering the 'thinness' of, for instance, the Warwickshire structure plan, which was accepted as meeting the basic definition of a structure plan, in this author's opinion it does not appear likely that the appraisal teams will dismiss many of these submitted plans at this stage. It seems as though the D.O.E. will rely on the public examination to bring up any inadequacies in the plan and institute any major revisions through reservation or modification by the Minister after the examination process is complete. As we shall see, however, this reliance may not be well placed, considering the requirement for public participation and the resources available within the D.O.E. to attempt major planning exercises.

THE SELECTION OF ISSUES AND PARTICIPANTS

In discussions with D.O.E. officials it became clear that both the initial acceptance of draft plans and the selection of issues which were to be discussed at the public examination was a process which was quite sensitive to local party-political concerns, with great attention being given to local groups. The public examination was viewed as an important part of the entire process, but clearly not as the be-all and end-all of the system. The initial changes in its format, with the absence of a right to be heard or to cross-examination, were designed to make the programme run as smoothly and as quickly as possible. Thus, according to D.O.E. policy, the examination is meant only to guide the entire process. To use a phrase often repeated: 'It's important, but its importance can be exaggerated.'

The public-examination panel consists of three members – a chairman who has some independent and important role in the community, one member from the D.O.E. regional office who must come from either the Housing and Environment or Roads and Transport Branches (not the directly involved Plans and Planning Branch), and one member who has served as a planning-inquiry inspector. This panel is selected well before the examination is to take place, and the D.O.E. assigns to it a secretary, a career administrative officer of middle or principal rank, whose job it is to organise the public-examination meetings and serve as a conduit of information between the participants and the public-examination panel. The panel secretary and the technical person who has been working with the appraisal team draw up the list of matters which will be discussed at the examination. The secretary does the final drafting of this list and submits it to the panel chairman, who can add items to it. The panel chairman and members may not delete issues from the list, but in practice the published list (including the very important order of presentation) is discussed by the panel, its secretary, and the technical men to reach an agreed agenda. It is important to note here that the Town and Country Planning Act of 1971, as amended by the 1972 legislation, provides that: 'The person or persons holding the examination shall have power, exercisable either before or during the course of the examination, to invite additional bodies or persons to take part therein if it appears to him or them desirable to do so' (sec. 9, sub. [5]). This gives the panel the final say as to which parties can appear, and thus gives some degree of independence to the examination.

The avowed purpose of the D.O.E. during this public examination is to clarify, explain, expand and explore the

160

relationships of various parts of the structure plan. It serves as a forum to clarify which parts of the plan have to be modified or 'reserved' and, not incidentally, it allows the local authority itself to suggest changes that might be acceptable to both levels of government. One of the central problems, at least in the initial examinations, is to get the local authorities to separate their political policy choices from their methodology and growth predictions. At the moment the structure plans are coming in as self-fulfilling prophecies, for there is no way to distinguish the survey-based facts, which have been loaded to favour the final strategy chosen, from the policy itself. Some observers would say that this problem is inherent in the process, but it has been magnified by the fact that most authorities have used a number of factors, such as housing estates, or green-belt allocations, as fixed commitments on which to base their plans. They are not only committed to these because of the political decisions of the locality, but they treat them as given to direct even further policies for the area.

The drafting of the list of issues for discussion is crucial because, since the outside public do not have the right to appear or speak on whatever they choose, the selection defines the perimeters of public access and discussion. Turning to the *Code of Practice*, the basic criteria as to what will be examined are: clashes between the plan and national or regional policies, or those of neighbouring planning authorities; any conflicts between the various general proposals in the plan; issues involving substantial controversy which has not been resolved – 'an examination will not be concerned with every provision in a plan, any more than with pursuing all comments on it.' (CODE OF PRACTICE, 3.13)

It is important to note here the major areas of review with which the examination must deal. First there is the local authority's interpretation of national policies. Basically the examination provides a place to question parts of the structure plan that might conflict, say, with national employment or agricultural policy. The plan must be in general compliance with major government policies as enacted either in legislation or through the publication of White Papers or circulars. Secondly, the plan must give a fair interpretation of regional strategy and policies. This criterion is clear from the T.C.P.A., which requires that the survey include an appraisal of major

161

changes in not only the local authority but also neighbouring authorities (T.C.P.A., 1971, sec. 6, sub. 3). Similarly, Section 7 requires that the local authority shall have regard to 'current policies with respect to the economic planning and development of the region as a whole'. (T.C.P.A., 1971, sec. 7, sub. 4a)

The difficulty here is that few regional strategies have been completed and that regional policy statements vary considerably. Thus, in each area, the criteria for regional interpretation will be different depending upon the state of the local regional plans. There is a third area of examination, which is the consistency of the structure plan with those of neighbouring authorities. Under the statute the local authority is under an obligation to consult with neighbouring authorities (sec. 6, sub. 4) and to state the relationship of their proposals to the general proposals for the development and other use of land in neighbouring areas (sec. 7, sub. 3b). Further, when the final structure plan is submitted, it must contain a statement listing the consultations with neighbouring authorities and indicate the considerations underlying any major items of policy affecting neighbouring authorities and the extent of agreement on major items (sec. 8, sub. 3b; and Regulations 1972 [no. 1154] schedule 1, part ii[xi]). Here again the D.O.E. will have no easy task at the public examination because not only are the regional plans not agreed upon but often the neighbouring local authorities will be submitting their plans years apart. Thus, it will be quite difficult to see where the conflicts may occur.

A fourth area of review is the internal coherence or consistency of the plan. Generally this means that the aims and objectives relate to the problems and that the policies match the forecasts and estimates. Under the legislation the plan must include a reasoned justification of the policy and general proposals (REGULATIONS 1972 [no. 1154] schedule 9[3]). What is involved here then is an investigation of the gaps or contradictions present in the plan.

Finally, the examination will consider the provisions for the implementation of the plan. This will entail an analysis of the resources available and the general feasibility of the major policies. A major problem here is that, since the central government maintains annual checks on the capital expenditure of local authorities, it will be very difficult to know with a realistic basis the actual level of spending resources available to the local authority in the next three to four years. While it is possible at the examination to ascertain whether the demands on financial resources controlled by central-government departments are in line with the current estimate of expenditure, it is impossible to know future expenditure levels, since these are linked to national considerations of inflation and the balance of payments. Another aspect of the implementation, besides the financial one, which will be considered is the relationship between the structure plan and the future production of local plans. Here the examination panel will have to consider whether there is enough material to guide local plan preparation without being in such excessive detail as to take the local planning function out of the hands of the districts. The last aspect of implementation which will have to be considered is the local authority's proposals for monitoring its structure plan over time. Section 6(1) of the T.C.P.A. requires the local authority to keep its plan 'under review' and the examination will have to consider how this will be done.

The matters which must be considered are then compared with the matters that have come to the attention of the panel secretary through review of the public-participation exercise and the formal representations and objections to the plan. The controversial matters which come up through public participation are supposed to be set down in the local authority's statement about publicity and public participation: 'this statement will help the Secretary of State to appreciate what issues have proved controversial, and do not appear to have been suitably resolved . . . to consider which of these give rise to matters which should be selected for examination' (CODE OF PRACTICE, 3.16). Also the representations and objections to the plan 'will help him to appreciate which are the matters he should select for discussion at the examinations'. (CODE OF PRACTICE, 3.20)

The selection of issues to a large extent predetermines the success of the public-review exercise, where the public at large does not have the right to appear and thus select the issues by their participation in the review. In the first public examinations a great deal of attention seemed to be paid to the selection of issues of public controversy. Since the documents were so broadly drafted it was difficult to delineate the issues. The first

163

two considerations, about national policy and regional strategy, were fairly easy because these were the matters that the Department itself was concerned with. If the officials had conflicting plans between neighbouring authorities, or conflicts between plans and their own central-government policies, they were creating large administrative problems for themselves in the future, so they sought to remedy the situation as soon as possible. Similarly, it was not particularly difficult to point out internal inconsistencies in the plans. The difficulty that arose was how to judge the other issues which were not important to the D.O.E. administration of the planning system, but which were perhaps quite important to the various members of the public. The *Code of Practice* stressed that the examination 'will be directed to the matters which the Secretary of State considers need to be further investigated . . . it is the occasion for covering in public the matters to be examined, and for doing so in depth, but not for endless argument or for pursuing points of detail for their own sake' (CODE OF PRACTICE, 3.1). But it did not really explain what this probe meant or what matters should be included.

It should be apparent that the importance of representations and objections in selecting issues would vary dramatically depending upon one's view of the function of the public examination. If the examination is not to serve as a forum for disposing of grievances, nor as a place for the ventilation of differences of opinion, then it would not even be necessary to include highly controversial local issues if they did not directly affect the gathering of information for the Secretary of State's decision on modifications or reservations. Under some sort of pure theory of examination any matters that were in line with national and regional policies and presented in a coherent and consistent manner would not need to be discussed in spite of, say, strenuous opposition from a minority within the local authority. On the other hand, if the examination is thought of as a method of legitimising the structure plan – for allowing its basic logic or policies to gain public acceptance – then one would have to include local controversial matters even if they were not of strategic importance to the plan. Evidently in the West Midlands the latter opinion prevailed, for a number of items were included in the list of issues for discussion which were strictly local in importance but which seemed to be included, at least in this author's opinion, for the sake of building public confidence in the openness and fairness of the examination procedure. A number of items were included among the issues that were being considered elsewhere on appeal by the Ministry. For instance, major out-of-town shopping centres, new villages, electricity-generating plants, and even motorways were considered at the examination. Evidently it was felt too impolitic to inhibit discussion of such contentious matters, in spite of the fact that they did not affect the relationships between authorities and were being handled elsewhere.

After the submission of the plan, it is the authority's responsibility to make copies available for inspection, publish notices of this in the local press and then allow a minimum of six weeks for representations and objections to come in (CODE OF PRACTICE, 3.21, sec. 8, T.C.P.A. 1971, reg. 5 1972 Statutory Instrument no. 1154). Evidently this is being treated as both a minimum and a maximum time limit. A look at the representations and objections submitted for the first two examinations shows that the public is having great difficulty grappling with this 'strategic concept'. While some are policy documents prepared by major lobbies or conservation groups, others are simple letters from neighbours worrying about a particular field, road or footpath.

Turning, for instance, to Worcestershire, to discern the type of representations or objections that the D.O.E. had to sift through, of the initial twenty-two representations received, eight opposed the policy of growth for one small town, Kidderminster, six argued for and against village development in various villages, and eight were miscellaneous complaints. For nstance, one lady wrote to complain that she objected to the purchase of her front garden as public open space. Another person wrote to complain that an incursion into the green belt would hurt his home in an adjoining village. Another tried to discern whether his land was 'diagrammatically' chosen as 'built up' or green-belt land. The representatives of large organisations, such as the National Farmers' Union or the Council for the Protection of Rural England, tended to be more abstract and deal with more general concepts, such as village-development policy, or the scale of the green belt. Often there was some overlap between the particular landowner and the organisations, but the most emotional letters seemed to come from the single individual. For instance, while there was a great deal of comment on the expansion of the central Worcestershire villages, it was the comments by the particular residents, who saw the possibility of their villages turning into towns, or their back-garden view into houses, that caused the most heat.

The D.O.E. has allowed itself a relatively brief period to try to integrate these representations and objections into the list of issues, for under the *Code of Practice* (3.34) the preliminary list of matters to be examined, and participants, comes out within four weeks of the expiry of the objection period. As it turned out in the first examinations, the issues that were selected were quite different in the different areas and, as might be expected, the participants selected tended to be the spokesmen of the large group and of private interests.

In the Warwickshire examination the list of issues started with an area-by-area discussion of growth, an analysis of transportation, and then green belt, recreation and shopping facilities. Although the process received substantial press coverage, the only private individuals represented were either interested academics or major property holders. The more typical participant was, say, the National Chamber of Trade, the Birmingham & Midland Motor Omnibus Co., or the Midland New Towns Society. In Worcestershire the D.O.E. started with the question of employment availability, then the housing that would be needed to meet this employment, and then the area-by-area growth proposals. This was then linked to the transportation needed to support that level of housing supply. Finally the countryside problems of village growth, recreation, power stations and out-of-town shopping areas were dealt with. In the urban setting of Coventry the matters for discussion were the particularly poor areas of the city, and how to meet the needs of particular or special classes of city resident.

This preliminary list, to which, it must be remembered, the panel chairman can make additions, is published, and there is again a four-week period for representations or comments on the list of matters and participants. It was at this point that a number of would-be participants first realised that the statute (T.C.P.A. 1971, sec. 9) allowed for the exclusion of some people. For instance, one local residents' group in Worcestershire, the Greenhill Residents' Association, wrote:

We . . . do most strongly object to not being included as an organisation which will be represented at the examination in public of the . . . structure plan . . . we have put in considerable time and effort (and) we therefore demand, as a reasonable body of citizens (800 members) the right of representation at the examination. . . . It would appear most unjust that with all this support we are not entitled at this moment of time to a hearing at the examination. (WORCESTERSHIRE REPRESENTATIONS)

We see here then that it is possible, within the workings of the system, for views both to be ignored by the local planners during the participation and then not brought up at all by the D.O.E. as an issue. Looking at the internal D.O.E. treatment of this important decision, the feeling seemed to be that 'sufficient weight should be given to those people who have taken the trouble to make representations or objections . . . but the examination is not for hearing objections. Participants are there to clarify issues.' Once chosen, participants also seemed to have trouble with the order of discussion: 'My difficulty arises, Sir, in the breakdown that you have suggested for this discussion, because it does not seem to cover all the matters I wish to raise.' (TRANSCRIPT, Mr Blennon Hasset, 29 Nov 1973)

Since it is the Government who has to make the decision on issues and participants, a number of things are lost. In the normal adversarial process of, say, a public inquiry the parties themselves decide what it is they wish to discuss, that is the selection of issues, and they also usually arrange the order of that discussion. The adjudicator in such a system simply accepts the information given to him and decides on the basis of that information. However, under an inquisitorial method of inquiry such as the public examination it is the adjudicator or, in this case, the D.O.E. and public examination panel who select the issues and decide the order of discussion. The chairman is supposed to restrict 'off the point' remarks that might open up wider discussions, and it is the panel members who in fact control the debate rather than the parties themselves through examination and cross-examination. For instance, it is the D.O.E. which has to determine which are 'genuine associations' and which are merely fronts, and which has to 'balance' the discussion to get what it and the panel consider a fair discussion.

By having the government body which is doing the public review select the issues, it may well be that there is more likelihood of including matters that might be missed in the bluster of confrontation-style adversarial inquiry. This is very likely since, under the statute, the D.O.E. or the panel can call in outside participants who have not made representations and ask them to contribute to the examination. For the first public examinations this was done, and people appeared who might not otherwise have participated. However, it might equally be true that the D.O.E. or the panel, despite its good faith intentions, might not choose to discuss matters that would be of extreme importance to some members of the local community. While it may perhaps be unlikely that the D.O.E. would choose not to have any participants on issues on which there have been representations, the Department is clearly entitled to do so under the statute. It is important to see, then, that the discussion of such issues depends, not upon the parties' ability to bring them forward, but upon the government officials' good faith and administrative efficiency to do so. The worrisome thing, then, from this discussion of the selection of interests and participants, is that it might be the case that the D.O.E. could omit a crucial issue or person, and the system does not seem to allow for the fact that the community of interests and disagreements between the local authorities and central government might in fact not include all the important matters for the planned-for public.

THE EXAMINATION IN PUBLIC

After the publication of the final list, a notice of the examination is published and then, some six weeks later, the examination itself begins – approximately six months after the original submission. According to the *Code of Practice* published by the D.O.E., the examination 'will be designed to create the right atmosphere for intensive discussion but to get away from the formalities of the traditional public local inquiry. . . . The panel should not sit apart from the participants, but that the panel and participants should, whenever possible, sit round the same table' (3.50), and the essential feature of the examination 'will be that of a probing discussion, led by the chairman and other members of the panel.' (3.45)

In order to start this process in the correct atmosphere there is first a preliminary session, the purpose of which is to stress the different nature of an examination *vis-à-vis* an inquiry, the lack of counsel, and the 'probing' nature of the panel's role. It is here that the participants are introduced, the programme dates and times established, and the mechanics of the appearances clarified. The hope as expressed by one D.O.E. spectator is that when the first session actually begins, 'the whole atmosphere of the examination is established in the first ten minutes. . . . [It will be] a totally different pattern . . . a human atmosphere'.

The idea is that the examination will inform the D.O.E. decision-makers about the various factors to be taken into account, and allow for some measure of legitimation through public discussion. This is all to be done rapidly enough to get the process completed before the plans become obsolete. The first examinations certainly were speedy and they were very different indeed from the normal, almost judicial, style of the public inquiry. They were held around squares of tables and they kept strictly, almost rigidly, to their published timetable.

There were, however, some difficulties, expressed by the participants:

> We find as participants here that few of our questions seem to be the right ones. On the one hand the questions are detailed and cannot be answered in this forum. We [also] tend to be told that our points are too general and are not really structure plan issues anyway, and it makes one wonder why we are all using the tax-payers' money to go through this sort of procedure (TRANSCRIPT, Mr Herson, 12 Dec 1973, p. 21),

or

> the way the conversation goes, the way the agenda each day, and what you tell us you are going to discuss, doesn't give us much opportunity to decide exactly what we are going to say. We are following a probing discussion are we not. (TRANSCRIPT, Mr Stone, 4 Nov 1973, p. 17)

The difficulty seemed to be mainly that because there was no cross-examination the level of discussion varied dramatically. At some times the panel followed up (probed) questions them-

169

selves, and there was in fact a discussion in the true sense of the word. In other situations, questions that were of vital interest to the participants would simply be left hanging:

> It depends whether there is a free and fair discussion of all points. At the moment Warwickshire's policy seems to be not to answer any of the points at all. I think it is fair to say this depends on the chairman. (TRANSCRIPT, Mr Braithwaite, 16 Nov 1973, p. 32)

> [Mr Chairman] you yourself [should] ask, make, the city council's representatives justify their proposals. Because quite honestly sir, we can continue to shell up arguments, points, queries, statistical questions, comments about blight, but as long as we are getting no answers to them we are speaking into a great void. (TRANSCRIPT, Mr Waddington, 12 Dec 1973, p. 28)

THE ROLE OF THE CHAIRMAN

It seems then that the reliability of the process depends upon the chairman taking a very interventionist role. The D.O.E. told the first chairmen that the examination 'will involve much more intervention than is customary on the part of inspectors'. However, the role played by the first two chairmen seemed to differ dramatically. The first, a retired civil servant, was not what one would call a great 'inquisitor' and when the 'probing' was left to him it often fell flat: 'I mean I don't want to get into the situation of having a statement and counter-statement and a sort of reply and then another' (TRANSCRIPT, Chairman Heaton, 4 Nov 1973, p. 19). He would often even follow up requests for specific questions by bringing in someone else to say something, or simply by saying 'I do not think that we can usefully take this part of the discussion any further at the moment.' (TRANSCRIPT, 15 Nov 1973, p. 15)

The other chairman, a barrister, took a very different approach. He felt that, if lawyers were not to be allowed into the process to sort out the detailed issues and clarify the facts, someone had to sift the facts, and the obvious person was the chairman, sitting almost as a continental judge, asking questions, calling on participants and pinning statements down. Not surprisingly there was very little dispute and a great deal more praise from the participants for his handling of the examination.

170

There is perhaps no little irony present in the fact that a process that is designed to eliminate lawyers and cross-examination should work best when it is a lawyer who is running the procedure.

These chairmen had a further problem beyond that of monitoring the factual content of people's statements and that was to dissociate themselves sufficiently from the D.O.E. to take on an independent role. In the first public examination the panel sat with the D.O.E. at its right-hand side at the same end of the table. By the time of the second examination, even this physical association was eliminated and the D.O.E. officials sat out amongst the other participants, well away from the panel. This emphasised the D.O.E.'s role as a participant like the others present. In the first examination, although the secretary was a D.O.E. employee and one of the panel members was a member of the regional office, the panel went to great lengths to play an independent role. During the examination the chairman would rebuke anyone for associating them directly with the D.O.E.:

'I think copies are with your department, sir.' (Mr Swann)
'You must not talk about my department. I have no department.' (Mr Heaton)

The D.O.E. personnel did not discuss the examination privately with the panel members during the proceedings, and it was understood that, even at the regional office, the examination would not be discussed until after the panel report had been submitted. In interviews with local authorities' planners this autonomy was felt to be legitimate in spite of the fact that the panel received its oral and written briefing from the D.O.E. throughout the pre-examination period. One planner said how good the chairman was, how he had asked just the correct questions to give the proper form to the discussion and how he seemed, far from being a puppet of the D.O.E., to be particularly hard in questioning their men. Nor did the planners seem to be worried by the fact that at least two members of the panel could not oppose government policy as stated by the Minister or in ministerial circulars.

One interesting innovation was attempted at one examination, which will presumably be attempted again. When the participants could not agree on particular methods they withdrew for a 'side-room discussion' to reach an agreed-upon statement of the differences between them. The idea of this is to allow for the discussion and, hopefully, the resolution of questions of a technical nature where there is disagreement between the authority and another participant. These side-room discussions are open to all who might be interested, and it is hoped that this will provide a means of settling technical disputes in a rapid manner while the more general discussion continues:

> Since there was some disagreement on employment-fore-casting the chairman requested the Worcestershire County Council and the Department of Environment and the Department of Employment to hold a side-room discussion on the methods appropriate to forecasting employment. (DAILY NOTES, 15 Jan 1974, p. 3, para. 10)

In this case the side-room discussion allowed government departments to question the local authority's puffing of employment statistics which were based on interviews with industrialists and reach a compromise figure of possible employment growth.

The question arising from this description of the format of the public examination is what good qualities does it possess. First, of course, there is speed, for in the context of planning there seems to be a need for some popular exposure in as short a time as possible. If policy cannot be articulated and reviewed quickly, then decisions are taken solely on the basis of unarticulated policy which is not reviewed in public at all. A comparison of the carefully orchestrated public access in a public examination with the complete lack of involvement in the development of unstated policy under the obsolete development plans shows the examination in a considerably better light. Development-control decisions on the basis of current policy documents that have been aired in public are certainly better than decisions being made entirely inside the administrative structure.

A second virtue of the examination process is that it allows the central government to prod the local authorities into reappraising their ideas, and it removes some of the static or rigid nature of drafting land-use maps. Being nurtured and guided by the D.O.E. officials seems to produce an element of compromise upon the part of the local officials that would, perhaps, not be there without this form of presentation. For instance, when asked to compare the examination with an inquiry, one chief planner said: 'I really found the examination to be valuable. There was a form to the discussion, a way to talk about the issues that seemed to be lost under a deluge of local issues in the old town map type inquiry.' Instead of producing something final called a plan, which is then met by a barrage of criticism, the carefully orchestrated, almost contrived, review perhaps allows policy to evolve or progress.

One final point that is mentioned by the system's supporters and detractors alike is that the local man with a very small or detailed complaint is purposely excluded. This, of course, gives the speed but there seem to be grave doubts as to whether some 'policy' matters might necessarily be made up of an aggregate of very small and local issues, issues that will not be raised at all if they are not brought forward by the local owner. Even one of the chairmen expressed the view that the 'little man was not there to bring up the localised policies'.

This then brings up some of the system's obvious inadequacies, and points to some possible changes. The problems with the process are the general offensiveness to one's sense of fair play by excluding some private individuals, the lost order of presentation and the lost internal ordering of arguments, and of course the already mentioned lack of cross-examination to determine the validity of statements. Now these matters, which are the very strengths of the other process, have been excluded deliberately, but it seems that there are some changes needed to buttress the inquisitorial style.

First, as already mentioned, the chairmen should be chosen for their experience in questioning and sorting out facts. This points to individuals either in the legal profession or in executive or administrative positions which require skilled verbal 'probing'. The style of the examination depends, not upon a person being conversant with the particulars of the planning issues involved or the workings of the civil service, but upon the person's ability to make the participants clarify and give meaning to their statements.

Secondly, a vital change is needed in the administration of the panel's activities. Since the issues to be discussed, and the people discussing them, are all set by the D.O.E. and presented to the panel through the panel's secretary, an objector's or representer's secretary is needed, who would have a very different brief. He could be called in from outside, being a planner or a lawyer, and would be able to make suggestions as to participants or issues which, while not of interest to the D.O.E. or the local authority, might be of keen interest to some members of the public. While the panel chairman would have the final say on adding participants, as he does now, this would allow a very different view to be presented to the panel as to what was important. This advocate might also help the panel to pinpoint items that need clarification or more probing.

Thirdly, following up this idea and the frequent calls for some type of 'planning aid', this objector's secretary would not only have a brief to help the objectors, but also a fund to give financial help, at his discretion, for the presentation of necessary but under-represented views. One of the frequent criticisms by the participants in the process was that the best-argued cases were given by the large interests, and

> How difficult it is for the ordinary man in the street to make representation on these structure plans. . . . if we had financial and expert resources as ordinary citizens to call on we could have mounted all cases which have been submitted. . . . during this examination we have not been asked any probing questions or arguments about the view we have expressed. Therefore, perhaps we feel a little frustrated. (TRANSCRIPT, Mr Peek, 20 Nov 1973, p. 5)

The objector's advocate would see to it that certain representative local individuals or local groups were given the resources and, incidentally, that they were 'probed' for their views.

THE PANEL'S REPORT

After the examination, the panel's chairman prepares a report, making recommendations on what action the central government should take on the plan. The original idea was that there would be a daily transcript of the examination and that the chairman would be saved from a detailed summarisation of the factual disputes, merely making a report much like a select committee report in Parliament with the evidence attached. As it turned out, the transcripts ended up costing some £5000 for each examination, and there came to be long delays in publishing the transcript. It may well be that the transcripts will be eliminated entirely, and at the moment the panel secretary has begun to make daily summaries to accompany the panel's report.

It is not insignificant that the opening words in the first panel report published are those of Anthony Trollope in his novel *Can You Forgive Her?*:

> 'I like to have a plan', said Mr. Palliser.
> 'And so do I,' said his wife, 'if only for the sake of not keeping it.'

The three members of the panel, who sat for some 20 examination days in November and December 1973, were not uncritical of the structure-plan documents for the county of Warwickshire, the city of Coventry and the county borough of Solihull (PANEL REPORT). While they acknowledged that these authorities had suffered from a number of disabilities, not the least of which was the local-government reorganisation, and the fact that these were the first attempts at the new system, the panel's comments were not exactly laudatory. In looking at this first structure-plan public-examination-panel report there are two important aspects of the exercise which must be considered. First, the report contained a number of criticisms of the approach and methods of the plan-makers which are reminiscent of the comments of the Layfield Report on the Greater London Development Plan. These criticisms should thus be seen in the context of the types of difficulties which will face all government officials who are set the difficult task of making such a structure plan. These criticisms also tell the observer something about the difficulties with the structure-planning concept itself. Secondly, the report contains a number of recommendations concerning possible additions or changes in the plans. These changes will form the basis of the Secretary of State's action on the structure plans in terms of modifications or reservations. The changes recommended by the panel in the first report thus give a valuable insight into the role which the panel considers it and the public examination should play in the evolution of the structure plans.

Turning first to the criticisms, the panel found three basic difficulties with the planners' approach. The first and perhaps most disturbing for those who believe in the utility of the final structure-plan document was a lack of content in the plans. The panel was critical of the council officials for both changing their figures or projections dramatically within the time of the examination and also for putting meaningless statements in their plans. On the one hand Coventry City Council doubled its estimate of net migration out of the city between 1973 and 1986 within a few months of preparing the document. On the other, Warwickshire defended its plans by giving them no content at all. As the panel put it:

> Nor should flexibility be used as an excuse for not having a plan at all. For example, a statement by Warwickshire County Council that 'the plan is completely flexible as between the public and private transport sectors' seems to us to mean only that the role of public transport has not been considered. (PANEL REPORT, 2.7)

A second and related criticism was that even where there was content it often lacked a precise meaning, one that an intelligent reader could understand and apply. Often what appeared as firm policy in the documents was shown during the examination to be a flexible guideline subject to frequent change or reversal. The drafting of the structure plans was thus imprecise and according to the panel often did 'not reflect the Council's intentions' (PANEL REPORT, 2.9). This imprecision put the panel in an unenviable position in that they were required first to translate the document and then to attempt to see whether what was meant was realistic in the setting. According to the panel such a realistic approach was often lacking.

The problem which the panel met in these two criticisms is of course the central problem with such a strategic document. It must have content, yet be flexible enough to guide growth in the future. As the panel put it:

> A structure plan should be flexible within clearly understood policy decisions. It should not need to be changed dramatically but the authority should be prepared to change the plan, at least to a lesser degree, if monitoring suggests this to be necessary. . . . it must be sufficiently firm to enable people to know what to expect. (PANEL REPORT, 2.8)

As we saw the experienced planners in London were not, according to the Layfield Committee, particularly successful at this difficult task. It would appear from the first structure-plan public-examination-panel report that the provincial planners cannot be expected to perform in a categorically different manner. It is perhaps not a coincidence that the over-ambition one saw in the G.L.D.P. was mirrored in the over-bidding for growth that one saw in these three structure plans. (PANEL REPORT, 3.10)

The question of how much information the document would actually cover was one which seemed to trouble the panel a good deal, particularly in the context of the requirements for public participation. It was this problem which was the focus for the third major criticism of the planners. While the panel began from the position that the Secretary of State had already approved the public participation as adequate, they did not seem particularly impressed with the efforts of the authorities. The most forceful argument of the panel was that it would have been difficult for the public to participate meaning-fully on the basis of the structure-plan documents irrespective of the forum or format of the public-participation exercises. The public was not presented with statements in the documents which related their actual problems to the policy of the council. According to the panel the public often had difficulty in under-standing the possible policy alternatives, the relevant considera-tions pertinent to those alternatives, or the particular reasons why the councils chose one policy over another (PANEL REPORT, 2.12). Often the policy choices were presented as irrevocable conclusions and rarely were the reasons presented in a manner that would allow members of the affected public to comprehend those reasons and make meaningful comments. The panel was of the opinion that a great deal of the trouble was not the lack of logical reasoning but the obfuscation of that reasoning behind a curtain of planning jargon which made parts of the documents incomprehensible. To quote the panel:

We consider that planners will have to develop a greater mastery of the art of expressing themselves in plain words if public participation is to be effective. This aim would be further assisted if the relevant documents, of which there tend to be a great quantity, could be expressed in terms and issued in a form which did not put them beyond the reach of all but the addicts and the affluent. (PANEL REPORT, 2.13)

177

The question that comes to mind is whether the policy choices of the government officials would be as easily acceptable if stripped of their patina of professional language.

The panel's criticisms of the structure-planning process served to reinforce the importance of the panel's own function. If the plans lacked content, or needed clearer definition, or were unintelligible to members of the public then the public examination took on new importance, for it provided the best format for allowing central government to take an active role in ensuring meaningful and realistic policy statements. If one looks at the role of the examination and the recommendations of the panel it becomes apparent that the examination is crucial to the success of the process of making a structure plan, and is the only setting in which the various competing interests of the neighbouring authorities and parts of the community can be reconciled.

Turning to the public-participation function of the examination, the first panel itself recognised that the examination was perhaps the only setting in which the planners and the various spokesmen for groups in the community could communicate on an even footing. The panel itself was asking the questions, and the issues were already outlined by the D.O.E., but it was the presentations of various groups which brought the points home to the council officials. The panel clearly recognised that the examination performed an ancillary role beyond that of providing information to the Ministry, the panel was the final court of appeal for the public to express its views. The panel concluded that this was a very valuable role, not only for the sake of the integrity or legitimacy of the process in the eyes of the body politic, but also for the sake of the formulations of policy in the documents themselves. As the panel put it: 'Indeed, there have been occasions when we had the impression that different participants were listening to and understanding each other's views almost for the first time' (PANEL REPORT, 2.14). It went on to recommend that the participation function of the examination should be expanded, if anything, and that a wider range of participants be woven into the format. It also recommended that more representatives of industry, commerce, and local residents' groups, and particularly more women, be included in the examination process. What the panel seemed to be doing then was recognising that the examination had the unique role of synthesising the views of the community, the D.O.E., and the local authorities into one policy document.

The first panel went about this synthesis in a very defined and deliberate manner and was not timid in its recommended changes of the submitted structure plans. For instance, the county borough of Solihull in its structure plan allowed for only a limited population increase (some 18,000 over the time of the plan consisting of 12,000 natural increase and 6000 from immigration from other areas). Solihull is a middle-class well-to-do suburb of Birmingham and in its public-participation attitude surveys it found a definite no-growth sentiment among its populace. On the other hand the neighbouring county of Warwickshire foresaw a need for growth near the Birmingham urban area and planned for a large part of that growth, based on people moving to the area, to be located in Solihull (the natural increase plus 13,000 from immigration from other areas). The problem was that one council was refusing to take the increase that the other council felt they should have. The panel analysed the various costs and locations and concluded that Solihull's reasons for declining to plan for the extra amount of growth (that is some 7000 people they did not want) were based, not on monetary or geographical constraints, but on a commitment to 'no growth' for its own sake. The people living in the pleasant, rather attractive town, had no desire whatsoever to have it changed. The panel, however, in the context of the examination, could see that other communities which would have to accommodate this growth were equally disinclined to have the newcomers in their towns or villages. The panel concluded that the views of the local residents could not be the sole determinant, and then proceeded to recommend to the Secretary of State that the structure plans be modified to allow for a greater population in Solihull than they proposed in their structure plan (PANEL REPORT, 3.29). The panel then selected the particular area in Solihull which could accommodate the growth, and recommended the necessary changes in employment policy, manufacturing-industry location and transport policy to allow for such growth.

Another example of the types of change the panel recommended concerns the allocation of growth between the northern

179

and southern parts of the county of Warwickshire. As was mentioned previously, this issue was one which a number of academics had brought to the attention of the D.O.E. and which they articulated at the examination. Basically, the issue was that the county consists of a number of smart, wealthy communities in the south and working-class towns with few amenities in the north. The structure plan made no attempt to reconcile the differences between the areas or to plan for more balanced communities with more middle-class residents in the north of the county. The panel concluded that the county was making no attempt to direct or plan towards reducing these differences and that there was much that it could do in the way of providing infrastructure and amenities in the north: 'We take the view that there should be a positive planning policy to put growth in (the northern part of the county) with the twin objects of rectifying the present social and environmental imbalance between the north and south of the county and of reducing development pressures on the south.' (PANEL REPORT, 3.49)

What is of special importance here is that this policy, an attempt to help local depressed areas within a given county, had not been developed in any national forum or any local authority. It took the unique chemistry of the public examination to develop the idea of compensatory planning within a given locale. As the public examination panel put it: 'At the level of national policy it is common practice for less well-off areas to be given preferential treatment and, if conditions are already better in the south of the county, we cannot see that it would be unfair to spend more in the north.' (PANEL REPORT, 3.52)

The final area of the panel's recommendations which helps one to understand the first panel's view of its role and function is that of transportation. Transport is one area within which the local authorities have the actual power to spend money in such a way as to influence development. The authorities construct and maintain the various local road networks, and they have the power to subsidise the local public transportation services. The problems were, however, that the councils either had no policy at all (Warwickshire) or else had uniformly ignored public transport. Each of the plans contained elaborate road plans but none of the three contained, in the view of the panel, adequate discussions of the means of transport for those without automobiles. In its report the panel recommended that each should attempt to do something about the lack of public-transport policy (PANEL REPORT, 4.26). However, unlike the case where the panel could pinpoint where development might go in terms of a population compromise, there was no attempt upon the part of the panel in its report to delineate what the public transportation sections of the structure plans should contain. It could not recommend a new approach when little was said about the issue at the examination beyond the fact that the structure plans were completely inadequate.

This then shows that although the panel can establish inadequacies it cannot serve as a plan-drafter. It can compromise between competing approaches to a given problem, but it cannot assemble totally new information and impose that on the council. One wonders what the Secretary of State for the Environment is expected to do with the plans, when faced with the choice between approving an inadequate plan or reserving the transport section of the plan until the councils investigate the possibilities. The effect of the latter choice is that the Government would be re-affirming the *status quo*, that is, that there would be no public transport plan at all. It seems logical to assume that the third possibility, namely that the D.O.E. investigate and propose a public transportation plan itself, would be beyond the manpower capabilities of the regional office and, for that matter, beyond the design and purpose of the structure-planning system.

Drawing conclusions from the first panel's report may be a bit premature, but it would seem that there are some themes which are likely to be repeated, for they are some of the same issues raised by the G.L.D.P. review. On the one hand there are the criticisms concerning lack of content, imprecise drafting (or thinking), over-ambition, and a lack of meaningful consultation with the affected public. It was only in the public examination itself that some of these difficulties were overcome and various compromises between groups and neighbouring authorities arranged. It was the public examination which allowed for the creation of new policy (such as for the allocation of resources to less well-off parts of the counties) out of the draft plans, and the discussion of such policies between officials and interested members of the public. It is

181

important to note that the first panel was in an especially advantageous position for reaching such compromises because it was reviewing more than one structure plan. It is perhaps only in such a situation that any type of sub-regional policy can be thought out and implemented. Finally, one must conclude that while the public examination can serve as a forum for compromise or even the creation of new policy out of established information and policy choices the examination cannot create entirely new parts of the plans. If part of the structure plan for a given area is fundamentally lacking in content, supporting research or policy alternatives, it is not possible for the examination panel to do much more than point out that inadequacy.

THE D.O.E. DECISION-MAKING PROCESS

We have now reached the final stage of the administrative review, when the examination report is submitted and the final decision must be taken. Under the *Code* the panel's 'report following the examination will form an important element in the Secretary of State's decision-making process' (3.58). He has the choice, under the statute, of rejecting or approving the plan, with or without modifications or reservations (T.C.P.A. 1971, section 9 [1]). His decision letter, officially called notice of approval, combined with the submitted plan, becomes the statutory structure plan. We know from the *Code of Practice* that reservations will probably be the preferred form of tampering with the plans, since they do not require the advertisement and opportunity for objections or representations (but not more public examinations) which are needed for formal modifications. What we will explore now is how the administrators go about this delicate task.

As we saw, the appraisal team within the D.O.E. has been working with the local authority throughout the draft-plan and public-participation stage, and it is the appraisal team which focuses on the problems in the plan at the draft-plan presentation meeting. This same group briefs the panel once the final structure plan is submitted and, based on their technical appraisal and public objections, helps to advise the panel and the panel secretary on the important question of the selection of issues for examination. It is also this group which prepares the D.O.E.'s own presentation as a participant at that

182

examination. Once the panel submits its report, this same group within the D.O.E. regional office prepares a list of detailed points either omitted by the panel report or not dealt with in sufficient detail. Based on these matters and the report itself, the panel secretary produces a draft D.O.E. analysis of the panel report together with a tentative decision letter.

This analysis and recommended course of action must take into account a number of factors. First, there will presumably be a predisposition upon the part of the D.O.E. to accept the findings of the panel, since it was created by statute to be the major source of information for the Secretary of State's and thus the Department's decision on the acceptability of structure plans. Secondly, the analysis will have to take into account the report's implications for other aspects of government policy. If the panel has made recommendations that conflict with other stated policies or programmes, the Department would want to justify its rejection of this aspect of the panel report. For instance, if the report strongly condemned, say, peripheral growth in a White Land area, the Department might want to reaffirm its policy of encouraging housing development in that area. Thirdly, the analysis would have to take into account both the possible courses of action by way of modification or reservation and the effect of such action on other parts of the plan.

Since the various parts of the structure plans are linked, a major modification in an increase in the number of houses in an area would have to result in an increase in industrial sites, in shopping and recreational facilities. One important point that became clear through the interviews was that, in spite of some people's hopes for a national co-ordination of land-use through the public examination vehicle, this departmental analysis centred mainly on compromising the disputes between neighbouring authorities. In this author's opinion the D.O.E. took a reasonably constrained view of its role in producing a national strategy of land-use. It evidently felt that, since the responsibility for land-use planning is placed by statute on the local planning authorities, there should not be any attempt to introduce a 'grand scheme' of the central government's manufacture. The county councils had the responsibility of making the plans and the D.O.E. seemed to leave them fairly free to follow their own local aspirations. The D.O.E. seemed to view its function as the co-ordinator between authorities rather than as the innovator of new national policies at the local level.

Once this analysis and draft decision letter has been prepared, it is circulated extensively throughout the regional office both within the planning division and other divisions and, where relevant, within other government departments. This process generally takes some four to five weeks after the panel report has been received, although in the first examinations it took a good deal longer. After these comments are considered, the appraisal team and the panel secretary prepare a revised draft analysis for approval by the Regional Director. Once he has approved the analysis a draft of the formal notice of approval of the structure plan can be prepared by the same group, and this decision letter is then sent on to the London headquarters of the D.O.E. for consultation and review. Again the headquarters' office may seek comments from other government departments and, in discussions with the regional office, make changes in the draft report prior to submission to the Minister (in this case the Secretary of State for the Environment) for consideration and approval.

The D.O.E. has a difficult task in selecting which matters must ultimately be reserved or modified by this notice of approval. For one thing, since the structure plans are so all-encompassing and the factors are so interrelated, any major change in one part of the plan will have effects on other parts of the plan that may be difficult to appraise. Further, in situations where the D.O.E. has accepted a poor effort by a local authority as being an adequate structure plan for submission, it is extremely difficult to initiate major revisions. While the making of structure plans is supposed to take two to three years, the review process is a matter of weeks, and the burden on the regional office for any major redraft would be significant.

One problem facing the regional teams is that if they attempt to alter or rewrite a plan radically, without detailing the changes at the public examination, they are presumably creating a document without any public participation. So they must try to modify the plan without incorporating fresh matter. They can amplify and clarify issues in the plan, but once they introduce ideas that have not been discussed at all in public they lay themselves open to severe criticism, and they may violate the statute's requirements for 'adequate' public participation.

Another problem to be dealt with was the use of reservations, which are an innovation under the structure plan legislation. According to the *Code*: 'It is [the Secretary of State's] aim that, where he needs to differ from the plan as submitted, he should do so as far as possible by expressing reservations in his reasoned decision letter: and that modifications of any formal kind [which entail altering the plan itself] should not be proposed unless essential' (CODE OF PRACTICE, 3.47). The idea is to increase the flexibility of approach and the speed of issuing the decision letter. The reservations would withhold parts of the plan, but they carry with them, by definition, a lack of a plan for a given area. In a process already marked by its breadth and lack of concreteness, the reservations will introduce a new element of uncertainty. If wide use is made of reservations the local officials will presumably go about development control as they did before, basing it either on the obsolete development plan or on *ad hoc* policy-making.

The Secretary of State can of course direct that parts of the structure plan be resubmitted, as well as using the power of reservation to invalidate sections of the plan. Again, though, this may simply result in a lack of any plan and lead to further delays. There does not seem to be any way that the central government can force rapid redrafting, and the D.O.E. does not seem particularly well-suited to doing the task itself, either in terms of public participation, its statutory mandate, or manpower and facilities. If the D.O.E. is really, as it publicly professes, only supposed to act as an adviser, it is in a quandary. Either inadequate plans (and some of the plans already submitted would, in some people's estimation, fit into this category) will have to be left as they are, thin and yet grandiose, full of over-estimation, and yet weak on real guidance, or else the D.O.E. will have to make large parts of them inoperative, through reservations, and thus create a 'non-plan'.*

---

* It is significant that in the Warwickshire Structure Plan case this did in fact occur. The D.O.E. and the County are still disputing (July 1975) the list of 9 draft modifications and 4 reservations to the plan. They include such fundamental matters as the placing of 6500 more people on the eastern edge of the conurbation, the establishment of sports and recreational facilities in the green belt, and the possibility of major shopping centres outside urban areas. Further, the D.O.E. required the County, by reservation, to prepare and submit a comprehensive

Once the Secretary issues the tentative notice of approval, which contains the modifications or reservations, the local authority then meets with the D.O.E. to discuss the changes and any possible instructions for resubmission of parts of the plan. It then publicises the notice of approval, and the public may make objections for a period of six weeks. It will be during this time that the public will first learn of any major redrafting done by way of modification by the D.O.E., and if there is a controversy concerning major new material the Secretary of State has the option of re-opening the public examination to reconsider it.

The public-participation section of the T.C.P.A. places the local planning authority under an obligation to take such steps as will, in their opinion, secure 'adequate publicity is given . . . to matters which [the local authority] propose to include in the plan; that persons who may be expected to desire an opportunity of making representations to the authority with respect to those matters are made aware that they are entitled to an opportunity of doing so and that such persons are given an adequate opportunity of making such representations' (T.C.P.A. 1971, sec. 8 [1] a, b, c). If the D.O.E. introduces a new 'matter' after the preparation of the draft plan and the public examination, such a person would not have been allowed an opportunity of making any representations about it or in fact be allowed to do so. If a section of the structure plan was inadequate and the Department significantly modified it, these modifications would become such a new 'matter'. The affected person could then challenge in High Court the notice of approval as a violation of the rights contained in Section 8. Under Section 244 of the 1971 T.C.P.A., any person aggrieved by a structure plan or any alteration of such a plan may question the validity of the plan within six weeks of the publication of the first notice of the approval or adoption of the plan by making an application to the High Court. By claiming that the requirements of the Act in Section 8 were not met, and that he had been personally affected, the member of the public could seek to have the Court quash the plan. There seems to be a major

---

transportation policy and noted that they had given 'serious consideration to the possibility of rejecting the whole plan' because of the inadequacy of the original plan's transport policies. The D.O.E. statement (unpublished June 1975) said that they did not 'take this drastic step only because it would lead to renewed uncertainty on other questions'.

difficulty here for the D.O.E. because it would seem to be the case that Section 8 was designed to ensure that the local authority would provide adequate notice and facilities for representations. It should be noted that Section 8 leaves the determination of adequacy not to the D.O.E. but to the local authority ('in their opinion secure'). Now we mentioned earlier that this may be an inadequate guide to public participation at the local level but it does clearly leave the responsibility with the local authority. In the circumstance we have just described, it would appear that it was the D.O.E., not the local authority, which would be determining the adequacy of publicity and public participation on the modifications. It would seem, then, that all the challenging party would have to do to prove lack of compliance with the Act is obtain a statement from the local authority that the local authority did not find the matters proposed in the modifications had been given adequate public discussion. At the end of the day, the Court would have to decide whether the Department's approval or rejection power over the structure plan included within it the right to determine the adequacy of its own public-participation matters or whether such new matters had to go back to the local authority for them to determine such 'adequate publicity'.

What this discussion does is to emphasise the difficult position the D.O.E. is in where it has accepted a 'thin' structure-plan submission. Not only might it be difficult to arrange for extensive modification, but there might come a point where such modification was an abrogation of the statute. In the great majority of cases, though, such extensive work will not have to be contemplated and the publication of the final notice of approval, which is issued after the six-week period, will become, along with the submitted plan, the total approved structure plan for the area.

It is perhaps appropriate, at this point, to end the discussion of structure plans and the problems in their approval, and to begin a discussion of the less abstract, less general, more localised and specific process of plan-implementation and development-control.

187

10 Reforming the Control Process

The title of this chapter is *not* 'reforming plan implementing' because that would imply that there was in fact a causal relationship between the development plans, in their shiny new armour, and the day-to-day decision-making process at the local level on planning applications. Since such a supposition is tenuous to say the least, we will start the discussion from the premise that we are investigating a bureaucratic process dealing with applications on a case-by-case basis. While there are frequent attempts to lump all public-development decisions together under the rubric of 'planning control', we will leave aside the decision-makers in charge of their own public purse and concentrate on the area where public officials attempt to control the use and development of land which is not directly in their ownership. Britain's attempt to control private development piece by piece is at the heart of the system, and if policy is not being realistically formulated in the structure plans, then, if it exists at all, it must be within the process of development control.

By returning to the local and particular decision we have come full circle from the idea of strategy and policy in an abstract sense to an arena of very concrete particularised decisions. We are back to particularised rights in relation to specific parcels of land, with personal property interests being affected by the decisions. The rather hazy, over-generalised nature of structure plans, and the intra-government disputes which seem to be looming on the local planning horizon, point to the fact that the attempts to re-arrange radically the approach to planning attempted under the P.A.G. and the 1968 legislation have not particularly altered the importance of the individual caseworker's decision. We are back, then, to the problems we saw in Chapter 5, only with the reorganisation of local government, and the time-consuming development of structure plans, the problems of the ability to man the casework part of the process are in even more serious doubt.

POSITIVE PURPOSES IN A NEGATIVE PROCESS

Compared with the lofty aims of the development plans, and the positive development ideas present in, say, the arranging of a New Town or the compulsory purchase and comprehensive redevelopment of land, development control is concerned solely with what one can *not* do on one's land. Although some 80 per cent of the 615,000 applications received in 1972 were permitted, development control is the focus for the criticism of those who cannot expand their homes, build their shops, find inexpensive homes to buy, or stop their neighbours from erecting an ugly addition to their property. Since the development-control caseworkers can only negotiate – they cannot force owners to build or develop in some way that the owner does not desire or think profitable – they often find it very difficult to convince themselves or the public of the value of their work. While there is some hope of using planning conditions to mould development more positively, this is not the usual procedure. Perhaps, then, we should start by looking at the particular facets of the goals or purposes of planning which the control officers have to believe in in order to justify a process which can only bear fruit in the *non*-appearance of development.

First, we have to take as an article of faith the proposition that a review by a local-government employee will prohibit more development that the 'public' would consider 'bad' than it will development that they would consider 'good'. The reason this has to be accepted on faith is that nowhere in the legislation are the criteria of 'goodness' or 'badness' of deciding on a particular development actually laid out, and no studies have been made (or perhaps are possible) which can show that this piece-by-piece review is having beneficial results. Perhaps Lewis Keeble, writing almost fifteen years ago, expressed the tenets of the faith most lucidly:

As always with statutory planning, a great deal of the greatest success cannot be seen on the ground, but consists in the prevention of evils. If one were to add up the total amount of good done by preventing damage to quietness, privacy, safety and general pleasantness in residential areas

189

through excluding unsuitable uses, it would add up to a total sufficient alone to justify the whole elaborate code of legislation and the large and unwieldy planning machine which is operated. (KEEBLE, p. 58)

In order to accept this almost religious sentiment, we have to return to those goals mentioned previously which form the underpinning of the planning legislation. We must accept the notions of the 'goodness' of physical order, the idea of constraint of urban areas, the provision of 'amenity': in a phrase, the garden mentality. At the particularised level the judgement which the caseworker exercises has to be guided by what he or she thinks does not offend the public consciousness. In the words of the Parliamentary Secretary to the Ministry of Town and Country Planning, in the first years of the Act's implementation: 'If a man seeks to build an isolated home in the countryside it is clear that he is entitled to do so, so long as it does not affront the eye, absorb farm land or create some other public mischief' (in HARRISON, p. 258). It is this concentration on the nuisance quality of development which, in fact, the caseworker must ultimately fall back on. In the same way that a court can weigh the competing claims in a neighbourhood and eliminate a land-use that is a nuisance, when reviewing an application the caseworker must look to the particular surroundings, weigh the claims against notions of the planning legislation's aims (which, as we have seen, include conservation or amenity), and reach a conclusion.

At the start of an analysis of the control process it should be borne in mind that a number of commentators do not accept this fundamental creed at all. Apart from the growing number of journalists who criticise the green belts for depriving people of cheap housing land, there is a body of academic opinion which holds the view that the underpinnings of the planning system were, in fact, geared to the protection of the affluent and upper-middle class and that the aggregate effect of the control decisions has been to deprive the great mass of people of homes, gardens, jobs, or even accessible amenities. Peter Hall's massive two-volume work on the containment of urban England is perhaps the most erudite exposition of this view:

The main theme underlying [the ideas of urban containment and what I have called the garden mentality] is the un-

190

desirability of rapid or profound change. This is not surprising as a slogan for a group which was securely in possession and which felt a threat to the status quo. . . . This was easier because as possessors they could manage the political system. . . . [The policies lead to small cramped housing but] perhaps only a few yards from the new estate, at most perhaps a mile or two, the open countryside extends uninterruptedly. Here and there stand meticulously preserved villages or isolated cottages, long since deserted by their original agricultural owners and bought by the more fortunate citizens of exurbia. . . . Rural England was of course always a place of segregation, of social status, where the social hierarchy was finely but firmly drawn. By and large, it has remained so. The more prosperous members of the old county society, joined by selected newcomers from the cities, have sought to defend a way of life which they regarded as traditionally their right. The weapon they have used, and it has been a powerful one, is conservationist planning. (HALL, 1973, vol. 1, pp. 626–8)

Perhaps, with this dispute as to the purpose of what the caseworker is doing in mind, we can proceed to the way in which he approaches the refusal or granting of a planning application. It must be remembered that, compared with his colleagues in structure-plan work at the county level, for example, the caseworker in the new district planning authority is of a markedly lower calibre. He has less academic training, fewer professional qualifications and a lower salary. Further, it is generally conceded that, with each new set of recruits, it is rarely the man with the top qualifications who takes a position in development-control work. There may be many factors to explain this phenomenon, but a crucial one is the character of the work itself. The mundane parcel-by-parcel review, the servicing of the development clientele, simply is not of the type that stimulates or attracts the recent graduate. In Harrison's words:

Younger planners would perhaps rather work on more academic tasks where they can be insulated from the real political processes and can also retain illusions about the social and economic benefits of planning. The limits encountered in implementation can be ignored and there is no

need to face up to the real image of planning with the public.
(HARRISON, p. 269)

It is no wonder, then, that the caseworkers feel like second-class citizens in their jobs.

Turning to the job itself, we must start by looking at how the process functioned under the old local-government system and from there we can proceed to how it will function under the new system. Under the old system, with all the planning power located in the counties, it would seem likely that at least the location of casework would be clear. As it happened, however, the counties, although they were prohibited from delegating away all their planning functions, worked out with the old local districts a series of bilateral agreements to delegate the casework of development control and enforcement. Various types of districts entered into such agreements. Various sizes of districts could enter into such agreements with the counties, and all boroughs of more than 60,000 population could insist on such a delegation agreement (T.C.P.A. 1971, sec. 3, Circular no. 58/ 59, Town and Country General Regulations 1969 Statutory Instrument no. 286). Some counties relied heavily on delegation, while eleven counties had no such system at all. The delegation agreements allowed a flexible arrangement between the counties and districts, but with the counties always maintaining the final say and always receiving notification of all planning applications. It also led to a great many conflicts between the upper and lower tiers, a duplication of effort and a lack of speed in processing. The old process, described at length in Professor Mandelker's study of green-belt application processing in East Sussex, starts with informal contact between the caseworker in the local council and the prospective developer. After this consultation, and various advice as to the best way to submit an application, the developer submits an application for planning permission. The caseworker both views the site and talks with various people in his department, and reaches a personal decision on the 'goodness' of the development. Under the statute, the local authority 'Shall have regard to the provisions of the development plan, so far as material to the application, and to any other material considerations.' (T.C.P.A. 1971, sec. 29)

This leaves the caseworker reasonably free to reflect what he thinks is the view of the 'public' and in particular what the views of members of the local council's planning committee might be. The caseworker makes up the recommendation on the application in a short paragraph or two and submits this, along with similar recommendations on a long series of applications, to that committee. These recommendations tend to be automatically approved *pro forma* unless a particular political complaint has been made to one of the council's planning committees, in which case there might be a short discussion. Although there may not be contentious issues in the great majority of the cases, it is the caseworker's decision which is actually the controlling one. As Mandelker said: 'In the counties which I visited, the planning committee followed the advice of its technical officers in at least 95% of the cases.' (MANDELKER, 1962, p. 69)

The existence of the delegation agreements meant that the wise developer would make his preliminary consultation with both the county and district officers. When the application came in, copies were sent to both levels of local government and the county would decide whether this was a matter that was to be decided by them or left to the districts. While there are a number of different models for liaison between the two levels – joint efforts, successive review, or mixed application review teams – a fairly typical one would be the situation in the city borough of Rye. There the County Area Planning Officer would consult with the Borough (district-level) Surveyor on the site and help to formulate the recommendations to the Town Planning Committee. The Town Planning Committee would either approve or not approve that recommendation at one of its meetings every six weeks and this decision, in turn, would be ratified by the entire Borough Council. Under this particular delegation agreement, in cases where the planning committee and the full council disagree the county makes the final decision. In an unpublished study by Graham the relationship between the county and the borough was explored and the supremacy of the county's role was underlined. The county could call in any important planning applications, and the caseworker could pay close attention to important matters. Also, due to the small economic base of the borough, any major disagreement which might result in an inquiry or a compulsory purchase order had to have the backing of the county, or else the cost could conceivably endanger the financial position of the small borough. Graham goes on to point out that, since the old development plan merely said about the town of Rye 'the county will continue to be predominantly agricultural, residential and recreational in character' and the town map for the area only covered existing use up until 1967, the case-by-case decisions depended very much on the particular views of the caseworkers. He found that in some cases the town map was pointed to as the primary reason for a decision, while in others it was ignored completely. (GRAHAM, p. 12)

This then leads to the crucial question: under the old system what was the basis of the decision? Graham points to the personal feelings of the development-control caseworkers. Mandelker states that 'as the departmental liaison between the county and district councils, the area officers' judgment on the individual application will often be controlling' (MANDELKER, 1962, p. 87), and he goes on to say that 'the technical planning officer appears to predominate. Vagueness in the county development plan and in the green belt concept allows him to use a wide degree of discretion in reaching his decision.' (p. 89)

McLoughlin, in an extensive survey of seventeen local authorities, framed a questionnaire which revealed that the caseworkers themselves felt that the development plan really was the most important factor in their decisions, followed by 'local policies, the site and its surroundings, precedent, experience and common sense and personal judgement and philosophy' (MCLOUGHLIN, 1973a, pp. 99–100), but in his own analysis the 'written matter of development plans' (like the structure plan) ranked well below the inputs of the personal site view or an up-to-date local town map. What this means, then, is that the very 'technical' task of reviewing a particular application for development is in reality a very subjective process, not capable of being defined in terms of standards, but only a matter of subjective revelation from the caseworkers.

INFLUENCES ON THE CASEWORKERS: POLITICS, CENTRAL GOVERNMENT AND LAW

There are three external influences which must figure dramatically in the caseworkers' general approach, the first being the role of political opinion, either ideological or party-political, the second being the views and influence of central government, and the third being law. Political views exert their influence at the juncture between the caseworkers' recommendations being presented in the planning committee's agenda (either the county or delegated to the district) and their recommendation to the entire council. According to most of the studies undertaken, and my own interviews, the personal view of the committee chairman is usually the key ingredient in approval. The control officer will often keep very close control over the information coming to the chairman and the view he expresses. Since, by definition, the chairman is an elected and thus an 'amateur' planner, the caseworker attempts to create a relationship which requires him to act as an interpreter or teacher to the chairman. Graham described how in Rye the discussion at committee meetings was always guided by the chairman and caseworkers acting in concert. In Dennis's study, when his group of fairly provocative residents attempted to supply information directly to the committee members and bypass the antagonistic caseworkers, they were met with statements like:

Look, the proper and decent thing to do is to write to the planning department. The chairman [of the planning committee] has asked you to write through the paid officials. . . . Any normal decent transaction should be done through the officials. The officials advise on policy. The councillors generally, not always, but generally, accept the advice of the officials. (DENNIS, 1972, p. 209)

Dennis goes on to criticise this attempt at information control, and makes rather stirring pleas for local democracy, but this leads to the second aspect of the relationship between party politics and caseworkers' decisions.

In Britain the unified centralised nature of the political process guarantees any individual government figure at the local level a certain level of anonymity. While local issues are the caseworker's bread and butter, his elected counterpart on the planning committee knows that his political future will, to a large extent, reflect national party performance, *not* local issues. It is this anonymity which, in part, led to the recent local-government scandals. The representatives are interested in the occasional application, but they know that they will not be held responsible at the local polls. The caseworker will keep track of what he considers to be major changes in political policy such as, for instance, a national need for residential building plots, but will not necessarily be guided in his day-to-day decisions by the particular nuances of local party sentiment.

The next influence on the local control official is central-government policy, as expressed through either the ministerial directives and circulars or the planning-inquiry procedure. The circulars and directives tend to be abstract and open-ended. Mandelker found that on the green-belt decisions the circulars could not develop or articulate criteria with enough precision to guide the caseworkers (MANDELKER, 1962, p. 125). Similarly, on planning appeals against refusals of planning applications, the D.O.E. always tends to approach the process in an *ad hoc* way, its professional civil servants concentrating on the problems of keeping their own workload running smoothly rather than attempting the formidable task of national co-ordination of policy through the appeals decisions. Great credence is given the inspectors' decisions at inquiries, and they are more or less left to their own judgement: 'Decisions do not serve as precedents, and only the most general guidance is provided by the circular. In 95% of the cases the inspector is affirmed, even though his judgment is largely an individual reaction to the planning site and to the arguments of the parties.' (MANDELKER, 1962, p. 138)

It should not be overlooked, however, that the major vehicle for having the planning officials reconsider their planning decisions is the public inquiry. For both the planner and the lawyer it is the inquiry that provides the focus for whether or not any given decision is 'best'. The report of the Franks Committee in July 1957 led to a code of procedure for these inquiries, which is drafted by the Council on Tribunals (Tribunals and Inquiries Act, 1971). These rules establish the groundwork for the quasi-judicial format of the inquiries and are laid down in the Town and Country Planning Inquiries Procedure Rules, 1969 (1969 Statutory Instrument no. 1092). These public re-evaluations applied to a great many situations beyond merely the refusal of a planning permission, such as the pre-1968 development plans, the designation of New Town sites, advertising display decisions, and so on. The rules established the rights of the people who appear at inquiries to make written submissions, to have site inspections, and to call evidence. The planning official will presumably go about his decision-making job keeping in mind the type of procedure he may have to go through if his refusal is challenged. It should be stressed that, under the Rules (Rule 7[1]), the people who may appear as of right are the applicant, the local planning authority (including affected New Town development corporations and the district council where the land is situated), and a limited category of third parties who must be notified. These include the owners, or agricultural tenants, or persons who have made representations within the time limit about an application for development which requires public advertising under section 26 of the 1971 T.C.P.A. These are again the various unneighbourly uses laid down in the General Development Order.

This public inquiry procedure has not been altered fundamentally and it still serves as the primary forum for the review of specific decisions. Provisions have been made for the inspector's decision to be final in a prescribed category of planning appeals (T.C.P.A. 1971, Schedule 9). This, in many ways, simply formalises the accepted practice in the great majority of the cases anyway. There was an as yet unused major innovation introduced in inquiry procedure in the 1971 T.C.P.A., which allows the D.O.E. to establish something called a Planning Inquiry Commission (T.C.P.A. 1971, secs 47–9). This was, in many ways, the forerunner to the public examination process in that it was an attempt to see a wide public evaluation of major land-use decisions. The idea was to have a team of investigators (three to five members), rather than one inspector, who could look at not only objections and representations but also national or regional considerations and technical and scientific aspects of the development. The Commission could thus identify a wide range of policy considerations. Since it has not been used, however, we cannot yet evaluate its ability to live up to its potential, and at the moment it is not a viable consideration on the caseworker's horizon.

The third and perhaps most important factor of the caseworker's function is the framework of the planning law itself. The complexity of the legislation juxtaposed with the British judiciary's characteristic aloofness from reviewing 'policy' in administrative decisions have contributed to the caseworker's ability to go it alone, within the general limits of a process which only allows him the choice of approving or disapproving applications for someone else's idea.*

The complexity of the process is formidable, and the applicant, member of the public, or elected representative on the local council, are all equally at the mercy of the caseworker as to the particular categorisation of a development idea and its relationship to the statutory framework. For instance, there is a scheme for central-government review of 'substantial' departures from the development plan, but it is possible that the official may consider it not to be substantial and approve the application, so it will not even come to the notice of the D.O.E. Similarly, the scheme has provisions both for changes of use of a structure to a similar use (under the Use Classes Order) or the erection of minor structures or alterations (under the General Development Order), but even in these areas of development, as of right, the caseworker's categorisation may, to a large extent, be controlling.

The courts are capable of reviewing actions which are beyond the scope of the statute, but generally it seems that the intervention of the judiciary has strengthened the powers of the caseworkers to make binding decisions. For instance in the case of *Lever (Finance), Ltd.* v. *Westminster Corporation* [1970] 3 All E.R. 496 the caseworker had sanctioned variations from the originally approved planning application over the telephone, and the developer continued with the development. After a demonstration at the council level caused the council to override the planning-control official the developer went to court. Lord Denning, in supporting the developer's reliance on the officer, said:

> It should not be necessary for the developers to go back to the planning authority for every immaterial variation. The permission covers any variation which is not material. But then the question arises: who is to decide whether a variation is material or not? In practice it has been the planning

---

* In the Dobry review of the development-control system discussed below the final report suggests that the traditional scope for judicial review, namely that the court can review the administrative action only if the action is 'not within the powers' granted in the legislation, should be extended to cases where the administrative decision was ambiguous or 'unreasonable in a comprehensive sense'. (DOBRY FINAL REPORT, p. 146)

officer. This is a sensible practice and I think we should affirm it. (p. 498)

Generally, the local authority is bound by the statements and actions of the caseworkers when they purport to act upon the authority's behalf, *Wells* v. *Minister of Housing and Local Government* [1967] 2 All E.R. 1041. In fact, the 1971 T.C.P.A., section 4, allows the local authority to delegate authority in a variety of situations directly to the officers of the authority; 'where any functions have under this section been delegated to an officer of a local authority, any determination by him . . . shall, if it is notified in writing to the applicant, be treated for all purposes as a determination of the delegating authority' (sec. 4 [5]). The same legislation that had brought in the new structure-plan system, the 1968 T.C.P.A., also established a number of provisions to strengthen the caseworker's hand in dealing with the control of development and the non-compliance with permissions granted under that system. First, in the enforcement area, the officials had complained that it was difficult to stop a use of land before the unauthorised development or use had irrevocably changed the character of it. Part II of the Act provided for a system of 'stop notices' which could be used immediately to prohibit use pending a decision on the validity of the enforcement notice. Section 19 allowed the imposition of fines for the violation of such stop notices.

Further, the planners were given a stronger set of powers governing buildings of historic or architectural interest. Under a system of listed buildings, rather than individual building-preservation orders, the planners were given wider powers of preservation, including the power to preserve the building themselves for six months pending a central-government decision on the suitability of permanently protecting the building. Further, the authority is given the power to acquire such buildings compulsorily if they are being allowed to fall into disrepair. If the disrepair can be shown to be deliberate compensation will not take into account any redevelopment value of the site.

Over the life of planning legislation there can be seen the gradual expansion of these types of powers with the planning authority. Trees may be preserved (T.C.P.A. 1971, sec. 60), caravan park sites controlled (Caravan Sites and Control of

199

Development Act 1960, and T.C.P.A. 1971, Part v), and the display of advertisements regulated (T.C.P.A. 1971, secs 63, 64, 109). The problem has been that, while the government has seen fit to expand this negative-control power of the local offices and thus strengthen the caseworkers' position, they have not been particularly helpful in supplying the caseworkers with new positive tools to make new land-uses occur. The most notable example of this is in the area of conditions attached to planning permission.

CONDITIONS

While the 1971 T.C.P.A. allowed for the conditions to speed up developments applied for by use of completion notices (sec. 44), the general rule, as most recently laid down in Circular no. 5/68, is that conditions can only be used to serve 'some genuine planning purpose in relation to the development permitted'. And planning purposes have been strictly defined to mean the particular land-use needs of the particular project. For instance 'permission to extend a building cannot properly be granted subject to a condition that a car park shall be provided large enough to cater for the employees in the extension and the existing building' (Circular no. 5/68[9]). Similarly, the court in *Hall & Co., Ltd.* v. *Shoreham-on-Sea U.D.C.* [1964] 1 All E.R. 1, struck down a condition requiring the construction of an ancillary road to an industrial plot, saying:

> Under the conditions now sought to be imposed, on the other hand, the plaintiffs must construct the ancillary road as and when they may be required to do so over the whole of their frontage entirely at their own expense. . . . In this circumstance, although I have much sympathy with the object sought to be achieved by the defendants, I am satisfied that conditions 3 and 4 are so unreasonable that they must be held to be ultra vires. (p. 7)

The most recent case concerning conditions, *R.* v. *London Borough of Hillingdon, ex parte Royco Homes, Ltd.* [1974] 2 All E.R. 643, again highlighted the limited extent to which the courts will allow local authorities to use planning conditions to mould development. There, the local authority had given planning permission for seven blocks of three-storey flats subject to a series of conditions that restricted the cost, design,

type of residence, and type of resident of the development
(basically to create housing for low-income tenants on the local
council's waiting list). The court declared that the conditions
were so unreasonable that they were beyond the powers of the
local authority under the planning legislation. Lord Widgery
said of the conditions that

> they undoubtedly in my judgment are the equivalent of
> requiring the private developer to take on at his own expense
> a significant part of the duty of the local authority as housing
> authority. However well intentioned and however sensible
> such a desire on the part of the planning authority may have
> been, it seems to me that it is unreasonable . . . [and] clearly
> ultra vires. (p. 651)

THE COURTS AND THE ROLE OF THIRD PARTIES IN LOCAL PLANNING DECISIONS

One of the most fundamental issues with which the courts have
had to deal is the position of members of the public – neighbours, amenity groups, special interest groups – in the process
of making planning decisions. In the same way that there has
been a judicial emphasis on the strength of the caseworkers to
police, but not to enforce, new development, there has also been
a general reluctance upon the part of the courts to define the
role of third parties in the process or give them any legal right
of access to that process.

When the caseworker approaches any given planning
application to decide whether it is in the public interest he
must, among other things, look to the views of the particularly
affected neighbours. The particular view that would be spoiled,
the regency building that would be placed next to a garish new
development, or the noise and bustle that would be created by
a new group of stores, all must enter his mind when he evaluates
a permission. The legal question is do the caseworkers or the
council have to go out and solicit those views or, in fact,
consider them when making the decision. In a practical way
this question is reduced to one of whether the third party has
the right to have the courts question the process of decision-
making at all.

The basic tenet of the planning legislation has been that its
purpose was, to quote Salmon in the classical case of *Buxton* v.
Minister of Housing and Local Government [1960] 3 All E.R. 408

201

'To restrict development for the benefit of the public at large and not to confer new rights on any individual members of the public' (p. 411). The *Buxton* case was concerned with a local-authority refusal of planning permission for a chalk-pit operation, which went to appeal before a public inquiry. Interested third parties, namely neighbouring landowners who feared the nuisance of the chalk dust, appeared at the inquiry. The inspector recommended that the local decision be maintained and that planning permission be refused. The Minister rejected the inspector's report, and the party actually involved, the local authority, did not challenge the Minister's finding under the provisions for a statutory review in the courts under what was then section 31 of the Town and Country Planning Act of 1959 (now incorporated in T.C.P.A. 1971, section 245). The neighbours attempted to appeal against the Minister's decision in the High Court under this section. That statutory right of appeal to the court was restricted to persons 'aggrieved by any action on the part of the Minister' and the court held that those neighbours were not such aggrieved persons. The result of this decision was that third parties, individual members of the public, had no legal rights to challenge the decision-making process of either the local planners or the Minister.

Returning to the caseworker, this gives him a rather wide rein when exercising his powers and at the same time leaves the role of the third parties rather ill-defined. This was especially true in regard to the granting of permissions as opposed to refusals. If there were a refusal the applicant could request a ministerial appeal, a public inquiry before an inspector. Interested third parties could make written representations and it came to be the general customary, although not legal, rule, that they could appear at the inquiry and participate. However, in the granting of permissions the only check was the call-in procedure of the Ministry. Not only might the third party not be notified, since he possesses no legal rights, but there would be no guarantee that the Minister, namely the D.O.E., would actually consider a submission that some application was ripe for a review.

The recent changes in the legislation in some ways strengthen the third parties' position. For certain categories of development the application for planning permission must be accompanied by an advertisement and site notices. (T.C.P.A. 1971, sec. 26)

These unneighbourly uses are specified in the General Development Order and include such unsightly things as turkish baths, public conveniences, sewerage operations, and slaughterhouses (General Development Order 1963, amended in the General Development Order 1969). What is important here is that these requirements of newspaper advertisements and site notices may in fact be some of the most important reforms introduced into the process. To the outsiders these requirements, along with the requirement that the planning authority keep a public register of planning applications and decisions, are the method by which they can have cognisance of the local planning ideas and bring their views to the attention of the planning official. For the official they are a way to acquire knowledge about the public interests actually involved in any given decision. Such reforms take the process out of the realm of the planner's individual competence and put it up for public scrutiny. At one time the decision was so secret that even the owner of the land in question might not know about the application. Presumably such owners had valuable information for the decision-maker, but they were often ignorant of applications made by developers for large areas of land including their own. Now under section 27 of the 1971 T.C.P.A. the application for planning permission must include a certificate stating that any owners or agricultural tenants have been notified of the application for permission to develop.

This notion that third parties' views are at least relevant, if not amounting to a legal right to use the statutory judicial appeal procedure of the T.C.P.A., has been buttressed by various cases that have established that it is legally valid for the planning decision-makers to take into account particular rights of members of the public. For instance, in the case of *Stringer* v. *Minister of Housing and Local Government* [1971] 1 All E.R. 64, the court allowed the particular needs of one private owner, the Manchester Radio Telescope, to be taken into account when refusing the application for permission.

The problem then has been that, although the third party's views might be relevant to the caseworker, there is no guarantee that they will be considered because the individual cannot go to court to enforce such a right. In perhaps the most egregious example of this, the case of *Gregory* v. *London Borough of Camden* [1966] 2 All E.R. 196, neighbours rightly complained that the local authority had allowed the erection of a school in the land facing their back gardens in direct contradiction of the residential land-use laid down in the old County of London Development Plan without notifying the central government of this substantial departure from the plan, as required by Ministry directive. The neighbours only found out about the school when construction began and they sought a declaration that the planning permission was *ultra vires* of the local authority. The court said they did not have the ability to use the court to question the governmental activity: 'the plaintiffs have no legal right to step in at all. They may have suffered damnum, that is to say, loss in one way or another, but they have not suffered injuria, that is to say, any legal wrong' (p. 203). Thus, while the neighbour might be able to use a Parliamentary question or the Parliamentary Commissioner (the Government Ombudsman), to investigate local malfeasance, it does not seem to be the case that he can use the statutory right of judicial review established in the Act (T.C.P.A. 1971, sec. 245), nor can he even come before the court to seek a declaration that the local planners' actions were beyond their powers.

There is one possible area of access for third parties that has not been fully explored by the amenity groups, and that is the use of the prerogative writ of certiorari to protect their interests. While *Buxton* established that such a third party did not have sufficient legal interest to come before the court and challenge the planners' decisions under the T.C.P.A., the case seemed to leave open the question of whether the third party might challenge illegal or *ultra vires* activity under the traditional certiorari proceedings: 'It may be that the words "person aggrieved" for the purposes of certiorari do not necessarily mean the same as "person aggrieved" within the meaning of Section 31 of the Act of 1959' *Buxton* v. *Minister of Housing and Local Government* [1960] 3 All E.R. 408, at 413. The various legal commentators have assumed that in situations where the Minister has exercised his discretion so unreasonably as not to amount to an exercise of discretion at all, or made a fundamental error of law, this remedy might be available to the third party. (HEAP, pp. 127–8)

It is interesting to note that the recent case of *R.* v. *London Borough of Hillingdon, ex parte Royco Homes, Ltd.* [1974] 2 All E.R. 643, lends support to such a possible avenue of judicial protection of third-party interests. While in *Hillingdon* the party seeking to have the conditions quashed was also the party seeking planning permission, the case did establish that the traditional remedy of certiorari (with its wide, common-law notion of 'person aggrieved' and thus possibility of a wide range of third parties) was not precluded because of the provision for a statutory right of review. Lord Widgery, in the *Hillingdon* case noted that such a request for common-law certiorari had never arisen under the post-1947 legislation, and surmised that this was perhaps because the lawyers had been under the mis-apprehension that certiorari could only be applied where the administrative body was under a requirement to act judicially, and the exercise of planning discretion would not seem to be of such a character. This point was cleared up in the famous administrative law case of *Ridge* v. *Baldwin* [1963] 2 All E.R. 66, and Lord Widgery plainly states that he 'can see no reason for this court holding otherwise than that there is power in appropriate cases for the use of the prerogative orders to control the activity of a local planning authority' [1974] 2 All E.R. 643, at 648. Now if the remedy is available it may well be that third parties could qualify for its use in situations where the courts would traditionally not give them standing to bring either a statutory review or an action for a declaration.

It is perhaps useful to make the comparison here with the position in the United States, where the judiciary takes a very strong position on the review of official discretion and allows a wide variety of interested third parties to question government activity in the courts. Under the myriad of federal programmes, the federal courts have, since the mid-1960s, widened the notion of an aggrieved person (under the 1970 Administrative Pro-cedure Act, sec. 10, 701–6), to include virtually any affected member of the public. Private individuals have used the courts to question administrative lawlessness in a wide variety of settings. Private parties who have been deprived of 'rights' to such intangibles as television viewing, conservation interests, or relocation housing counselling, have all been allowed into federal court to challenge the administrative agencies' handling of the legislative scheme (ROBERTS). There has also been a similar expansion of the 'standing' rules in most state courts in pursuance of the interests of third parties under state-zoning and conservation schemes.

205

Once in court, the third parties in the United States are allowed a thorough examination of the nature of the discretion exercised by officials, and the administrators' decision is, not infrequently, overturned on the grounds that it did not co-incide with the purpose of the statute. It must be kept in mind that, unlike the situation in Britain, the court is under an obligation to consider whether various legislative schemes constitute a 'taking' of property which would necessitate the payment of just compensation under the Constitution. Since this consideration is at the centre of many disputes, and since an evaluation of the extent of administrative interference with proprietary rights carries with it an examination of the arbitrary character of administrative action, there is often a very thorough analysis of how administrative decision-making occurs. Whereas in the United States the administrator knows that he may be subject to a review on the basis of his approval of an activity in a judicial as well as an administrative forum, the development-control caseworker would make his decisions against just the opposite setting – his approval would most probably not be challenged in any forum.

THE EFFECTS OF THE REFORMS ON LOCAL ORGANISA-
TION AND PLAN-MAKING PROCEDURE:
MAGNIFYING THE PROBLEM?

In some ways the development-control worker's lot was improved under the previous reforms. The Report on Management of Development Control (DEVELOPMENT CONTROL STUDY) and the Bains Report opted in favour of more discretion being vested in the local caseworker. Under the 1968 Town and Country Planning Act it became possible for the elected council to delegate a great many small matters to the officials. While this perhaps only formalised the existing reality, the purpose of the change was to speed up the process and eliminate some committee approvals. The legislation also allowed the Minister to delegate to his inspector the right to make the final decision in some types of cases. By the 1970s 60 per cent of the appeals were being decided finally on the inspector's decision (POOLE). Also a system of allowing the use of inspector review, based solely on written representations (thus eliminating the need for lengthy oral testimony), was instituted in certain cases. Generally then, apart from a few minor changes which buttressed the rights of the public (such as the right to a site notification of a planning application for development in conservation areas or of listed buildings) the procedural changes enhanced the power of the non-elected official to make final decisions on applications.

On the other hand the changes in government form and plan-making have not improved the control worker's position. In the new district planning authorities the applicant will apply directly to the district, and it will be the caseworker who must clarify the application as to whether it is a county or a district matter. Now, due to a last minute change in the 1972 Local Government Act (Schedule xvi, paras 15–33), the county will at least receive copies of the applications classified as non-county matters, but the possibility for inter-authority rivalry is tremendous. While the system is in some ways similar to the old delegation agreements, the supposed responsibility at the lowly district level is bound to cause friction on most contentious issues. Part of this will arise at the stage of the creation of the development plans scheme and the counties' certification of acceptability of local plans (Local Government Act 1972, Schedule xvi, paras 2, 3, part LX, para. 183) but most officials interviewed felt that there would probably be a day-to-day conflict far in excess of that under the previous delegation arrangement.

Under the new system the district will prepare the written recommendation on applications for the district–county planning committee, but there will have to be a great deal of consultation with the county throughout the process, both on initial classification, and on matters that might be considered county matters. The counties will send deputations to the district planning meetings on matters they feel are important and likewise the districts will send deputations to the county meetings. Irrespective of the major disagreements on what is a county matter, there will have to be an elaborate system of co-ordination and discussion throughout the whole range of local-service provision as well as planning-application processing. This procedure will most probably be slower, and there are various commentators who see the magnitude of the co-ordination problems as representing a possibility that the reorganisation is 'a step backwards in the management of community and environment problems and in particular the management of urban problems'. (STEWART, 1972, p. 451)

Added to the possibility of more conflict and greater processing time there is also a difficulty engendered from the establishment of some 400 planning authorities outside London, as opposed to the previous figure of county and county-borough planning departments of 141. The first result of this expansion has been a tremendous inflation of caseworkers' staff salary. Irrespective of the quality of decisions they will be costing the government more. The Royal Town Planning Institute, in one comment, pointed out that not only would there be a shortage of people with the requisite degrees but there would also be a great deal of personnel movement between authorities (R.T.P.I.). Also, many of the attempts to set up teams for particular public-works projects or renewal programmes at the county level might be hindered by the lack of available personnel.

This general manpower scarcity means two things. One is that there will be a continued emphasis on the expenditure and training of planning personnel, the other is that the new officials hired for the bottom-level day-to-day control work will, for the next few years, be of an even lower calibre. The education of planners is a continuing topic for discussion. Some, such as Lady Sharp, in her paper on the education of transport and land-use planners, emphasise the need to integrate the process of educating those who build public works and those who make land-use application decisions. Others throw the net still wider, and call for an education in public administration which will produce a planner acquainted with cost–benefit analysis, cybernetics, systems analysis and linear programming. Professor Hall: 'the capacity of the planner to accept, digest and process information will be many times greater in 1980 than it is in 1970. By 2000 the explosion in capacity may be almost unimaginable' (in COWAN AND DONNISON, p. 50). What this does not bear on directly though, is how one can educate a person to make a better decision on the local planning application, particularly when it is the caseworker who will have the least of this training.

According to the most recent evidence (KITCHEN), planning schools are expanding at a rate of 15 to 20 per cent a year, but the number of graduates is still only in the range of 500 a year.

208

This means that many of the new authorities just established at the district level will have had to hire more people with fewer degrees and fewer qualifications. Whether this lowers the quality of discretion exercised is problematical, but it would seem logical to assume that these people would be less likely to take planning risks. They, like their predecessors at the county level, would tend to rely on the routine tried-and-tested approvals in the area for their guidelines.

The major and perennial problem that was not eliminated by the reform was that of administrative overload, the slowness of application processing, and, particularly, of appeals. While the average percentage of application approvals has remained in the 80 to 85 per cent range, the time for processing, particularly appeals, has increased. As of 1973, only 70 per cent of the applications were being decided at the local level within the two-month statutory period (DOBRY INTERIM REPORT, 3.2.1) and the average time between when the appeal is lodged and the decision is made had increased to 51 weeks for ministerial decision and 36 weeks for direct inspector decision (POOLE). This will probably increase under the new local authorities.

The central government's concern with this facet of the problems in control work is a reflection of their own administrative workload, but it still is of crucial importance, since not only is processing time a visible government cost at local- and central-government level, but such delay represents a very real loss to developers. Since lead time represents money in terms of interest payments and administrative costs to the developer and, in the aggregate, a loss of efficiency to the country, it is perhaps fitting that the major reforms attempted in relation to the control process should concentrate on the speeding up of processing time, although it is to be pondered whether open access from 'third parties' is not equally important.

THE DOBRY REVIEW OF THE DEVELOPMENT-CONTROL SYSTEM

When the numbers of planning appeals rose some 123 per cent from 1970 to 1973, and reached a grand total of over 17,000, the harried and overworked D.O.E. persuaded the Government to establish a review panel to think up ways of speeding up the process.

The government chose an experienced barrister, George

209

Dobry, Q.C., as the group's chairman, and appointed an advisory group of sixteen people, over half of whom were planning officials, the remainder being lawyers, elected officials and academics. Mr Dobry's terms of reference were to consider the development-control system in the light of: 'the new re-distribution of planning functions between local authorities and the new system of structure and local plans' (DOBRY INTERIM REPORT, p. iii), and to review the appeal structure. Unlike various other reviews this one was meant to be very speedy. When appointed in October 1973 the chairman was instructed to produce a preliminary report within four months and the final report within six months. Clearly some immediate solutions were sought.

The circular announcing the review panel (CIRCULAR 142/73) prefaced the problem as one of crisis dimensions: 'Emergency steps have been taken to provide more inspectors and to train middle management planning staff of local authorities' (para. 2) and the D.O.E. even instituted some immediate measures to take the pressure off the department. They recommended separating run-of-the-mill applications from contentious appli-cations at the committee review stage, and expediting small decisions. The circular came out strongly in favour of im-mediate delegation of authority to the control workers from the elected committee: on matters of small-scale development, all matters nearly within the categories allowed as of right under the General Development Order (or specified advertisement control), section 53 determinations that planning approval is not needed, and certificates of established use. 'The Secretary of State considers that only in exceptional circumstances is . . . an absence of delegation justifiable' (para. 7 ii). The circular recommended the creation of a non-statutory guide to local-development control, which would eventually be incorporated in the structure and local plans. Also, it put the local authorities on notice that it did not intend to call in applications in very many circumstances, and 'not merely on the grounds of local controversy' (para. 11). Finally, the D.O.E. stressed its dependence on inquiry by written representations.

The review panel sent out a questionnaire to interested officials, lawyers, planners and academics, soliciting their views on the problems in control work. The aim of this questionnaire was to determine if categorisation of applications and the enlargement of as-of-right approvals might speed up the process. Throughout the questionnaire there was a tension between the speed of processing and the supposed expansion of the rights of neighbours and applicants. While people were asked to comment on ways to increase discussion with affected members of the public, there seemed to be an emphasis on how to decrease the obstruction to the control workers caused by those objections: 'Given the new rights [sic] in public participation at the structure and local plan stage, is there scope for a more robust approach at the development control stage?' (DOBRY QUESTIONNAIRE, III-6). The questionnaire asked about the whole range of fundamentals involved in the *ad hoc* procedure – applicants' lead time, the quality of the development, the need for 'positive' control, the delegation of decision-making from the committees to the control officers, and methods of changing the administrative review of appeals through, for instance, a regional planning-appeal tribunal, or inquiry by written representations.

The Review Committee received a wide variety of opinion from various sources. For instance the Town and Country Planning Association summed up the problems thus:

> The 1972 Local Government Act . . . will make matters worse by spreading limited staff resources more thinly between a larger number of planning authorities, and this is already causing the system to be overloaded with a growing backlog of appeals and delays in the processing of planning applications. (TOWN AND COUNTRY PLANNING ASSOCIATION, p. 4)

But the Association came out strongly against interfering with the range of discretion of planning officers (who compose their membership) through the enlargement of categorisation and as-of-right approval: 'Development proposals do not fall into a range of neat categories which can be universally applied' (p. 5). They were in favour, however, of more delegation of authority away from the elected officials to the caseworkers. Similarly, they objected to any 'inducement to challenge the local authority' (p. 7) coming from the central government in the form of 'policy', such as the freeing of white (undecided) land for residential use. Generally, the spokesmen for the caseworkers felt that delay was not really a problem, 'Delay is often very much in the public interest as, not only does it allow more thorough consultation and debate, but it is also tending to

211

slow down the speed of change in our towns and cities to a more human tempo' (p. 1), and that development decision-making entailed such expertise that the 'professionals' should not be interfered with. While the Association made a number of suggestions about increasing rather than decreasing public participation, they came out in favour of eliminating the right to appeal to central government in certain types of cases, and leaving the review to county-elected officials. Knowing what we do about the relationship between the 'professional' planners and the amateur elected officials, this would again increase the relative power of the local career decision-maker.

The panel received recommendations from spokesmen for various groups, and, as would be expected, those in the area of development and housing construction called for much speedier procedures and as-of-right approvals. Others, such as some academics, put in various possible plans for new approaches which might not necessarily be geared to the interest of either the local officials or the developers but which might make for a more efficient system. For instance, this author submitted a proposal that the applicants should be taxed on their applications and applications for appeal. In this way, those people receiving the benefits of the service, namely developers, would contribute to the maintenance of the service directly. The final report recommended just such a stamp duty on similar standard charge for planning applications (DOBRY FINAL REPORT, pp. 14, 78–9).

Professor McAuslan submitted a proposal which stressed that processing time and staffing budget allocations are clearly related. 'Any reform which has, as one of its aims, the speeding up of the process of development control at the appeal level will involve the use of more personnel' (MCAUSLAN SUBMISSION, p. 6). He took issue with the idea contained in earlier reviews, such as the Bains Report, that the local councillor could be eliminated entirely, or merely review the performance of the caseworkers, and not make individual decisions himself. McAuslan's major recommendation was for a regional series of panels to review decisions and filter those that should go to full appeal and those that should be refused. The panel, consisting of local-planning-authority elected members, would attempt to bring local knowledge to local problems under the direction of a D.O.E. chairman.

Dobry considered these various recommendations, coming from 165 various government bodies, professional firms, nationalised industries, amenity societies, development companies and individuals, and issued an interim report in a very short time. Basically, Dobry did not recommend any radical changes except that the procedures should be simplified and liberalised. While the interim report did not make any specific recommendations as to how those simplifications might be executed, the final report published in February 1975 contains a set of novel solutions to the control problem. Mr Dobry's proposal is that all applications be divided into two categories. One category (Class A) would deal with all of the run-of-the-mill applications, which would include those which comply with the current development plans or are of a simple or minor nature to which there are no significant objections. If the local authority did not reach a decision on applications within a fixed period (42 days) then the application would be deemed to be granted. According to the final report this first category of application would encompass some 70 or 80 per cent of all planning applications. There would also be a second category of application which would involve those controversial situations where the local authority chose to take more time to study the impact of the proposed development. In the case of this second category (Class B) there would be longer time limits (three months) and no deemed approval if action is not taken on the application within the time limit. (DOBRY FINAL REPORT, p. 11)

The initial problem with this approach is a rather fundamental one, namely how would the local authority determine which applications are controversial and thus in Class B and which are not and thus in Class A. It would seem that external factors, such as how far behind the local planners are in processing applications, would determine this designation, particularly in the light of the fact that a Class A application which was not rejected within the time limit would be deemed approved. There is a larger problem here, which is that the guidelines for determining this controversiality would presumably be the structure plans and local plans when they are finally drafted. The question is whether the final planning documents will be of sufficient specificity to cull out such important applications from the more mundane ones.

213

One of the most peculiar aspects of the Dobry recommendations, both in the interim and final report, was the ambivalent attitude taken towards the interaction of the control workers with members of the public, either applicants or neighbours. On the one hand, Dobry has stressed the need for consultation between the planners and the applicants (DOBRY INTERIM REPORT 2.11). The interim report stresses the need for discussion before the application is made, during review and during appeals. In the interim report it was recommended that central government should set up a consultative committee to help the applicants and local authorities communicate, and that there should even be planning advice centres to help explain the procedures to applicants and objectors (DOBRY INTERIM REPORT 2.14, 5.42). However, the final recommendation seems to have as its basis a recommendation that planning review should achieve greater dispatch at the expense of more local consultation or participation. The specific recommendations in the final report call for a strict time limit on consultations with the public for each category of application. Dobry does recommend site notice or neighbour notification for Class A cases and goes further for Class B cases in recommending 'the publication of lists of applications in local newspapers *or* on public notice boards *and* to registered local societies' (DOBRY FINAL REPORT, p. 11). While this would lead to more visibility for planning applications and thus more possibility of 'consultation' very little is said about how the unwilling local authority might be forced to listen to the public. 'The best method of involving the public must be chosen for each set of circumstances' (p. 20). Further, it would seem under the time limitation that there will be even less time for those groups to make their views known.

The third important aspect of the Dobry review was its recommendations in the area of appeals from development application refusal by the local authority. While the Dobry interim report called for only minor changes the final Dobry report made recommendations of a more fundamental nature. The interim report merely emphasised the need for an exchange of information and technical proofs of evidence prior to the inquiries into application refusals and the introduction of a system of grouping appeals and hearing them in sessions (DOBRY INTERIM REPORT 2.29). This idea was greeted favourably by the new Parliamentary Under-Secretary of State at the Department of the Environment, Gordon Oakes,* and thus there may well be a system of regional assizes which will hear whole sets of interrelated appeals.

While such a system of consecutive appeals related by location and content may be implemented, it is more doubtful whether the appeal recommendations contained in the final Dobry report will see the light of day. Following the bifurcation of appeals into a minor and major category the final report advocated that while the minor (Class A) application refusals could still be appealed on, the applicant would not be allowed legal representation and the appeal would be very 'informal' (DOBRY FINAL REPORT, p. 22). While the inspector would have to eventually give a written opinion, the initial decision could be given orally. This recommendation would presumably face strong opposition, for not only would some property-owners face the loss of development value without legal representation, but also the local authority would be given the chance to eliminate opposition by simply classifying the application as minor, refusing it, and thus eliminating the right to counsel at appeal even if the development was in fact of major importance. The elimination of counsel at Class A public inquiries, which would deal with what the Dobry group hoped would be 70 per cent of the development applications, make one wonder whether the Committee took the time to read the Franks Report and clearly understood the possibility of abuse and personal hardship with such a system. While schemes of orchestrated review are beneficial or perhaps even necessary in the setting of long-term structure-plan review it seems doubtful whether they are fair when the issues deal with a particular development or a particular owner.

CRITICISMS AND SUGGESTIONS ON THE DOBRY REFORMS

The difficulty with the Dobry reports is that they attempt to recommend internal administrative changes (that is consultation, the separation of minor and major applications) and variations of the rules of development control procedure (that is different rules as to time limits and appeal procedures) without really coming to grips with the realities of the day-to-day process or the supposed purposes of the process. The

---

* *The Times* (1 May 1974) p. 2.

interim report says that, 'Local plans, framed in the light of structure plans and national policies, and supplemented by policy statements and other guidelines, must provide the parameters for development control. So far as possible, development control decisions should be taken within this framework and "ad hoc" decisions reduced to a minimum.' (DOBRY INTERIM REPORT 4.53)

Similarly the separation of application into the A and B category as proposed in the final report is to be based on the structure and local plans. If that was in fact possible then there would not be even a need for case by case approval, a map could easily implement the planning for the particular parcel (as it attempts to do under the zoning system used extensively in the United States). However, the Dobry final report does not make this final jump and in fact leaves the caseworker to exercise his personal judgement.

The most striking contradiction present in the Dobry analysis is the absence of any commitment to allocate more resources, time, or money to improve the quality of the caseworkers' judgement. If the purpose of the planning legislation is to make a pleasant environment for the 'public interest', then development on any given parcel would have to include the view of the neighbours and affected individuals whether they live close to or far from the parcel. Beyond a plea for more notice, little was done to strengthen individuals' access to the decision-making universe of the caseworker. As we have seen, the purposes of the legislation are difficult to nail down: they stem from the British attitude towards gardens and the separation of industry from residential areas – the living of a pleasant life. What Mr Dobry did not do was to encourage access to the deciding caseworker for those most closely affected. Rather than increase the amount of access from outside, Dobry recommends closer liaison between the controlled and the controller and an automatic approval in the majority of cases (the A group) when a decision has not come down within the required time limit. Nothing was said about allowing for an appeal against the grant of permission by affected neighbours and it seems unlikely that the abolition of counsel at the Class A appeals would strengthen those neighbours' position when such an appeal occurs at the instigation of the affected applicant.

Perhaps the most cogent criticism of the Dobry approach was

given by Jeffery Jowell of the London School of Economics, writing as a spokesman for the Greater London Group in a submission critiquing the Interim Dobry Report:

> In our view a great deal of development is controlled for the express purpose of protecting immediate private interests . . . the public interest is made up of an accumulation of private interests, and a development frequently affects virtually only immediate neighbours, in other words virtually only identifiable private interests; [there should be more] thorough canvass of opinion of private interests . . . because knowledge of the accumulation of private interests will allow a more informed decision on the question of public interest. . . . We would further suggest that a strong argument could be made for widening the criteria governing decisions on development applications. (JOWELL, pp. 2–3)

The question then presented is what might be a better approach to control, and the following represents one possible approach. First of all, regulation is not desirable for its own sake. There is nothing inherently good about having a local-government official look at every set of architectural plans for the whole country. There are inherent costs in regulation, administrative ones such as salaries, and very real ones to the members of the public, who must live and pay for the delay. Besides the cost, regulation reduces innovation and encourages repetition. What is important then is to focus the administrative energies to reach the desired purposes, not merely to regulate them because it seems like a good idea.

It is important perhaps to mention here that the United States, which has had the model of Britain to examine for some twenty-five years, has definitely opted for a system of selective regulation. As Fred Bosselman wrote:

> The need is apparent for some method of concentrating state efforts on major land use issues if the burdens of regulation are not to exceed its benefits. Those who cry for comprehensive regulation of all development by the state merely show that they have not thought through the problem. (BOSSELMAN AND CALLIES, p. 27)

The way to focus government energies is first to eliminate control on a variety of developments. This can be done by the means investigated in Dobry (automatic approval of minor householder applications or the use of design criteria, DOBRY INTERIM REPORT, 4.8), or it can be done by the use of a number of dwelling criteria (for example development as of right of less than five houses in specified areas) or it can be done by 'planning' certain areas where permissions will not be needed for various categories of use. Under this type of change the local authority would have to make their decisions beforehand, but since that is what the word planning implies, it is perhaps not too far-fetched an idea.

Coupled with this, the planning caseworker should have a wide variety of tools which he does not currently possess to meet the problems that require attention. There are a number of important development decisions in every local authority and it would seem that far more attention might be paid to them. If the community is interested in high-rise buildings, the retention of a vital shopping and street life, or the provision of varied-cost private dwellings together, it is on these that the authorities should concentrate. To do this various mechanisms can be designed, but one of the most promising would seem to be the American idea of an 'environmental impact statement', recommended in the Dobry Final Report (p. 72). In the United States most major projects which receive federal-government aid require, under the National Environmental Policy Act, a statement describing the development's impact on the environment, and justification of the development in the light of local and national policies. Similar provisions have been adopted in various States for State projects and, under at least one jurisdiction, California, the courts have interpreted the California Environmental Quality Act 1970 as requiring environmental-impact statements for virtually all development, whether publicly subsidised or entirely privately financed. These impact statements have made the developer do a good deal of homework on the effect of his development on the area and have often forced him to make accommodations to allow for neighbouring land-uses. The statements have provided a focus for both government analysis and public discussion, by interested groups and affected neighbours, of the merits of particular plans. In Britian such a requirement might force the developers to supply the expertise which the local authorities at the caseworker level often seem to lack.

218

Jowell recommends that the applicant, in *all* circumstances, should 'demonstrate as fully as possible the impact of the development upon the land-uses and the social and economic character of his land and the surrounding area' (JOWELL, p. 4). But one could easily limit such research to a particular category of development, and make the developer hold a public meeting or publish and distribute a number of copies of the statement. Dobry recommends impact statements for only specially significant Class B proposals. (DOBRY FINAL REPORT, p. 71)

Another tool might be to change the legislation to allow for conditions in planning permissions which have been considered by the courts to be unreasonable or beyond 'planning purposes'. (*R.* v. *London Borough of Hillingdon, ex parte Royco Homes, Ltd.* [1974] 2 All E.R. 643.) Conditions on major industrial locations might provide for transportation to the site, on major residential developments they might provide for a percentage of low-rent accommodation, or on shopping centres they might provide for the relocation of existing shop tenants at similar rental prices. The idea would be that the conditions might allow the control officer actually to make something happen, as opposed to his usual role of stopping about 20 per cent of the applications.

A final suggestion for a tool to concentrate the energies of the control staff is to allow in more of those private interests of neighbours who are often so eloquent in pointing out the 'public interest.' Dobry recommends both an independent national system of advice centres for applicants and objectors alike, and also recommends the introduction of a Planning Aid Scheme (DOBRY FINAL REPORT, p. 115). Besides admonitions to the caseworkers to canvass the neighbours, write to surrounding residents and publish applications, it would seem that the third parties should be given further rights to challenge the local decision in this now limited area of intensive regulation. This could be done through both legislation to allow access to the courts to general members of the public, to challenge local authority approvals which were beyond the statute, and a right to request appeals and public inquiries on some important planning approvals. Under such a scheme provision would have to be made so that the initial local authority approval would not vest the applicant with a comprehensive right to develop.

219

Such third-party access would serve the purpose of guaranteeing that, on this limited range of discretionary review, the officers and the council had, in fact, carried out an investigation capable of being aired and justified in public.

When designing reforms, it must be kept in mind that development control cannot be separated from the plan-making process, and attempts at reform should not concentrate on either the general or the specific but on both. Even with an integrated approach there are a great many factors that are not within the control of the local authority. The public officials involved in the process should know the limited extent of their influence and set their horizons accordingly.

PART THREE

Some Conclusions and Solutions

11 Conclusions: An Evaluation of the Reforms

Throughout this essay we have thus far managed to avoid an iron-clad definition of the words 'planning', 'reform', or 'law', although all have been used in the title of the work. What we have been considering is the attempt to improve, change or remove the faults in something called the planning system. The planning system is at once an informational system, a structure for the diffusion of various attempts to arrive at patterns for future land-uses, a method of implementing those patterns through the decisions on applications to develop various parcels of land, and the interlocking, small societies of the various participants in the system: lawyers, citizens, planners, councillors and developers. What should be clear by now is that the laws involved, whether they be laid down by statute, regulation or decision, are the guidelines on how the various participants can behave. The laws lay down the constraints on both government and private action. It is changes in the law – for example, the introduction of the way of making a development plan as laid down in the 1968 T.C.P.A., or the method of holding a public review – which are the means of reforming the system.

By now we have seen enough of these attempts at change perhaps to understand how a system can best go about reforming itself. Since central government has the primary responsibility for introducing such changes, and since it is the level of government which reviews the effects of such changes (by, for instance, reviewing the new development plans, or by deciding appeals from refusals for planning permissions) we have been able to focus on the major innovator of reforms by looking at how central government functions. One of the things that has become apparent is that the central government's approaches to such reform have been influenced to a great

223

extent by the prevailing view of what is involved in the process of planning.

At the core of the prevailing view is a belief that the decisions concerning planning and the allocation of land can be, and are, made on an objective basis. Since this is a rational process what is needed is more expertise, greater ability in exercising such expertise, and more documents to lay out this rational framework. Chapters 1 to 10 have, hopefully, cast significant doubt on this rationale, with its emphasis on professionalisation. In this conclusion we shall seek to refine that doubt and suggest the most successful parts of the reforms, principally those which do not emphasise the expertise and competence of planning officials but, instead, seek to engineer new ways to bring forward values from throughout the community.

Tied to this belief in the objectivity of planning decision-making is the assumption that changes instigated by central government will radiate out to the subservient local authorities and change the actual functioning of the local implementers. For instance, it is assumed that an instruction to draft a structure plan will result in the local authority actually producing a plan that will be relevant to the final decision on whether a person may, or may not, build a house on his parcel of land. Since the central government cannot be present when such decisions are finally made, they have to concentrate on the end-product of the plans themselves. What often seems to have happened in the past is that the documents themselves have become the goal-orientation of the system. Linked with this, the central government's own definition of the problem as a bureaucratic one for their particular agency, has been the definition of the approaches to reform. For instance, overloads of their own review procedures have always been the moving factor in changes in the statutory law. Similarly, it has been the central government's departmental descriptions of the problems which have led to the compartmentalised reviews. The P.A.G. looked only at development plans, and Dobry looked only at development control, and the reforms ensuing from those two studies will define the solutions only in terms of their compartment of review.

What is ironic here is that this professionalised and depart-mentalised view tends to obscure the fact that the decision on any particular allocation or any particular planning permission will take into account a vast quantity of imponderable, only half-known factors: the effect on neighbours and the likelihood of industrial expansion, the demands on a school, the need for a footpath, the council's concern that year for house-building, or central government's rate-support largesse. Further, it will be the aggregate of the vast number of these individual administrative decisions that will determine the land-use of the area. By concentrating on, for example, the end-product of the plans, or by responding only to administrative overloads in one area, it becomes more difficult for ideas about what is a 'good' decision to surface. Ideas in planning have a way of changing over time; what was a valid approach ten years ago may not be so now. A simple list of sub-disciplines shows the currency of planning ideas: advocacy planning, environmental planning, urban planning, corporate planning, cybernetic planning. The reason for this is that almost any series of factors, or ways of ordering them, may become relevant because at the end of the day planning is really a way of applying the term 'public interest'. By not letting new ideas surface the professionalised approach of reforming governments may then guarantee that the planning decisions are not valid for the 'public interest' of the day.

In the broad sense, then, a tunnel-vision view of the reform process may lead to a suppression of the new ideas needed to make planning administrative decision-making viable. To keep the administrative process in tune with its represented public is important, not merely on the usual notions of fairness or democracy, but because it keeps the administrative process relevant to the areas it is supposed to administer. The reform of planning policy, as opposed to administrative structure, may begin not at the top, in central government, but at the bottom in, for example, the local feeling against high-rise council housing. It is important for the central government to ensure that the administrative system can learn rapidly enough about such policy ideas. To use Donald Schon's terms: 'A learning system must transform its ideas in good currency at a rate commensurate with its own changing situation' (SCHON, p. 116). In our case the reform should allow for the rapid digestion of policy ideas by the local planner. Reforms which start at the centre can be most efficacious where they do

225

not let that local decider or allocator hide behind his expertise, his notions of what is best. The purpose of reforms should be to guarantee that the local official rethinks the problems he is dealing with from time to time. The focus of the reform should be to guarantee that the experts not only do their job but redefine what their job is or should be as they go along. Since the experts cannot possibly have a monopoly on the relevant ideas, the aim of reform should be to bring in as wide a set of values as possible for the decision-maker to use when he makes his decision.

We can now turn to the reforms introduced thus far and see which of them seem to have the most potential for causing such re-evaluation. The standard of analysis is the ability of the reforms to make the entire planning system aware of the relevant considerations upon which to make decisions and able to assimilate new problems and new approaches to those problems creatively. In this study we have seen two methods of reshaping the system: the restructuring of the administrative units making the decisions, and the reshaping of the process leading to the end-product of plans. Interlaced with these has been a series of new procedures for allowing the system's interaction with the community, and it has been these procedures which seem to have been the most important. A brief look at each of these again, in terms of these ideas of a public process rethinking its premises in an open forum, will show which reforms have been most valuable thus far and what areas might be the most fruitful in the future.

REFORMING INSTITUTIONAL UNITS

On the face of it, the concentration on reforming the size or shape of the acting units has been decidedly unproductive. While there may certainly be valid excuses for local-government reorganisation with the system as implemented, there can be little excuse for the reform of local-government structure on planning grounds. While it may be argued that the 1968 changes in planning method were based on a unitary scheme of local government and that the 1972 Local Government Act was based on a two-tier government, this is not necessarily a state of affairs that can be written off as an expediency forced through by 'politicians'. Since the concentration in both areas was on a particular fixed state, for example, a redrawn, local-govern-

226

ment boundary or a new planning document, it is not particularly surprising that they were not entirely relevant when they finally appeared. In the case of reorganisation the central government had of course changed parties twice while the reform was under way but, by being a change which depended on a fixed state of things (in this case a boundary line), it was a reform that built in the possibility of immediate obsolescence. Due to the vicissitudes of politics, this obsolescence or inability to reflect the problems of the time just happened to appear much more quickly than might otherwise have been expected. As described above this lack of synchronisation between the problems and the units attempting to solve the problems is rather fundamental. The local plans are being drafted by different bodies from those who draft the structure or strategy plan. The counties who are supposedly drafting the strategy for the area in those structure plans are not the same administrative units who are making the administrative decisions on planning applications.

This example of the lack of co-ordination between two different but related reforming processes – local governments and plan-making – exemplifies the difficulties where the reforming energies concentrate upon a particular form or end-product rather than upon the procedures needed to allow the continual re-evaluation of policies in a given area. For instance, in the local government area it might have been far better to concentrate on the changes needed to make the provision of a given service more responsive to the needs of those serviced rather than attempt to find some final end-state for a local authority which would be efficient and responsive for all the services.

Typical of the distortion that comes about by concentrating on the end-product is the political responsiveness of the elected council members. One of the problems was supposed to be that the members were not fulfilling their duties to set policy for the council and reflect the wishes of the served public to the official administration. It was felt that the members tended to concentrate on the detail brought to them by constituents and that they were not able to relate such detail to the over-all policies of the council.

There are a number of ways in which this problem might be approached. The basic way chosen by the government was to

227

seek a final state of affairs in which there would be fewer councillors with larger constituencies and thus perhaps a broader view of the areas' problems, so under the reorganisation the number of elected members has been reduced. The difficulty is that there is no guarantee that fewer representatives are necessarily more prone to take into account policy matters than were the larger number. From the constituents' point of view, there are certainly fewer representatives to consider those opinions. There are a number of other ways of approaching the problem. Those that concentrate not on the form but on the way in which the councillors go about their job of representing their public seem to have had a far greater impact on council responsiveness already. For instance, the opening up to the press of committee meetings and the register of councillors' financial interests have both influenced the way the decisions are made far more than the size of the constituency. If these procedures had been pursued further there might perhaps have been wider possibilities for fundamental change.

It should not be overlooked that, although the reorganisation may not necessarily have created more efficient local councils or more responsive political bodies, it does allow for more efficient central-government control over those bodies. The new district units in particular will tend to be more nearly of the same size, making central-government comparisons of performance on services easier. While this means of comparison of efficiency and service between districts will also be available to the citizens of those districts, it will be of most use to the central government which is paying for a large percentage of the local authority's budget. What we may be seeing, then, is a centralising rather than a decentralising process. The reorganised form may be easier to manage and co-ordinate at the central level but, returning to our criteria for ensuring re-evaluation and interaction with ideas outside the government, the reorganisation may have done very little.

REFORMING PLAN-MAKING

When we look at the changes in the area of plan-making it seems that those changes which concentrated on the procedures of bringing forward unrecognised or undigested facts and values to the attention of the government official were the most fundamental. Those which concentrated on the particular end-product called the plan seemed to be the least important. As we said, it was perhaps not the structure plan itself but rather the *process* of having to make one that was significant.

To take the most obvious example, it may well be that the structure plans themselves vary drastically in their usefulness. By the time the document is prepared and then implemented by a different local authority at the district level, and then actually used as a reference in the administrative decision on approving a planning application, it may not be particularly relevant. However, the process of drafting it and particularly the survey done of the various factors may continue to be relevant. If the idea is to know what is happening, to ensure that the decision-maker has sufficient material available to make a particular decision, then the survey may be very useful. As with all social statistics the data in the surveys can vary dramatically. It would seem that the review of the survey divorced from the specific policies of the structure plan may have been the most important part of the D.O.E.'s entire participation in the public examination. In later years, when major unforeseen developments have taken place in an authority (for example a new industry, the cancellation of a motorway, the withholding of capital-loan sanction for a local-authority development), it will be the survey and not the structure plan that will still be referred to.

To take another example, the requirements for public participation laid down in section 8 of the T.C.P.A. of 1971 are not particularly extensive, but they do give the central government the power to reject the local authorities' efforts and thus to monitor its attempts to receive information from outside its own government structure. If the concentration of the reformist zeal had been on the process, not the end-product of the plan, then it would seem that it might be far more fruitful for the central government to concentrate on instructing the local authority on how to go about this process of public re-evaluation. What happened instead was that, at least with the first plans, there were no public castigations for inadequate attempts and no rejections of even the most pitiful attempts so far.

The most dramatic innovation in terms of procedure in the plan-making area has been the development of the public examination. It is in the case of the public examination that the central government's reformist energies were focused almost entirely on the procedures of interaction with the outside public and not upon the particular end-product. Irrespective of whether the public examination is thought to represent an advance over the notion of a public inquiry or the final defeat of the Franks Committee idea of full legal rights to appear before the administrative decision-maker, it must be acknowledged that it is one innovation that fundamentally affected the ability of the public re-evaluation and synthesis of ideas outside the ambit of the local officials' values. Once the central government became interested in the process it developed a whole series of innovations that will have a major effect on the static nature of some local officials' thoughts. The examination provides a rapid way to make local officials publicly account for their data-gathering and policy decisions. The D.O.E. can orchestrate a process which can force the local planners to reconsider various parts of their ideas; similarly, the panel can bring in outside parties to appear who have not even made objections but who may express values or know facts that neither the local planners nor the central government employees were acquainted with. We saw that this innovation could have been refined to provide a more even-handed public evaluation (for instance by introducing a second panel secretary to bring even a wider set of values than the D.O.E. panel secretary might do) but this reform in procedure has been reasonably successful. It allows for the concentration and distillation of the views of members of the public, it allows speed, and it allows an alternative forum for a discussion of local-authority policy decisions outside either the D.O.E. or the local authority. The public-examination procedure seems, then, to be a way to make plan-making appear less like a rationalised, professionalised, static process and more like an evolution of policy out of a welter of divergent facts and values.

THE IMPORTANCE OF PROCEDURAL REFORM

It was suggested in Chapter 1 that the idea of planning the way communities are to grow and change is, by its nature, too complex for any one rational administrative system, reformed or unreformed, to deal with. When it comes to the actual decision about an actual piece of land the decision-maker is bound to be dealing with a situation that was neither contemplated at the time the plan was drafted nor, in fact, knowable in all its facets at the time the decision was made. Schon makes a brilliant parallel between such a planner and the situation of Napoleon at the Battle of Borodino, as described by Tolstoy in *War and Peace*,

> From the battle-field adjutants he had sent out, and orderlies from his marshals, kept galloping up to Napoleon with reports of the progress of the action, but all these reports were false, both because it was impossible to establish what was happening at any given moment, and because many of the adjutants did not go to the actual place of conflict, but reported what they had heard from others; and also because while an adjutant was riding the couple of versts to Napoleon circumstances changed and the news he brought was already becoming false. Thus an adjutant galloped up from Murat with tidings that Borodino had been occupied and the bridge over the Kolocha was in the hands of the French. The adjutant asked whether Napoleon wished the troops to cross it. Napoleon gave orders that the troops should form up on the farther side and wait. But before that order was given – almost as soon in fact as the sergeant had left Borodino – the bridge had been retaken by the Russians and burnt. . . .
>
> An adjutant galloped up from the flèches with a pale and frightened face and reported to Napoleon that their attack had been repulsed, Campan wounded and Davout killed; yet at the very time the adjutant had been told that the French had been repulsed, the flèches had in fact been recaptured by other French troops, and Davout was alive and only slightly bruised. On the basis of these necessarily untrustworthy reports Napoleon gave his orders, which had either been executed before he gave them, or could not be and were not executed. (SCHON, p. 208, quoting translation by L. Maude, Oxford University Press, 1941, Book XI, ch. II, pp. 8–10)

Since the land-use decision-maker is faced with such an ambivalent series of factors, values and instructions, the reforms designed to help him in his task should be those that allow for the most current, most public and most thorough re-evaluation of his premises before he makes his decision. Thus reforms which concentrate on the end-products, the documents, and the speed

231

and room for him to exercise his 'expertise' are perhaps the greatest waste of intellectual administrative energy. Those which take him out of the shadow of his professionalisation and make him more aware of the glare of others' views are thus the most valuable investment in reform. We will now look briefly at the type of procedural reform which might go furthest towards creating a groundwork for such decision-making.

One of the basic difficulties which we have seen is that the elected officials are generally rather deferential to the expertise of the local planning officials. This has been amplified by the delegation of more of the final decision-making power to the elected official under the provisions of the 1968 T.C.P.A. and, while the owner may ask for the council to consider his planning application even though the council has specifically delegated that category to the officer, the council is under no such obligation to call in the application. Over-all, more and more decision-making is delegated, with a consequent drop in direct elected supervision on planning-permission decisions. This deference is equally true at the plan-making stage. As we saw, the survey work and the preparation of the tentative structure plans is done almost exclusively by local officials. By the time the elected officials can review the plan, the social statistics in the survey may already point directly to the conclusions on policy. One major problem, then, is how to guarantee the access of outside ideas and values where the representative democracy is not necessarily in a position to provide this function.

The traditional methods available are the lawyer's procedural techniques of notice and the right to be heard. The rights of notice and the post-Franks public inquiry on a planning appeal represent these procedural methods' coming-of-age in the planning area. While there were no third-party rights under the original legislation, gradually there came to be more third-party participation in the public hearing. The current administrative practice of the D.O.E. is that inspectors generally recognise third parties and even let them participate in the public inquiry, including cross-examination and putting forward their own case. The inspector will often summarise the third party's case in his report. Similarly, although third parties do not have a right to appear and thus are not given express notification of the substance of such appeal, there is a system of public notice in the press about appeals. In terms of notice, the law has evolved so that it requires site notices (notices posted on the site for at least seven days) for applications for certain categories of development such as 'bad neighbours' development and developments in conservation areas. Similarly, a system of placing planning applications in a public register which is open to public inspection has also evolved. The purpose of these various requirements is to give all members of the public an equal chance to bring forward relevant considerations to the attention of the local official.

The difficulty is that, while such notice and appearance before an inspector at an inquiry may be valuable in the application of policy in a particular land-use decision, it is not entirely useful in evaluating that policy for future reference. In situations where the primary consideration lies in articulating the way in which the officials will go about such decision-making, the requirement of notice and a right to be heard lead to inordinate delay. The Layfield inquiry into the Greater London Development Plan was, in the opinion of many, an example of these procedural reforms run amuck. Since practically everyone in London was interested, and since a vast variety of factors could be relevant, the possible list of factors to be considered, and the participants, took literally years to go through.

The problem with relying solely on traditional notions of procedural reform is only too easy to see. The participants feel a sense of futility because they think the minds of the decision-makers are already made up. The decision-makers feel their time is being wasted. The public as a whole loses because neither are the policy decisions made rapidly nor are the premises articulated sufficiently well to serve as a guide to them.

This is not to denigrate the usefulness of the traditional procedural tools but simply to suggest that what is needed, on the part of those interested in actually reforming the planning system, is attention to the moulding of these techniques to fit specific circumstances (for example, perhaps amenity groups that are members of the Civic Trust should be notified as of right of all planning applications submitted to the local authority) and, more important, to devise new procedural protections for various aspects of the system. The development of the public examination is the primary example of such an

233

invention being made to meet the new circumstances of a new type of planning document, but there could easily be others of a similar character. It is sad to note here that sections 47–9 of the 1971 T.C.P.A., which provide for a Planning Inquiry Commission to review large-scale planning applications, have not been experimented with extensively, for this is just the type of reform which might be of great value.

A possible variation on the theme is to set up various types of advisory forums for various types of local planning activity. If the examination is useful for structure plans, there may be a variety of forums that would be useful in bringing forward public values on other aspects of planning. One such possibility might be the idea of an area committee to advise on planning applications. With the disappearance of the parish councils in most urban areas and the lack of attention paid to them in the rural areas where they still exist, there is no possibility of discussing planning applications except at the large district-council meetings. As Stewart described the idea, such an area committee would be much like a town meeting held every month, which could publicly discuss major projects or developments for the area: 'Cities and counties have many levels, and we too often assume that a uniformity of approach at the centre is all that is required . . . a sensitivity to the needs of the locality within the authority is required as well as an awareness of general problems' (STEWART, 1973, p. 651). One such area committee, described by McAuslan, is actually in existence in Stockport, and makes direct recommendations to the council and acts in an advisory and consultative role to the council.

Along similar lines, the public-examination format might be adapted to fit particular circumstances. For instance, the local authority might orchestrate such an examination on any large development or renewal scheme. This could be supplemental to other types of public participation, and serve as a means of advising without having to have a full-blown public inquiry before setting down a plan for one sub-area.

One interesting development along these lines is the possible establishment of local advisory committees on various local problems. These advisory committees could be called together to deal with difficulties in their problem areas as they arose. There is a precedent for central government's introduction of such bodies. With the introduction of the listed-building

234

approach to building preservation in 1968 the Ministry of Housing and Local Government (now the D.O.E.) issued Circular 61/68, which suggested a variety of ways of going about the task of selecting buildings for preservation. In para. 21 the Ministry suggested, but did not require, that the local planning authorities should establish conservation-area advisory committees which would include in their membership people from the community who were not members of the local authority. The purpose of such an advisory committee was to offer advice on applications that would affect the character or appearance of a conservation area once established. The Ministry went on to suggest that residents, business-men, and members of both local and national amenity groups might be asked to join.

What is important to note is that such procedural changes would, in the first instance, be pragmatic methods of getting in more views and opinions, but could, in the long run, have the most fundamental impact on the ability of the planning system to function. For instance, the advisory groups could be a way to institutionalise the role of planning-interest groups in the plan-making and development-control process. Similarly, the use of a public-examination format for local projects could be a way to build in a search for the views of those members of the public who are affected but are not likely to be objectors. Thus such procedural innovations might in effect democratise the planning decision-making.

Flowing from this there might be procedural changes in the way local authorities consider plans or planning applications. In the same way that a public-examination secretary might play a different role if he were instructed to seek out and bring forward participants representing the objectors' interests, rather than those of the authorities involved, so might a branch of the local-authority planning department be given a different mandate to bring out different views. We suggested earlier that one possible approach was planning aid to support third-party objectors to the granting of planning permission. Perhaps as a corollary the authority could establish an internal department in effect to oppose the planning department's decisions before the planning committee in certain problem areas (for example, a local-authority department of existing communities). Charles Reich suggests just such an institutionalisation of

235

certain values for large administrative agencies, 'It is no longer a surprising thought that government must take measures to ensure a broad range of values and even to promote its own opposition. As government grows ever stronger, it must underwrite pluralism in ever more explicit terms.' (REICH, p. 1263)

We said at the beginning of this discussion that the best criterion for evaluating the attempts at reform was to see which changes caused those government employees who brought forward new values and ideas to redefine their reasons for acting. It would seem that the greatest potential for productive reform lies in changing the procedures, and the last few paragraphs have suggested possible lines of development toward that end. Such an emphasis would, however, cause substantial problems among the two professional groups, lawyers and planners, who are such important participants in the process.

THE IMPACT OF A PROCEDURAL EMPHASIS ON THE PLANNING PROFESSIONALS

Reforms along the lines just suggested carry with them a re-analysis of the role of the planners and lawyers involved in the process. Professionals are generally defined as a vocational group which manipulates a specific body of knowledge. Turning first to the local planning officials, one of the things that has been stressed throughout this book is that the actual decision-making involved in the drafting of a structure plan or the granting of planning permission is not based on what is best on technical criteria undiscoverable to the average layman but rather on the selection of the best course of action out of a series of competing public values. We have seen above how the most productive investment in reform would be to concentrate on those procedures which would allow for the most open and publicly reasoned selection of those public values.

For the local planning official, then, a redefinition of the profession would be necessary. The very basis of such reforms lies in the idea of stripping away the mantle of planning officials' professional expertise: the idea that the official can decide what is 'best from a planning point of view'. The areas of knowledge that would be professionally manipulated would not be learning which enables one to select public values but learning which allows those public values to compete for acceptance in an open forum. In a practical way they would have to redefine their task from being an attempt to order the future to being one of a broker for the various competing interests. Such a position would necessarily entail deference to elected officials and representative spokesmen, who would, on the surface, appear not to know very much about the techniques, words or methods of the planners. It would be difficult for the planning officials to realise that these people have just as much 'expertise' in public values as do the officials, and that what they do not have is the language or ability to relate those values to the raw data of the physical constraints (for example, the amount of land, the number of school children, the amount of water, and so on) and other public values. The planning officials' task, then, would be to translate these values into the jargon of the officials and the jargon of the officials into meaningful language for the representatives. It is here that the planning officials would have to go out of their way to avoid professionally manipulating the information to seek a value selection with which they agree. What we have done in the previous section is suggest administrative procedural changes which might guarantee this. (For instance, the suggestion that a local authority establish a department of existing communities would be a way to ensure institutionally that some of the officials would bring forward data in disagreement with other officials' information. Hopefully the resulting confrontation would ensure that it was not the official who made the choice of values but rather the elected representatives on the council.)

Since such procedural changes would carry with them a relegation of the role of the planner, it is to be expected that they will not receive widespread support from planning officials or their representative groups. We saw earlier how the Skeffington Committee's suggestion of just such an institutionalised or procedural change in the form of a community-planning representative was quietly eliminated from the central government's implementation of their proposals. It is important to keep in mind that often the most productive reforms will be opposed by the planning officials, and this opposition will be in direct proportion to the extent to which such reforms threaten the position and 'expertise' of those planners.

It will not only be the planners who will be subject to professional insecurity. When we turn to the lawyers we again see a situation where the concentration on productive procedural reform will have substantial effects on how the group will see its area of competence and its ability to manipulate that knowledge. Earlier we discussed at some length lawyers' inability to adapt their procedural competence to the benefit of individuals who have other than a property interest in planning. Lawyers have, until this point, excelled at developing the judicial style of public inquiry. As Professor McAuslan has pointed out, they have not been noted for their emphasis on procedural innovation once they have assumed positions of policy-making in the central government. (MCAUSLAN, 1974)

The lawyers too might have to devise structures for public value selection which would tend to relegate their positions *vis-à-vis* other professional groups. For instance if a public-examination type of hearing were used by the local authority when contemplating a major development – prior to a decision – the lawyers might be excluded entirely from representing participants but be used extensively as chairmen to 'probe', to find out policy rationale. This might occur particularly where the local council was considering a spending programme of some kind – the subsidy of a transport route, the purchase of a footpath system – where the councillors would be seeking general information rather than specific detail. The lawyers could appear later at the public inquiry once the council had made its decision, but it might be wise to limit their participation in the earlier procedure.

Similarly, the lawyers might have to concentrate on the development of procedures which would serve the same purpose as the traditional legal procedures in a different setting. For instance, one of the major difficulties with forums for the public review of policy decisions is the inordinate delay involved. In planning we have seen that public inquiries are often very time-consuming. What may be needed is for the lawyers to discard traditional notions in certain settings. To return once again to the public examination, it could be that the most important procedural change would be the establishment of a 'devil's advocate' type of secretary to serve such a panel, or the requirement that the panel chairman be a practising barrister. But the traditional ordering of issues by the participants'

238

lawyers, or cross-examination to determine 'truth' in a policy setting, may not be necessary. Such a reconsideration of role may be as difficult for the lawyers as for the planners.

A NOTE ON THESE CONCLUSIONS AS VIEWED FROM THE AMERICAN SIDE OF THE ATLANTIC

There are some important lessons to be learned by other legal systems if, as proposed here, the process of planning land-use is of such enormous complexity that no body of experts could possibly determine the shape of the communities' development very far into the future. What become important are not the planning documents or even the size and scope of the administrative apparatus but, as suggested above, the procedures for making specific choices based on various public values. For jurisdictions which do not have such elaborate administrative systems it should be stressed that more *ad hoc* reforms concentrating on a specific difficulty could be as efficacious as large, well-funded administrative changes.

For instance, local government reorganisation on a wide scale might not be as worthwhile as the specific exploration of procedures for the co-ordination of *ad hoc* service delivery, or public discussion of specific projects. Similarly, it may be more important to the financial efficiency of a local-government system to ensure a comparison of funding bases rather than the level of central-government support in any given year. Likewise, when establishing structures for dealing with certain land-use problems, reformers might do well to consider limiting the breadth of coverage and concentrating instead on the quality of decision-making in those areas of land-use selected for administrative control.

In the United States over the last few years a number of new programmes have been developed in various States to deal with various land-use problem areas under an administrative permission system. Typical are the California Coastal Protection Scheme, the Wisconsin Flood Plan Protection Scheme, and Maine's major site-location law. The purpose of these State-wide programmes was to create an administrative apparatus to take the place of a local zoning system, which had been unable to bring to bear enough of the necessary values to make a 'good decision' from the standpoint of the rest of the citizens in the State. It is somewhat ironic that these programmes seem to be encountering some of the problems that Britain experienced when it first introduced the T.C.P.A. of 1947. Again there has been a rush to give the administrators powers of control, without ensuring either that adequate surveys would be undertaken to present the administrator with sufficient information, or that there would be sufficient alternative forums for discussing the public values those administrators would select in making their decisions.

Without going into the intricacies of the various programmes, it is worth repeating that the community does not necessarily get 'better' land-use decisions if the expert professional decision-maker happens to work for the government rather than for the development company. This may be of special importance if the Americans ever actually pass one of the numerous Federal National Land-Use Bills that have been suggested over the last few years. The idea of such legislation would be to establish a federal body to give technical and financial assistance to the various States to develop land-use programmes. If such a body were to come into existence it would be extremely important to have it concentrate its energies on ensuring both that sufficient information is assembled by the States to enable a State to make decisions that affect it, and that there is concentration on the procedures for evaluating policy decisions.

Various aspects of the British experience might be valuable here. For one thing, the institutional arrangement of the administering agency is important. It was mentioned above that the fact that both highways and land-use come under the D.O.E.'s administrative umbrella was of great importance, since it allowed co-ordination between the two agencies. Similarly, it was suggested that a further possible change along these lines might be to consider ways of institutionalising divergent opinion at various levels of government. If the Americans place their programme under any one national department the programme may be given a distinct bias in favour of the particular expertise of the departmental area. For instance, if the land-use programme were to become part of the Department of Housing and Urban Development there would be no co-ordination with the highway-building section of the Department of Transportation.

Finally, the whole British experience with structure plans

and, in particular, the public examination of structure plans, is extremely pertinent to the birth pangs of American administrative development-control structures. What are needed are viable methods and procedures for evaluating public-policy choices. Reliance cannot be placed on traditional procedures, particularly on lengthy administrative hearings, to accomplish this. What is needed when the administrative system is still pliable and before the planning officials have secured a vested interest in protecting their own power to make decisions autonomously, is experimentation with different formats, advisory hearings, funding of amenity groups, institutionalisation of divergent views, advocates to seek out the non-involved public, advisory committees, area committees. It needs to be emphasised, in the United States as well as in the United Kingdom, that the methods of selecting courses of action for those methods are in fact the reality of the planning process.

Chapter 11 suggested that previous attempts to reform British Planning Law have not been entirely successful because they have concentrated on the forms of plans or administrative units rather than the procedures used in reaching particular decisions. The point was made that, where the reforming energies are focused on procedures (such as the Franks Report on the appeal process, or the attention given to the examination of structure plans), there often is a greater possibility of a reform which will affect actual land-use decisions and the way communities develop. It was this which led us to explore the various areas where a concentration on procedural reform might be worthwhile. However, it would seem from this discussion that further attempts to change the internal administration of planning (by establishing new management networks or by changing the geographical size of the planning units, for example), or the style of the various documents (that is regional plans, not-so structural plans, block plans), might not be the most fruitful method of expending intellectual and administrative energy.

There is, however, one aspect of the planning system which is so fundamental that changes in this area could have a wide-ranging effect on the actual pattern of land-use. What is being suggested here is that the system was initially posited upon a two-pedestal platform, both a negative regulatory system and a positive transfer of development rights to the nation, and that, in order to introduce any fundamental reform, one must return to the question of who owns the land that is to be used and how that ownership is to shape land-use.

MARKET VALUE AND THE TASK OF THE LOCAL OFFICIALS

The situation that existed in 1953, after the elimination of the betterment-levy sections of the 1947 legislation, left the planning system with the worst of both possible worlds. On the one hand the regulatory system of planning permissions had sufficient strength to encumber the market; on the other, the retention of land values in private owners' hands guaranteed that some owners' economic interests would prevail. Thus the value of land, while not determining all land-use, did, in many circumstances, lead the planners by the nose. A great many of the difficulties which we have seen in the planning system stem from the fact that the officials do interfere with people's ability to use land, but they cannot keep up with the external economic increases in land values that end up forcing them to give certain types of permission. The late 1960s saw a phenomenal increase in land prices throughout the country, with the price of land in the South-East increasing nearly four-fold between 1965 and 1970, from £5000 to £20,000 an acre (Drewett in HALL [ed.], 1973, vol. 2, p. 214). Some of the major difficulties flowing from the planning system, such as rapidly increasing values of housing plots with planning permission, and the local authorities' inability to pay the price to provide land for recreation or amenity, can all be traced to the planners' lack of control of the value and ownership of land.

There is, of course, major disagreement among economists and planners as to the relationship between the market-price structure and the role of the permission-granting official. The classic statement of what the market should do is best stated by Ratcliff:

The utilisation of land is ultimately determined by the relative efficiencies of various uses in various locations. Efficiency in use is measured by rent-paying ability, the ability of a use to extract economic utility from a site. The process of adjustment in city structure to a most efficient land-use pattern is through the competition of uses for the various locations. The use that can extract the greatest return from a given site will be the successful bidder. The outgrowth of this market process of competitive bidding for sites among potential users of land is an orderly pattern of land use spatially organised to perform most efficiently the economic functions that characterise urban life. (RATCLIFF, p. 369)

The problem is, however, that it does not do this. The market has major blockages and does not value, for any individual buyer, interests that the aggregate of land users might consider important. As Pigou puts it:

> Marginal private net product falls short of marginal social net product, because incidental services are performed to third parties from whom it is technically difficult to exact payment . . . [similarly] there are a number of others in which, owing to the technical difficulty of enforcing compensation for incidental disservices, marginal net product is greater than marginal social net product. (PIGOU, 1952, p. 184)

Thus, to step in and enforce the aggregate good of all the residents in the community is, it is argued, the task of the government official and thus of the planning system.

What has happened in Britain is that while there is political unanimity about the need for negative restrictions on how people can use their land, there is no such consensus on property owners' ability to gain from the increase in value of the land once they get that permission. Since the 1947 Act the pattern discernible is of the Labour Party continually trying to impose its concept of ownership of land – an owner may hold it or use it as it is but may not gain from its increase in value by the grant of a government licence or planning permission to develop. The Conservative Party, however, has been intent on keeping the increase in value and the ownership of land in private hands. The Conservative ideology, stated clearly as part of its 1970 campaign statement against the Labour Government's Land Commission, is that it has 'no place in a free society'. (CULLINGWORTH, p. 160)

As the government has changed hands between the two parties over the last two decades, this divergence of views has resulted in the Labour Government establishing mechanisms for transferring land values to the government and the Conservative Government just as quickly unscrambling those mechanisms. As we saw in Chapter 4, the initial attempt in 1947 to transfer the value of development rights to the national government was quickly changed under the Conservative Government which came into power in 1951. The next major development was the Labour Government's attempt in 1967 to establish a Land Commission to acquire land needed for development.

As in the 1947 situation, the Land Commission faltered because there were two very different reasons for its creation, one based on planning and the other based on taxation or wealth-distribution policy. The 1965 White Paper expressed the rationale thus:

> The two main objectives of the government's land policy are, therefore: (i) to secure that the right land is available at the right time for the implementation of national, regional and local plans; (ii) to secure that a substantial part of the development value created by the community returns to the community and that the burden of the cost of land for essential purposes is reduced. (LAND COMMISSION WHITE PAPER)

What the Government did was to create a central-government administrative structure to buy, or compulsorily purchase, land suitable for development. In terms of the future development of land, the Commission was designed to be an assembler, a super planning agency to determine land-use. It could manage, dispose of, or develop land itself, or use either private or public developers. Coupled with this was a betterment levy equal to a proportion of the development value on all land sold, either in the open market and paid as a tax, or in a sale to the Commission and used as a deduction against the market value. Initially this rate was to be 40 per cent, but in order to encourage early sales the percentage was to increase over time.

By creating a central-government agency to compete with the local authorities in the business of determining which land should be used where, and linking this agency to a tax which, while perhaps logical, was extremely unpopular with the politically influential landowners in the country, the Labour Government did little to ensure the programme's longevity under a different government. It is little wonder that not only did most landowning members of the public view its acquisition function as merely a goad to ensure collection of the betterment levy, but the local authorities, even the Labour-dominated ones, viewed it as an unwanted interloper seeking to interfere with local planning (see ASH, WELLS).

It is significant to note that even the Minister himself,

245

Richard Crossman, was aware that the final compromise which resulted was not exactly equipped to deal with the development land problem. In his controversial Diaries he made the following comment concerning the Land Commission's tumultuous beginings:

> [T]here is the difficulty that the Land Commission as envisaged is a sheer nonsense, a non-starter, because it is impossible to create a monopoly purchaser as was planned. And directly one gives up the monopoly purchaser and introduces betterment tax to deal with a two tier price system all the advantages of the Land Commission disappear. . . . [It] will increase prices, not reduce them, and hinder our housing policy, not help it. [A better alternative might be to] . . . simply improve the present planning Acts by the addition of new compulsory-purchase powers for local authorities.*

The Commission was supposed to provide land for development immediately, land that was being withheld from the market by owners waiting for further gains, and it was supposed to have local-authority planning permission for those parcels. As it turned out, the Commission, as shown by its reports, had extreme difficulty in agreeing with local authorities as to which land should be purchased and developed. In the areas of greatest need for development land the Commission and the local authorities were in direct confrontation, for it was the very policies of containment of urban areas in such places as the Midlands and the South-East that led to the shortage of development land in the first place. As the Commission expressed it in its second report, its lack of success in placing land on the market was mostly 'due to planning policies which are directed to the containment of urban growth and the preservation of open country'. (COMMISSION REPORTS, 1969, p. 4)

There were a number of reasons why the Land Commission was not judged a success. For one thing, as Roy Drewett points out in his excellent piece in the *Containment of Urban England* (HALL [ed.], 1973, vol. 2, chap. 7) the Land Commission may have actually reduced the supply of development land on the market and thus increased, not decreased, the price of land.

---

* The Crossman Diaries, *Sunday Times* (9 February 1975) p. 16.

'The Land Commission had made no contribution to loosen up the market or to supplying land to these particular companies (who needed development land). There was a general feeling that the Land Commission was just another force in the market which helped to push up prices' (p. 240). More important, the Commission was not well-suited for the job of a national land-use planning agency and, in the final analysis, that is what its task would have had to have entailed.

In 1971 the Conservative Government quickly 'swept the Land Commission away' and the property-owners, who had wisely waited through the Commission's short life without selling their land or paying the betterment levy, again were put in a position where they could reap the increase in land value.

THE AIMS OF A SYSTEM OF TRANSFERRED OWNERSHIP VALUE

The Land Commission, like its predecessor the 1947 betterment levy, was skewered on its inability to make its effects important enough to last through a change of government. While the negative system of control quickly gained wide acceptance, the transfer of ownership value showed little real value to either the local-authority planning agencies or the affected public. By mixing the planning rationale with a taxation rationale, and then muddling that between the divergent aims of lowering the price of all land to all consumers on the one hand, and of merely lowering the price of land to the purchasing governmental units on the other, the scheme was open to immediate and fatal attack.

What happened in the early 1970s was that the increased economic activity, the availability of housing finance, and the over-all demand for housing all led to a tremendous increase in the value of development land, sometimes of the magnitude of 70–100 per cent a year. With this increase came, of course, a great increase in the cost of housing and industrial sites, and land came to be one supposedly safe bet against inflation, which further pushed up this cost spiral. With the housing slump of 1974 and the evaporation of housing finance this situation levelled off somewhat, but the land values have not returned to the levels before the 'property boom'.

What is paradoxical about this increase in land prices is that, even if one were not a romantic, yearning for Henry

George, it is extremely difficult to deny that a good part of the increase in value is directly attributable to the social expenditure of government, both local and central. Not only do local governments direct the intensity of use through planning and augment the use through the infrastructure, but the central government also directs large amounts of money to specific land-use areas through its systems of industrial grants and New Town development funding. The central government, through the local authorities, supplies from 10 to 20 per cent of the private mortgage market and, starting in 1967, it has even stepped in to subsidise the mortgage levels of the rest of that market in order to keep interest rates politically acceptable.

Before turning to a possible solution of the ownership problem it is important to look at the reasons why such a system might be desirable in the first place. First, in terms of planning, if it is once accepted that there should be government interference in the allocation of what land is to be used for what purpose it is extremely shortsighted to give government officials the power to say only where development should *not* occur. If the aim is for officials to provide housing, recreational or industrial land, with ready access to the governmentally provided infrastructure of transport and support services, then it seems that the local authority should be able to say what land is going to be developed, and where. And it should be able to do this without having to justify its effect on the personal wealth of each parcel-owner.

Planning law is immersed in the ownership rights of particular parcel-owners, but as we have seen, seems to show a significant disregard for the rights of the affected public. One possible result of the transfer of increases in the value of land, due to its urbanisation or re-urbanisation, might be to shift the focus of public attention. Instead of concern for the excesses and arbitrariness of public officials' actions against landowners, public attention might centre on arbitrary action against other affected members of the community.

In terms of development costs to society as a whole, the transfer to the government of development value would significantly decrease the cost of the development of land for housing or industry. If the total land market were stabilised, and the scarcity element of land (the increase in price due to its location near to urbanising areas) eliminated, not only would

248

government development (roads, schools, sewers, and so on) be less costly to the rate-payer, but also the cost to the consumer would be less. Instead of transferring the increase in value due to the growth of the community to those private developers who happen to be fortunate enough to combine planning permission and ownership, the increase could go to either the local or central government or to the consumer himself.

The issue of who gets the value brings into focus the area of the most controversy for, at a minimum, such a system could freeze value at its immediate stage of evolution by taking over enough land to monopolise the market. Over time, if the government had enough land and allocated more land than the developers needed, the price could even be lowered. The controversy comes, however, when the aim of the system is seen as being to take away the increase in value that owners already feel they are entitled to. An owner whose land is a fair distance from an expanding city would not perhaps be too upset by a programme that would pay him a current value for his land and deprive him of the hope for an increase in that value when the town expands to meet his property. An owner already on the periphery of that city who expected to get planning permission would be extremely upset if he were to receive compensation only equal to the value of the land without the demand caused by the closeness to the city being taken into account. It is this goal, of transferring the development value which has already accrued to owners, that causes the deepest divisions between Labour and Conservative politicians.

A further difficulty is that there are a number of goals which are unstated but which colour the Labour Party's approach to transferring land values. One is that, as was mentioned in Chapter 1, the land speculator or greedy developer has replaced the landlord of the 1940s as the devil within the economic system. A programme which will cut speculators' profits while still ensuring development is one that would be extremely popular politically. Coupled with this is the fact that many of the particular programmes which the Labour Party is committed to, such as council housing, would be made budgetarily easier to implement by local Labour authorities if the price of land were decreased. While all authorities would benefit from less expenditure on land, those that sought to expand social programmes making intensive use of land would benefit doubly.

249

What this tends to obscure is that it might very well be the case that the private owners and developers who are producers, as opposed to those who merely hold assets in the form of land, may be the ones to benefit the most from a system which assures the rapid delivery of land with an adequate infrastructure at a low and constant price. While a system of transferring the increase in development value out of the hands of the particular owners will help local government with land developments, it is not necessarily the case that this would not be even more beneficial to private producers or consumers. The factory which does not have to spend a great deal of its investment capital would benefit, as would a private house-buyer who would pay only 6 to 10 per cent of his house-buying finances on land, as opposed to the current 20 to 30 per cent. (Drewett in HALL [ed.], 1973, vol. 2, p. 216)

THE EXAMPLE OF SWEDISH LAND STORAGE

There are various possible models available which could change the pattern of land-ownership. Local government's ability to develop land positively could be increased and the transfer of the increase in value due to urbanisation away from the particular owner to either the government or the consumer could be effected. What we shall do here is look at how such a system can work in a different political setting – Sweden – and then return to possible approaches here in the United Kingdom.*

Sweden has had a system of municipal land-ownership for most of the post-war years. Expressed in its most basic form, the local government simply buys land, holds it, and, after deciding which land will be used for recreation and which for development, sells or leases the land back to the private owner, not at a market price but at a price covering the cost to the authority. In order to obtain financing for the development through the state-guaranteed loan system the developer must not charge more than the land cost him (SWEDISH STATUTES). Throughout the following discussion it is important to remember that

---

* The following information is based on my study, which appeared in the *Modern Law Review* (March 1975) on *Land Storage: The Swedish Example*, undertaken during 1973, through a grant from Warwick University and the United States Department of Housing and Urban Development. It is based, to a large extent, on personal interviews with various Swedish administrators and politicians.

Sweden does not have the high density of land-use which, in other countries, so often leads to furious competition for the available land resources. This is because, by European standards, Sweden is relatively sparsely populated. Compared to Britain's 228 people per square kilometre, Sweden has a mere 18 per square kilometre. Although Sweden is highly industrialised, with some 80 per cent of the population living in the cities, it has still used less than 1 per cent of its available space for urbanisation, compared with Britain's use of over 8 per cent of its land. (ODMANN, N.B.U.P.)

Another factor to remember about land in Sweden is that, both historically and within the last few decades, land has been viewed differently in Sweden than in the continental or common-law countries. The 'right of all men' or right-of-way prerogative, which allows Swedes to walk over all land which is not directly under till or directly attached to a dwelling house, is not an aberration in the Swedish mentality but merely one of the most visible aspects of their different views. Moreover, Sweden has often made fundamental changes in ownership rights (such as eliminating the right of lumber companies to even own land) in order to meet wider social policies. In the last century changes were made to meet the needs of farmers; in this century they have been changed to meet the housing needs of the urbanised industrial population. (HEIMBURGER)

The other major point which must be kept in mind is that Sweden has had one political party in power for the entire post-war period. This continued political support has given the policy-makers within the party and the civil service a strong mandate to meet the problems of housing and rational urban development. While the particular goals have changed slowly, for instance from an almost total reliance on communal apartment-style living to a tolerance for single-family dwellings, the controlling political party has remained the same. The political popularity of the Social Democratic Party has allowed them the flexibility to introduce a wide variety of changes in the land and land-financing law, not a few of which might have caused serious controversy in other political climates. The best example of this is perhaps the recently enacted expropriation law, discussed below, the main point of which is to deprive future owners of compensation for their expectation of value due to urbanisation.

251

The Tools Available

Although the vast majority of the land which comes into public ownership is acquired through ordinary negotiation and purchase, this is only the result of a complicated array of legal and tax mechanisms which make these purchases possible. (FOJER)

First, the government bodies charged with the administration of local development are the kommunes or municipalities, which have been consolidated and strengthened to produce local governments of nearly uniform size and ability. There were 2365 kommunes in the 1940s, the number was reduced by the 1952 boundary reform to 904, and the second wave of reforms in the 1960s and early 1970s further reduced the number to a mere 275 municipal blocs. These units are based on a notion of city regions each with an urban community at its centre. With a minimum population of between 8000 and 10,000 people they are strong enough in terms of resources to carry on a land-buying programme.

The next point is that the income-tax structure of the country itself guarantees the local municipalities an autonomous and self-perpetuating source of funds; property tax constitutes only a small fraction of the municipal tax base. The basic form of tax is on income. The individual files one tax return through one organisation. His tax is made up of two parts: a steeply progressive national-income tax, and a proportional local-revenue tax at a flat rate. This means that each local authority sets its own rate depending on its needs. There is also a national equalising system, based on tax-paying capacity (not total revenue), which brings the resources of the poorer income authorities up to the national average. (STATISTICAL YEARBOOK)

This tax system guarantees the local authorities a uniform pool of resources, with no strings attached, for municipal improvement and planning. The first ingredient in land storage, namely how to pay for it, was thus strong from the outset. Combined with a political guideline of buying enough land to cover all projected development for a community for the next ten years, this lays the groundwork for the Swedish idea of community development. In the words of Peter Heimburger of the National Board of Urban Planning, 'a good and effective community development implies accordingly that

252

sufficient land is obtainable in the right place at the right moment and at a reasonable price'. (HEIMBURGER, p. 1)

The second aspect of tax policy which should be noted was that in 1968 the law concerning capital-gains taxation was changed. Prior to that time, in order to decrease speculation, capital-gains taxes at ordinary income rates had only been charged on profits on land held less than ten years, and gains made from land held longer than that were not taxed at all. In 1968 the rule was changed to provide for taxation of all gains, irrespective of the time the land had been owned. As might be expected, this made landowners in 1967 quite eager to sell prior to the imposition of the tax. (PASSOW)

The kommunes also have an entire system of local land-use planning based on negative control. Physical planning in Sweden is done both at the national level in the form of long-range planning and the co-ordination of local efforts, and at the local level. The kommunes develop both masterplans of the areas and detailed building plans and town plans. A private party who owns land and seeks to develop it must receive planning permission before he can proceed. These negative controls are further strengthened by a series of levies which allow the kommunes to tax infrastructure costs back to the owners of the benefited parcels.

This system of negative control has been buttressed by an elaborate system of land acquisition. In 1967 the central government decided to help the kommunes to meet the national goal of ten years worth of stored land, by augmenting their resources. From 1968 onwards the government has made available land-acquisition loans for land destined to be used for residential purposes. These loans are non-secured ten-year arrangements with interest being payable for only the first two years of the term. Starting with only 30 million Sw.Kr. (approximately £3 million) a year in central-government funds the programme is now up to a yearly loan availability of 85 million SwK.r. (£8·5 million). The central government controls the use of these funds through a permission system or a ceiling on the amount of municipal borrowing allowed. The central government can allow more borrowing in cases of rapid development and can curtail borrowing in areas which have acquired too much land for their immediate needs. Of course the municipality is always constrained by the fact that the payments on loans are reflected in the local tax rate, and over-investment in land with little return (such as when the kommune only leases its land) will result in an immediate jump in the flat rate.

The kommunes can use their funds, derived either from local income tax or these special funds, to purchase land (without stating its intended use) directly from landowners. Besides this obvious method there are two further devices which make the acquisition process easier. First the kommunes have, in certain circumstances, the right to step into sales which occur in the land market and take the place of the buyer. Under the Pre-emption Act 1967 (SWEDISH STATUTES, S.F.S. 1967, no. 868) and regulations therein, all sellers of land must notify the kommune of the intended sale. They keep a record of the sales volume and prices in the local land market, and thus not only have a constant source of knowledge for their own market buying but can also step in and take land on the same terms as the seller was willing to part with it, in all but certain types of transactions which are not covered by the pre-emption (such as very small parcels or transactions between relatives). For instance, if a farmer makes an agreement to sell land to a private builder who is thinking of buying the land and holding it, hoping to get planning permission at some future date, the farmer must record the intended sale with the kommune. The kommune, through its rights under the Pre-emption Act, can then step in and take the land on the same terms as the farmer was willing to sell it. The farmer would come out the same and the builder would only get his out-of-pocket expenses, but would not receive any compensation for any expectation value the parcel may have had for him.

The second major device which makes acquisition easier is the Swedish Expropriation Law. As early as 1949 the fact that land could be purchased compulsorily for the purpose of storage for a possible future use was specifically laid out in the regulations. A valid purpose under which a kommune could invoke expropriation was 'to ensure that land is available on reasonable terms for urban development and otherwise to transfer to municipal ownership undeveloped land for disposal on leasehold tenure'. (SWEDISH STATUTES, Expropriation Act, 1949)

If the owners were not in a position to exploit the land to

254

conform with the kommune's plans, or if the exploitation would lead to unreasonably high prices for the land, the kommune could purchase the land compulsorily. To give an example: in one area the kommune in its local plans had called for the area north-east of the major city to be used for recreational land with some residential areas. In its dealings with the major landowner to acquire this large parcel the kommune made it known that, although it would have no use for the land for perhaps many years in the future, it still might use its expropriation powers to acquire the land without actually stating what public or private use it might be put to in the future. As might be expected, to avoid the lengthy process of expropriation, the landowner sold the land voluntarily.

The possibility of expropriation and the growth of the amount of land stored by the kommunes provides the backdrop against which the negotiation process could take place with any individual landowner. Since the kommunes hold both the negative control power to say which land can and which cannot be developed, as well as the right to expropriate, they were in a very strong position when bargaining with recalcitrant landowners. Although expropriation is rarely used as the actual method for purchasing land (according to a spokesman for the Ministry of Physical Planning and Local Government, less than 10 per cent of the land bought for storage is acquired through the expropriation mechanism) it is the possibility (or threat) of its use which eases the kommune's task in actually buying the land.

The development of the basis of payment under the expropriation law is an interesting one, for when the cases did get to the special real-estate courts, the level of compensation to the landowner was not supposed to reflect any 'unearned increment', although it was meant to reflect market price and thus expectation value. This obviously ambiguous guideline came to be resolved in favour of the landowner, and, in the words of one government official who worked on the recent expropriation law-reform committee, the courts were very 'generous' to the owners. It came to be the political consensus that the owners were getting in too good a position compared with the municipalities and, as of 1972, an entirely new method of valuation for compensation has been developed. In Sweden, after nearly forty years of Social-Democratic political leadership, the expectation value of a change to urban use has been taken out of the expropriation compensation formula. Although owners are allowed any gains due to expectation up until the fixed date of 1 July 1971, thereafter no increase will be allowed for the owners' hopes of the possibility of development of the property.

The new legislation changes the burden of proof so that it is the owner who must show that his land has increased in value for the particular use it is currently being put to. To do this he cannot give reasons which show an increase in value due to social investment (for example, a subway being constructed nearby) or the possibility of a higher urban use (for example, the fact that neighbouring farm land is now being used for housing). His only method of proving worth is to show that the land's particular use has resulted in higher earnings and thus the land is worth more for that use (for example, if the price of food goes up a farm is worth more). According to Professor Seve Ljungman of the University of Stockholm School of Law, in a personal interview in 1973, the new formula will more or less stabilise the price of land at its current value. Although the new legislation will not decrease the value of land to current landowners, due to the fact that the legislation presupposes land values as of 1971, it will not allow the person who holds land, for say ten years, to benefit from the expectation of change of use generated by future growth. It will only allow adjustments for inflation and actual improvements to the land. The problem is that since the land price should stabilise, this brings into serious doubt the need for the municipality to invest in land prior to the time it is needed at all.

The last major set of mechanisms which must be understood is the way in which the municipalities release the land for urbanisation after storing it for a number of years. The land that is acquired is vacant land purchased at its raw, undeveloped value, and because of the change in the capital-gains law, and the generally low level of land prices, it is acquired at a very low price. Much of the land is acquired for recreational and open-space areas, but as the economy grows the municipality decides where and when the land shall be used for development. The most important point here is that, although there are generalised long-term regional and master plans, the only documents which actually set out the use are detailed town plans and housing plans. These plans deal with immediate plans for urbanisation and, for instance, the five-year rolling housing plan only sets uses that are, in actuality, being contemplated for immediate production. While the municipalities must have some idea of the ten-year future need for land, the five-year dwelling growth plan is the crucial document.

The municipal land can either be sold or leased, but in either case the price takes into account the initial costs of the parcels, the holding costs and the infrastructure costs, but not any increase due to the fact that it has changed use from raw land to land due to be developed. This is, of course, the problematic aspect of the system, because if the market does not locate the better parcels according to price, the allocation mechanism must use political criteria to dispense an item of tremendous economic worth. That is, if it is not the people or organisations with the most money who get the best parcels, they must go to those people or organisations who meet a different standard (such as need, size, social worth, and so on). It is the establishment of those standards in a very political situation which may, as we shall see, lend itself either to abuse or politically correct, but socially inefficient, allocations.

The reason that these low prices for land can be passed on to the eventual resident of either the single-family house or flat is that the central-government loan system of construction finance strictly controls the prices at which development will be financed and thus at which it will be sold. Expressed very simply, the central government guarantees the top 30 per cent of the loans for the purchase of most buildings (the other 'safe' 70 per cent coming from private sources) and those loans are not made on developments which have exceeded certain guidelines for land and construction costs. Since some 90 per cent of all construction is financed through central government, this price control is very effective.

The land-cost increment, in the government finance guidelines, is limited by the price originally paid to the municipality, or, in the case of leases, the cost of the yearly lease payments.

One interesting point to note is the interrelationship between the local taxation system, the central-government land-finance structure, and the local government's land-storage scheme. In order to have income-tax payers to finance local growth and amenity, and in order to meet local demand for housing, local authorities must supply adequate land. However, in order to finance the construction, the municipality has to meet the very low land-price increment in the central government loan scheme. A municipality with a shortage of cheap land would have to sell the land at a price lower than the combined storage and infrastructure costs. In other words the municipalities either have to store enough land to beat the price rise or else subsidise the price of building land itself in order to get housing developments built and financed.

For this system of loan and price control to work, the central government had to ensure that there was a sophisticated mechanism in charge of the valuation side of the production financing. The National Housing Board in Sweden provides this service through a central Stockholm office with some 150 employees, and 450 employees in regional offices. The central government, which ultimately supplies the financing guarantees for development, thus keeps track of local material, labour, and land costs. It develops a series of secret area-cost prototypes for various types of dwelling. The developers must then apply for financing with a given price. The development will not obtain finance if it exceeds the prototype, but it will if it meets it or goes under that price. In 1972 the Housing Board managed to have 32 per cent of the multi-family dwellings that it financed at below prototype costs, with 24 per cent below prototype for single-family dwellings. By not disclosing the method of computation and by not relying on any type of cost-plus-profit formula, the Housing Board kept the costs of housing production at a fairly stable level.

To qualify for this housing and these loans a resident of a community must place his name on a waiting list, either with the various multi-family housing enterprises (or municipal housing co-operatives) or for single-family housing on the municipality waiting list. As housing is produced the earliest name is given the first option on the dwellings produced. The allocation mechanism for newly constructed dwellings is really not a market one at all, but a waiting list. Once a person is selected for a house or a co-operative apartment he must go through the normal problems of finding the down-payment and arranging the financing, but the over-all price will already have been determined within the National Housing Board guidelines.

Most multi-family housing is allocated by a queue system,

258

even to the second or subsequent buyers. Thus, while co-operative owners will receive a return on their capital investment relative to their length of ownership, it is not usually set by the demand for that particular apartment. However, for single-family housing the situation is quite different. The new house-buyer must wait in the queue, and once he has received the right to buy a house he does not get that right again. He pays a price which does not reflect over-all urban demand for single-family housing or land, but one which simply covers the production costs. He can, though, sell his house to a second owner. There is a separate second-owner market for existing privately owned homes and, as could be expected, the prices of these houses, which reflect both over-all demand and particular land location, are considerably higher.

The problem arises that the price differential between the single-family housing production market and the second-owner market is substantial. People with one-quarter to one-third again as much money as their counterparts can buy a home without being in the queue for the requisite five to ten years. It also means that someone who is in the queue and decides he does not want the house the day after he buys it can resell it for a windfall gain of an appreciable amount of money. However, he cannot get a government-financed house twice, so he is permanently in the second-owner market where his 'windfall' is needed to get any type of comparable single-family house.

The Fruits of the Storage System

Sweden has managed to accomplish three major goals through its many-faceted integrated approach to municipal land-buying. First, and most importantly for countries experiencing rapid land-price rises, the price of land through the country has remained remarkably stable. According to Professor Erik Calegrim of the Department of Real Estate Economics at the Royal Institute of Technology in Stockholm, on the whole the levels of land prices throughout Sweden, and even central city land, is only rising somewhere in the region of 5 to 6 per cent per year. These figures were confirmed in interviews. While this is due in part to reforms in taxation, and particularly capital-gains structures, it is due, in no small degree, to the fact that the local governments control a great deal of the land, and thus the market. Secondly, the land-purchasing system has

259

ensured that physical planning on the ground should supply a group of assembled parcels with an adequate infrastructure and that existing private-ownership patterns should not necessarily direct future use. This planning through buying has also ensured that adequate recreational and amenity land will be available within development areas. Thirdly, municipal ownership has allowed the local governments to begin to make decisions regarding the type of community housing and thus social structure desired. A community can be created which can accommodate various types of development to cater for various levels of income, wealth, education and social structure.

These goals were accomplished through a land-storage system which, at least in the communities investigated, paid its own way. In no municipality investigated was the cost of the land-storage policy more than 0·5 to 1 per cent of the total municipal budget. As one development official stated, 'even though the community depends on land as long as you buy it as raw farmland, it really only makes up the smallest part of the entire community costs'.

There is one final point that should be made, namely that the system seems to produce its best results when an element of openness in the allocation (not the acquisition) process is used. The communities who used design competition produced better and cheaper developments, while gaining the added advantages of being free from any commitments for unnecessary development of a certain type.

THE LABOUR PROPOSALS FOR LAND STORAGE

A scheme similar to the Swedish idea has been proposed at various times by various parties. Most recently, the Town and Country Planning Association proposed that: 'The magnitude of the problem of development values is now [1973] such that it demands the creation of a public land bank. . . . The land must be acquired by the public in advance of development' (TOWN AND COUNTRY PLANNING ASSOCIATION LETTER). As might be expected, the Conservative Government which was in power between 1970 and 1974 was not interested in any schemes to transfer land-ownership. There was some emphasis on the taxation of 'windfall' or speculative gains in land with the introduction of the development gains tax idea, later to be implemented by the next government, and pressure was exerted on local authorities to release more land through the development-control procedures. The Labour Party, then in opposition, was interested in establishing as part of its platform a new approach to land-ownership, one that would not copy the mistakes of earlier Labour proposals.

During 1972 the National Executive Committee of the Party, through its Home Policy Committee, established a study group on land policy. Based on reports in the press and the publications of various individuals and groups, there was evidently a difference of opinion within the party on the question of how to implement a change in land-ownership. One school of thought, best represented by Barras, Broadbent and Massey, of the Centre for Environmental Studies (BARRAS), and a small group called the Campaign for Nationalising Land, called for a once-and-for-all nationalisation, a legislated change of the form of ownership which would apply to all freeholds. As the campaign's tract put it:

> We propose that from the appointed day all freeholds should be nationalised, and everyone who before the appointed day owned a freehold would be deemed to be a leaseholder on the terms of a statutory lease from the crown. . . . We think there should be no exceptions whatever to this legislation, it should embrace the land currently owned by public corporations, charities, the National Trust, the Churches, and the Queen herself. (C.N.L., pp. 4–5)

Among this group various possible management structures were then proposed to deal with the development of the new 'leasehold land'. Barras proposed a National Development Corporation to deal with it and David Lipsey put forward the idea of a series of regional Land and Development Corporations. (LIPSEY)

The other school of thought, which eventually carried the day, rejected this total takeover of all land, one that would perhaps affect the equity position of the 50 per cent of the electorate living in owner-occupied single-family residences, and concentrated instead on a gradual nationalisation of the development land. As Labour's 'Programme for Britain', the party platform presented at the 1973 annual conference, expressed it:

> We believe the country recognises that dealing with the

261

problem of building land lies at the heart of meeting our urgent housing needs and maintaining the character of our cities. . . . The explosion in the price of building land has reached frightening proportions. The official estimate for the country as a whole indicates a rise in the price of building land in 1972 alone of 60%. . . . No solution short of full public ownership of all land needed for purposes of development, redevelopment and improvement will suffice if the homeless problem is to be met . . . we therefore propose that planning authorities prepare rolling ten year programmes of land acquisition. Areas scheduled as suitable for development would be automatically publicly acquired. (LABOUR'S PROGRAMME, pp. 48–50)

It is important to note that the reasons put forward for this approach were, first, to deal with the injustice of property-owners' unearned profits, second, to lower the price of housing, and third, to buttress the planning system. At the heart of the scheme was the idea of paying the owners only 'existing use' value, not the current real-market value.

When the Labour Party was in opposition the particulars of this scheme could easily enough be left in a rather blurred state. The basic idea of a 'land bank' seemed like a reasonable platform policy. To publicise the idea one influential back-bencher, Frank Allaun (M.P. for Salford East), introduced a '10 minute' Bill in January 1974 to provide for the compulsory purchase of land by local authorities at existing-use value, for the creation of a 10-year land bank.* As might be expected the Conservative Government took no action on the private member's bill. As fate would have it though, a General Election was called within a month's time and the sudden elevation of the Labour Party to control of the government, albeit without a parliamentary majority, meant that the land policy had to take on a firmer silhouette.

In the Queen's speech, which opened the new Labour Government's parliament on Tuesday 12 March 1974, there was one short sentence which committed the government to action on the land policy: 'Proposals will be prepared for bringing land required for development into public possession and for encouraging home ownership' (QUEEN'S SPEECH, 1974).

---

* *Hansard* (29 Jan. 1974) vol. 868, col. 248.

The new Secretary of State for the Department of the Environment, Anthony Crosland, and the new Minister for Planning, John Silkin, both gave high priority to the implementation of the land policy. What had originally been the Conservatives' sole approach to the increase in development-land values, announced on 17 December 1973* – a change to taxing all gains on sale of development or land with planning permission at the individual or corporate tax rate (with no offsets), not the capital-gains rate – was quickly incorporated in the Finance Bill, published on 26 April 1974. This scheme taxes both increases in value due to a change of use and the granting of planning permission, at the time of sale or of the lease of the development. However, this was just the beginning, for there was intense pressure from the trade unions and the National Executive of the Party over a series of business ventures of certain acquaintances of members of the Cabinet. This political development resulted in Jack Jones, General Secretary of the Transport and General Workers Union, stating that: 'We want to see speculation stopped, and stopped from whatever source. There are too few homes and too many heartbreaks. It is intolerable that on the one hand we have bad housing, on the other unemployed building workers and declining living standards, while speculators still make profits.'† The landowners and builders holding development land sensed the urgency of the situation and in a series of meetings in May 1974 their lobbying groups, the House Builders' Federation and the National Housebuilding Council, called upon the government merely to discuss various alternatives through a Green Paper, rather than go forward with a White Paper of the government's intended course of action.‡

Due to the vicissitudes of politics the Labour Government chose instead to issue a White Paper entitled simply 'Land' as one of the government's final official acts prior to calling the General Election of October 1974. It is important to delineate the Labour programme as laid down in the White Paper, for it represents the third attempt in as many decades to transfer to the public domain some of the elements of the ownership of land.

---

* *Hansard* (17 Dec. 1973) cols 956–7.
† *The Times* (17 April 1974), p. 12.
‡ *The Times* (6 May 1974), p. 18.

The White Paper begins with eloquent quotations from both David Lloyd George and Lewis Silkin, the father of the 1947 legislation, about the evils of the value created by the community being transferred to the landowner, and then describes the two previous attempts, in 1947 and 1967, to transfer ownership to the government. It then describes the Labour Government's plans in very general terms. First, a central agency, such as the Central Land Board under the 1947 Act or the Land Commission under the 1967 legislation, is rejected for England and Scotland: 'the acquisition and disposal of development land is best left in the main to local authorities' (LAND WHITE PAPER, para. 24). The local authorities will be supported by a back-up organisation to advise them, and, in situations where they do not live up to their instructions, to act in their stead. The local authorities will acquire all land that is to be developed or redeveloped for a period of not more than ten years in the future and, under a rolling programme, will continue to acquire land as it is put to use. The White Paper calls for a blanket acquisition of all development land and presupposes that, after the initial transition period, no development will be allowed to begin except on local authority land (para. 27). Thus, even if a person wanted to develop his land and submitted a planning application, it would first have to be acquired and then resold to the developer.

Because of the split in planning functions between the county and the district described earlier in this book, the government was forced to allow both levels of local government the right to acquire land. The White Paper points out that the development-plan and development-control schemes are supposed to define the fields of operation of the two levels. It goes on to suggest that the acquisition schemes which determine which land the county acquires and which land the district acquires will be further techniques for defining their respective spheres. As we saw from the earlier discussion, it might just as easily provide yet another focus of antagonism between the two sets of government.

The White Paper presupposes a compensation system where the property owner could not object to compulsory purchase by the authority upon the basis of the validity of the authority's supposed future use of the land. This is similar to the procedure under compulsory purchase for New Town development

264

corporations where such objections can also be disregarded. The basis of compensation will be that of current-use value. Thus the provisions for a certificate of appropriate alternative development, whereby the local authority was forced to pay for the acquired land upon the basis of what development permission the land might have received had it not acquired the land compulsorily, will be eliminated. The White Paper, however, devotes very little attention to how this current use is to be determined beyond stating that it will not include any sum to represent the hope value that it might have if developed for some other purposes. It is perhaps not surprising that more attention was not devoted to this, for it is one of the most difficult aspects of the plan and would cause some individual landowners significant depreciation of their personal wealth. To deal with cases of hardship caused by this current-use valuation, the White Paper does describe a system of hardship tribunals to consider such cases and award additional payments.

The Labour Government went out of its way to emphasise that the plan was not a Draconian measure. First, for obvious political reasons, it exempted all owner-occupied housing from such public acquisition. Similarly, it allowed provisions for alterations and extensions of dwelling houses. Where an owner-occupied house does happen to have to be acquired by the local authority, the authority would have to pay full market value and the owner will continue to receive disturbance and home-loss payments as set down in the Land Compensation Act of 1973. To buttress this commitment further the Government made it clear that plots of land developed for owner-occupiers would result in the owner-occupier owning the freehold. It appears from the White Paper that the basis of such freehold transfer will be market value rather than the value it cost the local authority to assemble the land. But the document does mention that there will be some special provisions for those buying their first homes to allow them to benefit from the low land price.

Perhaps the most difficult aspect of such a programme would be the transition between the market-price system and the new acquisition and current-use value system. The White Paper acknowledges that, due to a shortage of skilled manpower (caused in part by the reorganisation of local government, the establishment of the great number of new planning authorities,

265

and the great deal of time spent on structure-plan making), it will not be possible to decide immediately which land should be acquired and then acquire it. The document thus acknowledges that the D.O.E. will have to give instructions by order to each authority to proceed as it is able. As a guarantee of the continuation of housing and industrial development during the transitional stage, the government would allow all land with planning permission and land owned by builders at the date of the White Paper to be developed and sold outside the acquisition system. Similarly, so as not to face those building companies with liquidity problems, the White Paper states that the move to current-use value will not be immediate.

The Labour Government proposes a taxation system to bridge this gap between market and current-use value. As mentioned earlier, the Finance Act of 1974 established a development-gains tax on the increase in value of land. This rate of tax varied, depending on whether the profit was made by a company (52 per cent or 55 per cent) or an individual (as high as 83 per cent for those in the highest brackets). Under the White Paper proposals this tax would be replaced by a Development Land Tax which would be fixed initially at 80 per cent (LAND WHITE PAPER, para. 43), but which would be subject to an increase up to 100 per cent through the time of transition. This tax would be a flat-rate tax imposed on all those who sold land or developed it. It would be based on the difference between the disposal price (that is, the sale price or market value in the case of development) and the price paid for the land, or the current-use value plus 10 per cent, or the price paid plus any increase due to the increase in the current use of that land. During the transitional period the local authority could buy the land net of the tax on development value that would have been payable by the owner had he sold his land privately.

The proposal presupposes that most non-owner occupied development will be released by the local authority on a leasehold, rather than a freehold, basis. Thus commercial property developers will not come out particularly well under the scheme. There is also a provision in the White Paper to allow purchase of office blocks (such as Harry Hyams's Centre Point) which have 'never been substantially occupied for a period of at least two years from the date of construction' (para. 62). And, in a rather unashamed election-eve closing

266

sentence, the White Paper states that the price to be paid upon acquisition will be the value payable had the premises been acquired at the date of construction.

The scheme is supposed to give local authorities more planning powers in a positive sense and to allow the community to benefit from the increase in value. However, at least in the White Paper, most financial benefit will go to the central government. 'The major part of the benefit will accrue to the taxpayer in general through the Exchequer; but a part will remain with the local community and part will be distributed amongst local authorities to help equalize the benefits of the scheme between ratepayers at large' (para. 59). Thus, although the benefits of the scheme would be shared between local and central government, the central government would still be the one to benefit most. It was this question which caused some of the greatest concern to the local authorities. The initial estimates are that the scheme will result in some £750 million a year being added, not to the speculators' accounts, but to the public's account.

In the confusion of the election these proposals did not receive widespread analysis. The White Paper had been curiously silent on the initial cost of the programme. Obviously the local authorities would not have sufficient funds themselves to buy all the development land at existing-use value and the central government would have to provide the seed money for the initial ten-year land bank. It was perhaps impolitic to mention a sum of money of this size within days of an election. The major difficulty of the plan, as expressed in the press, was that it did not seem to provide any vehicle for rapid acquisition of land. Since all landowners would be waiting for the next change of government there is a very real danger that the supply of land on the market would simply be drastically reduced. As Richard Milner wrote: 'Without determined compulsory acquisition, development land sales could simply dry up as they did after the 1947 Act and what started as a bold reform could end up as a bitter anticlimax.'*

When the Community Land Bill was introduced on 20 March 1975 this fear of inadequate compulsory purchase powers was met by the placing of a duty on the local authorities to acquire

---

* *Sunday Times* (15 Sep. 1974) p. 59.

compulsorily all development land once the initial transition period was passed. The Community Land Bill's basic premise is that after the transition stage all development as defined in the Town and Country Planning Act will take place on land owned by the municipality. In order to embark on the programme in each county, the county and district governments must reach an agreement on a land-acquisition and management scheme. The authorities will then be allowed to acquire land and after a specified date required to acquire all development land. The price paid will start as the market value less the 80 per cent development land tax and will eventually move towards the existing use value, or in effect a 100 per cent development tax.

The problem was that the very positive nature of the powers granted caused substantial opposition in that it did not seem that the Bill left enough public access to the public acquisition and planning process. Aside from the Conservative Party's basic ideological opposition to the idea (Hugh Rossi, the Conservative spokesman on housing, condemned the Bill as 'an infringement of a basic human right'),* there was also significant opposition from the professional organisations involved in the planning process. These criticisms were directed not so much at the idea itself but at the particular procedural form it had taken in this Bill. There were basically four types of criticism. First, the proposal to have the central government receive 40 per cent of the income generated was felt to give too great a share to the central government at the expense of the local authorities. Predictably, the Association of County Councils and the Association of District Councils voiced their displeasure with this allocation of the money generated.† Secondly, various planning groups pointed out that the split of municipal ownership between the bifurcated local authorities would cause a great deal of animosity. The fear was that the grant of another power to the authorities would intensify the rivalry built into the planning process through the 1974 Local Government Act. Thirdly, there were commentators who feared the secretive nature of the scheme which would abolish most of the need for planning inquiries but place nothing in its stead. In the words

* *The Times* (21 March 1975) p. 2.
† *The Times* (10 March 1975) p. 2.

of the Town and Country Planning Association: 'The Bill runs the risk of encouraging development which is not in accord with local planning policy and of creating a land acquisition process which is too secretive to be acceptable to the public.'* Finally the critics expressed a general distrust of the competence of the planners at the local level to handle the process. While the local-authority officials are to be trusted to grant planning permissions they are not felt to be competent actually to allocate land-uses through their ownership and decide when it should be developed. The Conservatives suggested that the Bill would 'greatly increase the possibility of corruption'.† *The Times*'s editorial stated that the local authorities 'have not the staff, or the funds, nor is their character such that they possess, or could acquire the imagination, judgement or motives, to fit them to exercise exclusive primary initiation in all development'.‡

The heart of the opposition to the scheme is that it will vest too much power over planning and land-allocation decisions in the local authorities without adequate procedural safeguards. While the arguments concerning which level of government gets what percentage of the moneys generated are simply the natural competition between these units for more revenue, and while the argument concerning the bifurcation of the planning process between the county and district level is endemic to the planning process under the 1974 Local Government Act, the two other criticisms are of a much more fundamental character. This is perhaps a prime example of how a concentration on the 'planning' aims of a scheme can bury the equally important procedural safeguards which could guarantee that scheme's success or failure. In the words of one critic in a letter to *The Times*: '[A]s both initiator of development schemes and the consenting power over them, the local authority will be judge and jury in its own cause'.§**

---

* Ibid.

† *The Times* (24 March 1975), p. 4.

‡ *The Times* (21 March 1975), p. 17.

§ *The Times* (24 March 1975), p. 15. Mr Lindsay Thomas.

** There have been significant developments during the debates on the Bill (up to July 1975) – the rolling programmes have been cut from 10 to 5 years, church and charity lands have been exempted, and compulsory purchases must now be supported by planning reasons. The original Bill did not require the authority to state the purpose for which the land was to be acquired, but after much criticism (particularly from the Law Society) it was amended in committee to require reasons to be given, which can be in the form of local or structure plans. It is

While the Bill is still in its initial stages at this point in time (March 1975) and will no doubt take some time to implement, it is perhaps useful to look at various ways in which the speedy procedures might be established to guarantee a better level of decision-making, more access by those affected in the community and less likelihood of hidden local-authority decisions which might lend themselves to special interests or corruption. The following model may be useful in the public debate of the legislation and its implementation.* In keeping with the general premise of this study, the discussion will concentrate on the procedural form such a scheme might take.

A MODEL SCHEME FOR BRITISH LAND STORAGE†

The first factor which must be kept in mind in designing a land-storage scheme is that the public sector already owns a significant portion of the land in the United Kingdom. The most recent survey done of the various holdings of the central government, nationalised industries, national trusts, and local governments showed that over 12 per cent of the surface area of the country is already publicly-owned (DOWRICK, p. 23). If roads, common land and leasehold interests are included, the figure may be as high as 18 per cent. Since the government already owns and maintains so much land, the question is should it assemble land for both future government and private-enterprise use. It should also be noted that the transfer of bonds for land will not necessarily cause the former owners to consume more goods and services and thus will not necessarily be inflationary.

With these factors in mind we can proceed to sketch a possible format and set of procedures for storing land, based on

---

somewhat disquieting to note that under Schedule 4 of the Bill as amended in committee the right to an inquiry can be dispensed with in cases where a structure or local plan exists which has met the public participation sections (8(1) or 12(1)) of the 1971 T.C.P.A. It seems then that there are those in central government who still think that the publicity requirements of the Act at the abstract strategy level are a substitute for the particularised review of planning decisions at the individual level.

* Due to the fact that the Bill was in its early stages at the time the book went to press no attempt has been made to compare the specifics of the Bill with the following model.

† This model was developed with the help of Professor J. P. W. B. McAuslan of the University of Warwick.

the premise that all development would be on public land and all land acquired would be paid for at existing prices. First the central government would establish the legislative authority and an initial fund of money in the form of long- and short-term securities. The size of this fund would be large enough to allow local governments to buy land to supply development needs for five to ten years in the future. Since the local governments would recoup their investment as the land came to be developed, this funding would be a one-time transfer from central to local government but it would have to be a substantial sum (informal estimates range from £300 million to £3000 million).

The power to acquire land for storage would be vested in the upper tier of the local government structure: the counties and the metropolitan counties. As we saw in the discussion of the split of planning powers between the counties and districts, there are already difficulties with a system of administration which posits the counties as the strategic planners and the districts as the implementers of those strategies. The counties would seem to be better agencies for making the strategic choice of which land was needed for development over a number of years. The difficulty, however, is that the districts have just established their own planning departments and they would need to receive ownership in order to carry out their local plans. The storage system would have to allow the districts to request the county to acquire land within the districts (or outside it for district use), and in the case of disputes between county and district on such matters the district should be able to appeal to central government for a review of any decision not to acquire land requested by the district.

The enabling statute would state that all undeveloped land, and developed land in respect of which certain types of redevelopment were expected, could be purchased by the county without having to state explicitly the possible future use. With the passage of the legislation, all local authorities would be placed under a duty to earmark for future purchase any land they considered worthy of development within a stated time. Basically, the county would earmark all land that has planning permission, is going to receive planning permission, or which might receive planning permission (white land). The county would then publish this earmarked land map and register a

271

notice of intention to purchase against all such land in the local Land Charges Register.

At this stage there would *not* be a right to a general public inquiry, but individual, affected owners would have a right to object to earmarking on three specific grounds: (1) the land is already developed; (2) the land is undeveloped but is part of the permissible garden or curtilage of a dwelling house; (3) the land has been acquired by a building company which will complete its development before a certain time limit. In order to keep a continuous supply of new housing building companies would have to be allowed to finish projects they were already engaged in.

All local authorities would be required to purchase a certain minimum amount of their earmarked land each year. This duty to purchase would be based, if statistics permitted it, on a formula which took into account the previous amounts of land developed yearly, the total amount of land already developed, and a factor to take into account radical deviations from past performance (for example if a major factory or airport were being built in the area). An alternative formula, cruder but recognising the lack of adequate statistics, would be based on the local authorities' housing stock; an amount of land would have to be purchased which would increase that housing stock by a certain percentage. These formulae would be fixed by the D.O.E. and could vary from region to region or authority to authority.

At the beginning of each fiscal year the local authority would select which of its earmarked land it would acquire that year. Provision would be made for consideration by the relevant committee of the county of any representations by groups or individuals as to which land should be acquired. This would help to ensure that the important political question of the type and location of land and thus of future community development was properly considered by the committee. It would be to this committee that the member districts would appeal for land to be purchased in their areas. Since they could appeal to central government, the committee's recommendation to the full council would have to include a reasoned justification for the selection of the sites and include evidence that all relevant representations had been properly considered. This process would have to be completed within three months. The counties would also be under a duty to purchase all land in respect of which an application was made for permission to develop or redevelop in certain ways (for example, an application for planning permission on land not earmarked, or earmarked but not purchased). Since the idea of the scheme is to have all development on public land some owners could not be allowed to develop their own land. They could develop it if they got permission, but they would have to pay the county the premium of the difference between the existing-use price and the value as developed land.

One major problem would have to be faced squarely: there would be a number of neighbouring local authorities who would not agree on developments on their periphery. Disputes of this type between the county and member district would be settled under the appeal procedure outlined above. There would have to be a similar procedure of appeal when a county-level authority wanted to buy land in the jurisdiction of a neighbouring county. One possible way of meeting this might be to allow any county to buy land within a certain distance of its periphery as of right, but require them to go through the already established method of seeking planning permission from that jurisdiction when the owning authority sought to develop it,

The purchase procedure under such a scheme would be designed to separate the transfer-of-ownership process from the evaluation-of-compensation process. If the land is registered the local authority would prepare a certificate of public purchase which, when registered at the land registry, would have the following effects: (1) title to the land would be automatically transferred to and vested in the acquiring authority; (2) all other interests in the land would be over-reached and transformed into claims against the county's acquisition-compensation fund. Under such a scheme the county could deal with the land at once and plan its use independent of any disputes about which owner is entitled to what amount of compensation for what interest. (In those cases where the land is not registered and the title is perhaps confused due to the documents being in various solicitors' and mortgagees' hands, or the exact boundaries being unclear, an unregistered acquisition certificate would be served on all known owners of interests in the land and these owners would be under a statutory obligation to hand over to the county all documents of title. The county could then

273

register the land and serve a public-purchase certificate. In case of disputes about title, owners could have right of appeal to the Lands Tribunal for a declaration of interest.)

The county would thus have the ownership of the land immediately, and could sell or lease the rights to use the land as it saw fit under the scheme. The county would, however, be under an obligation to offer the old occupier a licence to use the land for a short period of time if the county did not intend to develop the land within, say, eighteen months. The licensee would not have a property interest in the land, and upon termination of the licence would only receive compensation for improvements made to the land during his licensed occupation. By handling the land in this way the land would not fall into disrepair and would continue to be used economically.

The major difficulty with the purchase procedure will, of course, be the method of land valuation. Valuation is at least as much an art as it is a science, and the role played by the district valuer is substantial. He is an individual, schooled in surveying, whose unenviable job it is to guess or judge what a piece of land would fetch if the owner wanted to sell and a buyer wanted to buy. Under the scheme we are discussing, he would have to eliminate from that guess the 'hope' or development value beyond the value the parcel would be worth if it were restricted to its existing use. What would be important for the success of the scheme would be the establishment of legislated criteria restricting the discretion left to the valuer. The drafting of the valuation definitions would thus be of extreme importance. They might be based on either a positive formulation, a list of the only factors which could be taken into account, or a negative formulation, a series of factors which would be used to discount the market value that the district valuer already was familiar with. While this latter approach might seem a novel method of establishing valuation principles by statute, it might represent more nearly how a valuer would, in practice, value existing use, and could have the added advantage that the statute could enable the Minister to vary the percentages attached to different factors at different times and for different areas (for example, 20 per cent off for development potential, 10 per cent off for location, 15 per cent off to represent capital flow versus other assets, and so on).

Within one month of the registration of the public-purchase

certificate, the local authority would be required to pay 80 per cent of the provisional valuation of the land by the district valuer to the owner (in long- or short-term bonds). The district valuer would have another two months to firm up his valuation, after which the remaining 20 per cent would be payable, together with a 'bonus' of 10 per cent to owners who were not contesting the valuation. The bonus of 10 per cent can be justified as a rough estimate of the savings to the local authority of an uncontested claim. All owners would have a right to contest the valuation and appeal to the Lands Tribunal.

In respect of small claims a more generous approach to valuation could be provided for by statute, in order to mitigate the effects of the plan on the small investor. Coupled with this, there would have to be a hardship tribunal (presumably attached to the Lands Tribunal), which would have a small fund for paying bonuses to parties who are put in financial difficulties due to the purchase of their land.

There is one important point to consider here, which is the price the counties should pay to other governmental entities (such as British Rail, which holds a substantial amount of derelict land) for land needed for development. The nationalised industries might argue for the right to receive more compensation than the existing-use value for their land. In the past the nationalised industries have used their large land holdings as a much needed source of capital. However, it would seem that since the purpose of the scheme is to take all development land into local-authority ownership at existing-use value it would be fair and equitable to treat all owners similarly. To do otherwise would be to give the nationalised industries a subsidy at the expense of the local authorities; while this may seem like robbing Peter to pay Paul, it would in effect be a support for the transport and health sectors of public expenditure at the expense of the housing and local services sectors.

Up to this point we have dealt with a possible method of acquiring and assembling development land. That is only half the story, for there would also have to be a method for releasing and developing the land later in time when the particular area is ripe for development. This brings up two critical aspects of such a scheme: the method and price of disposal, and the procedures needed for public review of development on the land once it is released.

K

First, there is the question of the method of allocation. Since the local authorities use about one-fifth of all land, the counties will allocate a substantial portion of the land to their own or the member districts' projects. There is also a substantial amount of land used for other government projects (that is to say the central government and nationalised industries). It would seem logical to price the release of all that land as assembly cost, that is the existing-use value, plus interest costs, administrative costs of assembly, the cost of the infrastructure of street lights, sewers, and so on. The more important question is how to release the remainder of the land for private development. If the land were leased and not sold freehold, it would create a whole new category of home-owners without an equity interest in their land. The present owners of freehold would thus always be in a better position than all future owners, a situation which seems somewhat inequitable. The more logical system would seem to be to release the land freehold.

This freehold land could simply be auctioned off to the highest bidder from the building and development firms interested. Such sales could be made conditional upon meeting various planning and pricing criteria for the benefit of neighbours and future owners. The other option would be to sell the land at assembly cost to the occupier, not the builder, and to select the builder on the basis of an open competition with design and cost criteria of selection. The owners would have to contract either not to sell, or to pass any windfall profit (due to the difference in price between the market and the assembly costs) back to the county. Irrespective of the type of release, it would be crucial to the success of the plan to allow the county to impose positive obligations, either in the sale, as a covenant, or by way of planning conditions. This would mean that the legislation would have to be expanded to include certain specific matters (such as the provision of public housing, the percentage of open space, and so on).

There is a second side to this disposal problem, apart from the price, which would need careful attention, namely the procedural changes needed for the public review of development. Under the present scheme the Minister can call a public inquiry on public developments at his discretion. Similarly he can call in important, private development applications for review before a decision is made by the local authority. Besides this discretionary review there is the automatic review of planning-application refusals. Under a land-storage scheme the land would not be released until the county had decided, in conjunction with the districts, that the land should receive permission. There would thus be a dramatic increase in development where the council would both own the land initially and grant permission to develop before releasing that land. It becomes necessary to devise a procedure for the full public discussion of these new 'public' developments.

There would be two problems here, one the lack of release of land where either the community or, in particular, the developers thought it was necessary, and the other the review of positive decisions to develop. The lack of release, similar to a denial of planning permission except that the county owns the land, might be handled by the same planning-inquiry procedure that is already in existence. Instead of being an appeal against denial of permission, it would be an appeal against refusal of permission and willingness to sell. This would create some public discussion of a number of possible developments. However, the appellants would not have as much to gain as under the present system (that is, a vast increase in the value of their property) and there would probably be fewer of these public inquiries

As to the second problem (the review of positive decisions to develop) the present system of discretionary review by the Minister would not seem to be adequate. Since the great bulk of planning-permission-refusal public inquiries would disappear, there would need to be a substitute procedure to involve the public in important cases. One method of doing this would be to enlarge the method of review by statute, and enlarge the approaches to review available to the Minister. For instance, there could be a statutory list of categories of development where a public inquiry was needed. These could include (1) large-scale developments in relation to the size of the area in which they were to take place, (2) development on open space, particularly allotments, public open spaces or parks, and (3) unneighbourly developments (a category already the subject of statutorily required publicity, 1971 T.C.P.A., sec. 29), and others. Before the county could release land it would have to publicise such a release and any member of the community could appeal to the Minister on the grounds that the land fell

277

within one of the categories and required an inquiry. It might be possible to include here a category of appeal for occupiers of the county land under licence (that is, the old owners or tenants) who feel their present use is more reasonable than the new development contemplated by the county.

The legislation could also allow the Minister to use different types of review for different types of situation. For instance, if a county were engaged in a series of small developments which did not fall within any of the categories of automatic public inquiry, a procedure might be adopted whereby local residents could request a 'public examination' of current development policy in the county. This review could be instituted in problem areas or in areas where the regional office of the D.O.E. was worried about the soundness of county parcel-by-parcel decision-making.

Finally, a great deal of attention will have to be given to the procedures for dealing with cases of financial hardship for individual owners. Under the 1947 Act, a certain Mr Pilgrim in Romford had purchased a vacant lot through a £500 mortgage on his home. When the council purchased the vacant lot for £65 Mr Pilgrim promptly committed suicide. Naturally enough this created ill-will against the Act since some people thought there was a causal relationship between the two events (CULLINGWORTH, p. 154). In order to avoid similar problems under our scheme, there will have to be sufficient funds available and a wide enough discretion lodged with the hardship-review body to allow them to sift claims to find the small, high-risk property investor such as Mr Pilgrim. A limit in terms of either money or acreage will not be sufficient, for the screen must be able to look after the interests of the small investor who has gone into partnership, the small company dealing in land, the investor who has shares in a larger company, or the person of minor wealth who has had the misfortune to invest all his wealth in one large parcel. It will thus be of special importance to set up definite criteria relating the claim to the net worth of the individual, and allowing the hardship body to give the individual not only financial compensation but perhaps reinstatement in existing-use activity elsewhere.

This model represents only one pathway to reform, but it should at least give the reader a notion of the range of systemic changes that might lead to more fruitful results than the previous attempts at reform. The scheme would provide the local planners with a new type of mechanism to plot future development and might decrease the price of land for housing and recreation. Returning to the central theme of this study, its implementation would depend upon the types of procedure involved in the decisions made on what land is to be acquired and developed. Without public review of the new public development the scheme could have as many difficulties as the present system. However, real results could be seen if attention were paid to innovative methods of open-review structures. Three have been suggested: county committee written reports at the time of land acquisition; public examination of trends of parcel-by-parcel disposal in some counties; and public inquiries for certain categories of decisions to release and develop land. It is to these types of structures that we should direct our attention, for it is the procedure which will determine the success of any attempt at reforming planning law.*

---

* Readers interested in an analysis of the Community Land Act in the U.K. and its relationship to similar schemes in Canada, France, Germany, Sweden, Australia and the United States should look for *The Government Land Developers* by this author, to be published in 1976.

Bibliography

Unless given, the place of publication is London. The abbreviation D.O.E. stands for Department of the Environment.

ADMINISTRATIVE PROCEDURE ACT, 1970 (U.S.A.), *United States Code*, vol. 5, (1970).

ALDOUS, Tony, *Battle for the Environment* (Fontana, 1972).

ALLEN COMMITTEE, *Report of the Committee of Inquiry into the Impact of Rates on Households* (Chairman R. G. D. Allen), Cmnd. 2582 (H.M.S.O., 1964).

ARNSTEIN, Sherry R., 'A Ladder of Citizen Participation', *Journal of the American Institution of Planners*, vol. 35 (1969) p. 216.

ASH, Maurice, 'The Land Commission's Tragedy', *Town and Country Planning* (Dec. 1969) p. 542.

BAINS REPORT, *The New Local Authorities: Management and Structure* (Chairman M. A. Bains), D.O.E. (H.M.S.O., 1971).

BARLOW REPORT, *Report of the Royal Commission on the Distribution of the Industrial Population* (Chairman Sir Montague Barlow), Cmd. 6153 (H.M.S.O., 1940).

BARRAS, Richard, BROADBENT, Andrew, and MASSEY, Doreen, 'Planning and the Public Ownership of Land', *New Society* (21 June 1973).

BIRMINGHAM STRUCTURE PLAN, *City of Birmingham Structure Plan: Report on the Options*, by Neville Borg (City Engineer, Surveyor and Planning Officer's Dept, 1973).

BLUE BOOK, *National Incomes Blue Book* (H.M.S.O., 1960–70).

BOSSELMAN, Fred, and CALLIES, David, *The Quiet Revolution in Land Use Control: Summary Report* (Washington: U.S. Council on Environmental Quality, 1971).

BOYLE, L., *Equalisation and the Future of Local Government Finance* (Oliver & Boyd, 1966).

BROWN, Roger, 'Linking Local Planning with Structure Planning', *The Planner* (previously *Journal of the Town Planning Institute*), vol. 60, no. 1 (Jan. 1974) p. 505.

BUCHANAN, Colin, *Traffic in Towns*, Ministry of Housing and Local Government (H.M.S.O., 1963).

BUXTON, R. J., *Local Government* (Harmondsworth: Penguin, 1970).

CALIFORNIA ENVIRONMENTAL QUALITY ACT, 1970, *California Public Resources Code* 21151 (1970).

CARAVAN SITES AND CONTROL OF DEVELOPMENT ACT, 1960 (8 & 9 Eliz. 2, c. 62).

CENTRAL GOVERNMENT REORGANISATION WHITE PAPER, *The Reorganisation of Central Government*, Cmnd. 4506 (H.M.S.O., 1970).

CIRCULAR 9/58, *Report of the Committee on Administrative Tribunals and Inquiries*, Ministry of Housing and Local Government (H.M.S.O., 1958).

CIRCULAR 5/68, *The Use of Conditions in Planning Permissions*, Ministry of Housing and Local Government (H.M.S.O., 1968).

CIRCULAR 61/68, *Town and Country Planning Act, 1968 – Part V Historic Buildings and Conservation*, Ministry of Housing and Local Government (H.M.S.O., 1968).

CIRCULAR 2/70, *Capital Programmes*, D.O.E. (H.M.S.O., 1970).

CIRCULAR 52/72, *Development Plan Proposals: Publicity and Public Participation*, D.O.E. (H.M.S.O., 1972).

CIRCULAR 142/73, *Streamlining the Planning Machine*, D.O.E. (H.M.S.O., 1973).

CIRCULAR 98/74, *Structure Plans*, D.O.E. (H.M.S.O., 1974).

CIRCULAR 124/74, *Local Government Ombudsman*, D.O.E. (H.M.S.O., 1974).

C. N. L. (Campaign for Nationalising Land), *The Case for Nationalising Land* (Jack Brocklebank, Nicholas Kaldor, Joan Maynard, Robert Neild, Oliver Strutchbury, 1973).

CODE OF PRACTICE, *Structure Plans: The Examination in Public*, part of Circular 36/73, D.O.E. (H.M.S.O., 1973).

COMMISSION REPORTS, *Land Commission Report and Accounts* (H.M.S.O., March 1968, March 1969, March 1970).

COMMUNITY LAND BILL, *House of Commons Bill* 108, 12 March 1975 (H.M.S.O.).

CONDUCT IN LOCAL GOVERNMENT, *Report of the Prime Minister's Committee on Local Government Rules of Conduct* (Chairman Lord Redcliffe-Maud) (H.M.S.O., 1974).

CONURBATION, *The Report of the West-Midland Group on Postwar Reconstruction and Planning* (Architectural Press, 1948).

COVENTRY STRUCTURE PLAN (City Council, 1973).

COWAN, Peter, and DONNISON, David V., *The Future of Planning* (Heinemann, 1973).

CRIPPS, Eric I., and HALL, Peter, *Information and Urban Planning*, vol. 1 (Centre for Environmental Studies, 1969).

CULLINGWORTH, J. B., *Town and Country Planning in Britain*, 4th ed. (Allen & Unwin, 1972).

DAILY NOTES, *Worcestershire Structure Plan Daily Notes: Summary of Discussion*, D.O.E. (1974).

DAMER, S., and HAGUE, C., 'Public Participation in Planning: A Review', *Town Planning Review*, vol. 42 (1971) p. 217.

DAVIDOFF, Paul, 'Advocacy and Pluralism in Planning', *Journal of the American Institute of Planners*, vol. 31 (1965) p. 331.

DENNIS, Norman, *People and Planning* (Faber & Faber, 1970).

DENNIS, Norman, *Public Participation and Planners' Blight* (Faber & Faber, 1972).

DE SMITH, S. A., *Judicial Review of Administrative Action*, 2nd ed. (Stevens & Sons, 1968).

DEVELOPMENT CONTROL STUDY, *Management Study on Development Control* (H.M.S.O., 1967).

DEVOLUTION GREEN PAPER, *Devolution within the United Kingdom: Some Alternatives for Discussion*, Privy Council Office (H.M.S.O., 1974).

DEVOLUTION WHITE PAPER, *Democracy and Devolution Proposals for Scotland and Wales*, Cmnd. 5732 (H.M.S.O., 1974).

DISTRIBUTION OF INDUSTRY ACT, 1945 (8 & 9 Geo. 6, c. 36).

DOBRY FINAL REPORT, *Review of the Development Control System: Final Report* (H.M.S.O., 1975).

DOBRY INTERIM REPORT, *Interim Report on Review of Development Control System* (H.M.S.O., 1974).

DOBRY QUESTIONNAIRE, *Development Control Review Questionnaire*, D.O.E. (Oct. 1973).

DOWRICK, F. E., 'Public Ownership of Land – Taking Stock 1972–3', *Public Law* (Spring 1974), p. 10.

ECONOMIC COUNCIL, *The West-Midlands: Patterns of Growth*, West-Midlands Economic Planning Council (H.M.S.O., 1967).

EDDISON, P. A., *Plan Opportunity and Action*, Town and Country Planning Conference Document (Dec. 1971).

ELKIN, Stephen L., *Politics and Land Use Planning* (Cambridge University Press, 1974).

EVERSLEY, D. E. C., with D. Keate and U. Shaw, 'The Overspill Problem in the West-Midlands', *Studies in the Problems of Housing and Industrial Location*, no. 1 (West-Midlands New Town Society, 1958).

EVERSLEY, D. E. C., with U. Jackson and G. M. Lomas, *Population Growth and Planning Policy: An Analysis of Social and Economic Factors Affecting Housing and Employment Location in the West-Midlands* (Frank Cass, 1965).

FAIRLEY, Alisdair, 'The True Corruption of Local Government', *The Listener* (22 Feb. 1973) p. 229.

FINANCE ACT, 1974 (1974, c. 30).

FINANCE GREEN PAPER, *The Future Shape of Local Government Finance* (H.M.S.O., 1971).

FOJER, Lars, 'Local Authority Land Policy in Sweden', *Studies in Comparative Local Government*, vol. 6, no. 1 (Summer 1972).

FOSTER, C. D., and WHITEHEAD, C. M. E., 'The Layfield Report on the Greater London Development Plan', *Economica* (Nov. 1973) p. 442.

FRANKS, *Report of the Committee on Administrative Tribunals and Inquiries* (Chairman Sir Oliver Franks), Cmnd. 218 (H.M.S.O., 1957).

FRIEND, John, and JESSOP, Neil F., *Local Government and Strategic Choice* (Tavistock, 1969).

GENERAL DEVELOPMENT ORDER, 1963, *Town and Country Planning General Development Order, 1963*, Statutory Instruments no. 709 (H.M.S.O., 1963).

GENERAL DEVELOPMENT ORDER, 1969, *Town and Country Planning General Development (Amendment) Order, 1969*, Statutory Instruments no. 286 (H.M.S.O., 1969).

GENERAL RATE ACT, 1967 (1967, c. 9).

G. L. D. P., *Greater London Development Plan Statement* (G.L.C., 1969).

GODLEY, Wynne, and RHODES, John, *The Rate Support System*, Dept of Applied Economics, University of Cambridge (1973).

GRAHAM, R., 'Development Control: The Decision-making Process', unpublished paper (University of Warwick, 1974).

GREGORY, Roy, *The Price of Amenity: Five Studies in Conservation and Government* (Macmillan, 1971).

GRIFFITH, J. A. G., and STREET, H., *Principles of Administrative Law*, 3rd ed. (Pitman, 1967).

HAAR, Charles, *Land-Use Planning in a Free Society* (Harvard University Press, 1951).

HAAR, Charles, 'The Master Plan: An Impermanent Constitution', *Law and Contemporary Problems*, vol. 20 (1959) p. 350.

HAAR, Charles, *Law and Land* (Harvard University Press, 1964).

HAGMAN, Donald, *Urban Planning and Land Development Control Law* (St. Paul, Minn.: Wests, 1971).

HAGMAN, Donald, *Public Planning and the Control of Urban and Land Development* (St. Paul, Minn.: Wests, 1973).

HALL, Peter (ed.), *The Containment of Urban England*, 2 vols (Allen & Unwin, 1973).

HALL, Peter, 'The New Structure Plans: The West-Midlands Case', *New Society* (21 March 1974), p. 701.

HANCOCK REPORT, *Reports of the Local Government Commission* (H.M.S.O., 1958–65).

HANSON, Michael, 'Structure Plans Examined', *Municipal and Public Services Journal* (6 July 1973) p. 983.

HARRISON, M. L., 'Development Control: The Influence of Political, Legal and Ideological Factors', *Town Planning Review*, vol. 43 (1972) p. 254.

HART, W. O., *Introduction to the Law of Local Government and Administration*, 8th ed. (Butterworth, 1968).

HEAP, Desmond, *An Outline of Planning Law*, 6th ed. (Sweet & Maxwell, 1973).

HEIMBURGER, Peter, *The Use of Municipal Land Ownership as an Instrument in Influencing the Structure of Urban Development: Sweden's Experience* (Stockholm: National Board of Urban Planning [Sweden] 1973).

HELMORE, L. M., *The District Auditor* (MacDonald & Evans, 1961).

HEPWORTH, N. P., *The Finance of Local Government* (Allen & Unwin, 1971).

HILLMAN, Judy (ed.), *Planning for London* (Harmondsworth: Penguin, 1971).

HOWARD, Ebenezer, *Garden Cities of Tomorrow* (Faber & Faber, 1962).

JACKSON, R. M., *The Machinery of Local Government* (Macmillan, 1967).

JENKINS, Simon, 'The Politics of London Motorways', *Political Quarterly*, vol. 44 (1973) p. 257.

JOHNSON, Stanley, 'The Making of a Super Minister', *Spectator* (24 Oct. 1970), p. 494.

JOHNSON, Stanley, *The Politics of Environment* (Littlehampton: Tom Stacey, 1973).

JONES, G. W., *Borough Politics* (Macmillan, 1969).

JOWELL, Jeffery, 'Report of the Greater London Group – Evidence to the Review of the Development Control System' (unpublished, 1974).

KAPLAN, Marshal, 'Advocacy and the Urban Poor', *Journal of the American Institute of Planners*, vol. 35 (1969) p. 96.

KEEBLE, Lewis, *Town Planning at the Crossroads* (*Estates Gazette*, 1961).

KILBRANDON, *Report of the Royal Commission on the Constitution 1969–73*, Cmnd. 5460 – I, II (H.M.S.O., 1973).

KITCHEN, Ted, 'Planning Education in Britain – An Addendum', *The Planner*, vol. 60, no. 3 (March, 1974) p. 611.

LABOUR'S PROGRAMME, *Labour's Programme for Britain – Annual Conference, 1973* (Labour Party, 1973).

LAND COMMISSION WHITE PAPER, *The Land Commission*, Cmnd. 2771 (H.M.S.O., 1965).

LAND COMPENSATION ACT, 1973 (1973, c. 26).

LAND WHITE PAPER, *Land*, Cmnd. 5730 (H.M.S.O., 1974).

LAYFIELD, F. H. B., *Report of the Panel of Inquiry on the Greater London Development Plan*, D.O.E. (H.M.S.O., 1972).

LAYFIELD, F. H. B., and WHYBROW, Christopher, 'The Examination of Structure Plans', *Journal of Planning Law*, part I (1973) p. 516, part II (1973) p. 627.

LEFCOE, George, 'Notes on the Taxations and Re-organisation of Local Government in Sweden: Implications for Exclusionary Zoning and Revenue Sharing in the United States' (unpublished paper, University of Southern California, 1972).

LIPSEY, David, *Labour and Land*, Fabian Tract no. 422 (Fabian Society, 1973).

LOCAL GOVERNMENT ACT, 1929 (19 & 20 Geo. 5, c. 17).

LOCAL GOVERNMENT ACT, 1948 (11 & 12 Geo. 6, c. 26).

LOCAL GOVERNMENT ACT, 1966 (1966, c. 42).

LOCAL GOVERNMENT ACT, 1972 (1972, c. 70).

LOCAL GOVERNMENT ACT, 1974 (1974, c. 7).

LONG, Joyce, *The Wythall Inquiry* (*Estates Gazette*, 1961).

MCAUSLAN, J. P. W. B., 'Planning Law's Contribution to the Problems of an Urban Society', *Modern Law Review*, vol. 37, no. 2 (March 1974) p. 134.

MCAUSLAN, J. P. W. B., *Land, and Planning Law* (Weidenfeld & Nicolson, 1975).

MCAUSLAN SUBMISSION, 'Submission to Development Control Review' (unpublished, University of Warwick, 1973).

MACKINTOSH, John P., 'The Report of the Royal Commission on the Constitution 1969–73', *Political Quarterly* (Jan.–Mar. 1974) p. 115.

MCLOUGHLIN, J. Brian, *Control and Urban Planning* (Faber & Faber, 1973a).

MCLOUGHLIN, J. Brian, 'Warwickshire: The Reality of Structure Plans', *The Architect's Journal* (25 July 1973b), p. 184.

MACMURRAY, Trevor, 'Strengthening Our Approach', *The Planner* (Jan. 1974) p. 493.

MALLABY REPORT, *Report of the Committee on Staffing of Local Government* (H.M.S.O., 1967).

MANDELKER, Daniel, *Green Belts and Urban Growth* (University of Wisconsin Press, 1962).

MANDELKER, Daniel, *The Zoning Dilemma* (New York: Bobbs-Merrill, 1971).

MANUAL, *Structure and Local Plans – A Manual on Form and Content*, Ministry of Housing and Local Government (H.M.S.O., 1970).

MARCUS, Susanna T., 'Planners Who Are You?', *Journal of the Town Planning Institute*, vol. 57, no. 1 (Jan. 1971) p. 54.

MASTERS, Peter, 'Public Involvement in the Planning Process', *The Planner*, vol. 59, no. 10 (Dec. 1973) p. 459.

MEACHER, Molly, *Rate Rebates: A Study of the Effectiveness of Means Tests* (Child Poverty Action Group, 1971).

MITCHINSON, J., 'Public Participation Since Skeffington', *Local Government Chronicle* (1972) p. 61.

MOYNIHAN, Patrick, *Maximum Feasible Misunderstanding* (New York: Free Press, 1969).

NATIONAL PARKS AND ACCESS TO THE COUNTRYSIDE ACT, 1949 (12, 13 & 14 Geo. 6, c. 97).

N.B.U.P., *Physical Planning in Sweden*, The National Board of Urban Planning, Information in English, no. 2 (Stockholm, 1972).

NETWORKS, *Management Networks – A Study for Structure Plans*, D.O.E. (H.M.S.O., 1971).

NEW TOWNS ACT, 1946 (9 & 10 Geo. 6, c. 68).

NEW WATER INDUSTRY, D.O.E. (H.M.S.O., 1973).

NORR, M., NOORNHAMMAR, N. H., and SANDELS, C., *The Tax System in Sweden* (Stockholm's Enskilda Bank, 1969).

NORTH CITY AREA WIDE COUNCIL INC., 'Maximum Feasible Manipulation', *City* (Oct.–Nov. 1970) p. 30, reprinted in Hagman (1973), p. 188.

ODMANN, Ella, and DAHLBERG, Gun-Britt, *Planning Sweden*, National Institute of Building and Urban Planning Research (Stockholm: Ministry of Labour and Housing, Ministry of Physical Planning and Local Government, 1973).

P.A.G., *The Future of Development Plans – A Report of the Planning Advisory Group* (Chairman I. O. Pugh), Ministry of Housing and Local Government (H.M.S.O., 1965).

PANEL REPORT, *The Report of the Panel on the Examination in Public 13 Nov–19 Dec 1973 on Warwickshire County Structure Plan 1973, City of Coventry Structure Plan 1973 and County Borough of Solihull Structure Plan 1973* (D.O.E. publication, West-Midlands Regional Office).

PASSOW, Shirley S., 'Land Reserves and Teamwork in Planning Stockholm', *American Institute of Planners' Journal* (May 1970) p. 179.

PAYNE, Pamela, 'Planning Appeals', *Journal of the Town Planning Institute*, vol. 57, no. 3 (March 1971) p. 114.

PERRY, John, 'Approach to Local Planning', *The Planner*, vol. 60, no. 1, Feb. 1974) p. 492.

PIGOU, A., *The Economics of Welfare*, 4th ed. (Macmillan, 1952).

PIGOU, A., *Public Finance* (Macmillan, 1962).

POOLE, F. T., 'The Weight of Planning Applications and Appeals', *Journal of Planning and Environmental Law* (Feb. 1973), p. 96.

PREST, A. R., *Economics* (Weidenfeld & Nicolson, 1967).

PREST, A. R., *Public Finance* (Weidenfeld & Nicolson, 1970).

PUE, John F., *Government Finance: Economics of the Public Sector* (Homewood, Ill.: Irwin, 1968).

QUEEN'S SPEECH, 1974, *Her Majesty's Most Gracious Speech to Both Houses of Parliament, 12 March 1974* (H.M.S.O., 1974).

RATCLIFF, R. U., *Urban Land Economics* (New York: McGraw-Hill, 1949).

RATE SUPPORT GRANT ORDER, 1972, *The Rate Support Grant (Increase) Order, 1972, Local Government Finance* (H.M.S.O., 1972).

RATE SUPPORT GRANT ORDER, 1975, *The Rate Support Grant*

(Increase) Order, 1975, Local Government Finance (H.M.S.O., 1975).

RATING ACT, 1966 (1966, c. 9).

REDCLIFFE-MAUD COMMISSION REPORT, *Report of the Royal Commission on Local Government in England* (Chairman Lord Redcliffe-Maud), Cmnd. 4040 – I–IV (H.M.S.O., 1969).

REDCLIFFE-MAUD COMMITTEE REPORT, *Report of the Committee on the Management of Local Government* (Chairman Sir John Maud), 5 vols (H.M.S.O., 1967).

REDCLIFFE-MAUD, Lord, and WOOD, Bruce, *English Local Government Reformed* (Oxford University Press, 1974).

REES, L. B., *Government by Community* (Knight, 1971).

REGULATIONS, 1971, *Structure and Local Plans: Memorandum on Part I, Town and Country Planning Act, 1968*, Circular 44/71, D.O.E. (H.M.S.O., 1971).

REGULATIONS, 1972, *Structure and Local Plans Regulations, 1972*, Circular 72/72, D.O.E. (H.M.S.O., 1972).

REICH, Charles A., 'The Law of the Planned Society', *Yale Law Journal*, vol. 75 (1966) p. 1228.

REORGANISATION WHITE PAPER, *Local Government in England: Government Proposals for Reorganisation*, Cmnd. 4584 (H.M.S.O., 1971).

RHODES, G., *The Government of London: The Struggle for Reform* (Weidenfeld & Nicolson, 1970).

RICHARDS, Peter, *The Reformed Local Government System* (Allen & Unwin, 1973).

RIPLEY, B. J., *Administration in Local Authorities* (Butterworth, 1970).

ROBERTS, N. A., 'Homes, Roadbuilders and the Courts: Highway Relocation and Judicial Review of Administrative Action', *Southern California Law Review*, vol. 46 (1972) p. 51.

ROBERTS, N. A., 'Land Storage: The Swedish Example', *Modern Law Review* (March 1975).

ROBSON, W. A., *The Development of Local Government* (Allen & Unwin, 1958).

ROBSON, W. A., *Local Government in Crisis* (Allen & Unwin, 1968).

ROSE, Barry, *England Looks at Maud* (Chichester: Acford, 1970).

ROYAL COMMISSION ON LOCAL GOVERNMENT, 1923–9, *Final Report*, Cmd. 3436 (H.M.S.O., 1929).

289

R.T.P.I., 'Planning Services and Staff – Observations of the Royal Town Planning Institute', *Journal of the Town Planning Institute*, vol. 58, no. 10 (Dec. 1972) p. 460.

R.T.P.I. MEMORANDUM, 'Royal Town Planning Institute's Memorandum on the Local Government Bill', *Journal of the Town Planning Institute*, vol. 58, no. 4 (April 1972) p. 151.

SAMUELS, Alec, 'Town and Country Planning Act, 1968', *Public Law*, vol. 19 (1969).

SCHON, Donald A., *Beyond the Stable State* (Harmondsworth: Penguin, 1971).

SCOTT REPORT, *Report of the Committee on Land Utilisation in Rural Areas* (Chairman T. E. Scott), Cmd. 6378 (H.M.S.O., 1942).

SEEBOHM REPORT, *Report of the Committee on Local Authority and Allied Personal Social Services* (Chairman F. Seebohm), Cmnd. 3703 (H.M.S.O., 1968).

SELF, Peter, 'Nonsense on Stilts: Cost–Benefit Analysis and the Roskill Commission', *Political Quarterly*, vol. 41 (July–Sep. 1970) p. 249.

SELF, Peter, 'Planning by Judicial Inquiry', *R.I.B.A. Journal* (July 1971) p. 303.

SENIOR, Derick, *Strategic Planning in the New Metropolitan Areas*, Town and Country Planning Conference Document (Dec. 1971).

SHARP, Evelyn, *Transport Planning: The Men for the Job* (H.M.S.O., 1970).

SHARP, Thomas, 'Planning Planning', *Journal of the Town Planning Institute*, vol. 52, no. 6 (June 1966) p. 209.

SHELTER, *Condemned: A Shelter Report on Housing and Poverty* (Shelter Action Group Report, 1971).

SKEFFINGTON REPORT, *People and Planning* (Chairman A. M. Skeffington), Ministry of Housing and Local Government (H.M.S.O., 1969).

SMITH, G. (ed.), 'Redcliffe-Maud's Brave New England', *Local Government Chronicle* (Knight, 1969).

SOLIHULL STRUCTURE PLAN, *Structure Plan: Written Statement* (Borough Engineer, Surveyor and Town Planning Officer's Dept, 1973).

SPENSER, P., 'Party Politics and the Process of Local Democracy in an English Town Council', in *Councils in Action*, ed. A. Richards and A. Kuper (Cambridge University Press, 1971).

STAFFORDSHIRE STRUCTURE PLAN, *Staffordshire County Structure Plan*, 2 vols (County Council, 1973).

STANYER, Jeffrey, *County Government in England and Wales* (Routledge & Kegan Paul, 1967).

STATISTICAL YEARBOOK, *Administrative Districts of Sweden, 1973* (Stockholm: National Central Bureau of Statistics, 1973).

STEWART, J. D., 'New Separatism or New Co-operation', *Local Government Chronicle* (17 March 1972) p. 451.

STEWART, J. D., 'Area Committees – A New Dimension', *Local Government Chronicle* (22 June 1973) p. 651.

STEWART, J. D., and EDDISON Tony, 'Structure Planning and Corporate Planning', *Journal of the Town Planning Institute*, vol. 57, no. 8 (Dec. 1972) p. 460.

SWEDISH STATUTES, relevant statutory material information of interest is: *Building and Planning Act, 1947* (S.F.S. 1947, no. 385); various *Housing Acts* (S.F.S. 1947, no. 523; S.F.S. 1959, no. 605; S.F.S. 1962, no. 655; S.F.S. 1967, no. 309); *Building Code 1959* (S.F.S. 1959, no. 612); the *Pre-emption Act* (S.F.S. 1967, no. 868); and the various *Expropriation Acts* (S.F.S. 1917, no. 189; S.F.S. 1949, no. 663; S.F.S. 1966, no. 258).

TELLING, A. E., *Planning Law and Procedure*, 4th ed. (Butterworth, 1973).

TETLOW, John, and GOSS, Anthony, *Homes, Towns and Traffic* (Faber & Faber, 1965).

T.C.P.A., 1947, *Town and Country Planning Act, 1947* (10 & 11 Geo. 6, c. 51).

T.C.P.A., 1953, *Town and Country Planning Act, 1953* (1 & 2 Eliz. 2, c. 16).

T.C.P.A., 1954, *Town and Country Planning Act, 1954* (2 & 3 Eliz. 2, c. 72).

T.C.P.A., 1959, *Town and Country Planning Act, 1959* (7 & 8 Eliz. 2, c. 53).

T.C.P.A., 1962, *Town and Country Planning Act, 1962* (10 & 11 Eliz. 2, c. 38).

T.C.P.A., 1968, *Town and Country Planning Act, 1968* (1968, c. 72).

T.C.P.A., 1971, *Town and Country Planning Act, 1971* (1971, c. 78).

T.C.P.A., 1972, *Town and Country Planning (Amendment) Act, 1972* (1972, c. 42).

BIBLIOGRAPHY

TOWN AND COUNTRY PLANNING ASSOCIATION, 'Development Control Review: Reply to Questionnaire' (unpublished).

TOWN AND COUNTRY PLANNING ASSOCIATION LETTER, 'An Open Letter to Geoffrey Rippon: Statement by the T.C.P.A. on Development Value and Land Assemblies', *Town and Country Planning Magazine* (1973) p. 258.

TOWN CENTRES BULLETIN, *Town Centres: Approach to Renewal*, Ministry of Housing and Local Government and Ministry of Transport, Planning Bulletin, no. 1 (H.M.S.O., 1962).

TOWN DEVELOPMENT ACT, 1952 (15 & 16 Geo. 6 and 1 Eliz. 2, c. 54).

TRANSCRIPT, 'The Examination in Public of the Coventry–Solihull–Warwickshire Structure Plans', *Notes of Proceedings* (D.O.E., 1973).

TRIBUNALS AND INQUIRIES ACT, 1971 (1971, c. 62).

U.S. NATIONAL ENVIRONMENTAL POLICY ACT, 1969, *42 U.S. Code Annotated 4332* (1969).

UTHWATT, *Report of the Expert Committee on Compensation and Betterment* (Chairman Baron A. A. Uthwatt), Cmd. 6386 (H.M.S.O., 1942).

WADE, H. W. R., *Administrative Law*, 2nd ed. (Oxford: Clarendon Press, 1967).

WARWICKSHIRE STRUCTURE PLAN, *Draft County Structure 1972*, 2 vols (County Council, 1972).

WELLS, Sir Henry, 'Town Planning and the Land Commission Act', *Journal of the Town Planning Institute*, vol. 53, no. 8 (Sep.–Oct. 1967) p. 334.

WEST-MIDLANDS REGIONAL STUDY, *The West-Midlands: A Regional Study*, D.O.E. (H.M.S.O., 1965).

WHITE PAPER, 1967, *Town and Country Planning*, Cmnd. 3333 (H.M.S.O., 1967).

WISEMAN, Victor, *Local Government In England, 1958–69* (Routledge & Kegan Paul, 1969).

WORCESTER STRUCTURE PLAN, *The Preparation of an Urban Structure Plan for the City of Worcester: Report of Survey*, 12 vols (City Architect and Planning Officer's Dept, 1973).

WORCESTERSHIRE REPRESENTATIONS, unpublished representations made to the county of Worcestershire, 1973–4.

WORCESTERSHIRE STRUCTURE PLAN, *Draft County Structure Plan* (County Council, 1972).

BIBLIOGRAPHY

WRAITH, Ronald Edward, and LAMB, G. B., *Public Inquiries as an Instrument of Government* (Allen & Unwin, 1971).

ZETTER, Roger, 'Progress in Structure Planning', *The Planner*, vol. 59, no. 8 (Sep.–Oct. 1973) p. 372.

Index

New Towns 4, 5, 8, 41, 42, 67, 119–
20, 130, 145, 189, 196; development corporations 197, 248, 265
New Towns Act 66
New Zealand, ombudsman 45
non-metropolitan counties 39. *See
also* Counties
Norman Conquest 17
North Sea oil 3
notice of approval 186
Nottinghamshire 151
nuisance, actions for 5

Oakes, Gordon 215
Odmann, Ella 251
offices: buildings 8; development
certificate 120; unoccupied blocks
266
ombudsman, *see* local government
ombudsman
optimal size of local unit 30–2
Osman, Arthur 151
overspill 41, 42, 119, 127
owner-occupied houses 265

Page, Graham 91, 112
panels, examination 116–18; 160,
163, 166–8; chairman's role 170–
4; reports 174–83
parish meetings 18
parishes 7, 18
parks 18, 55
Parliamentary Commissioner (Ombudsman) 45, 46, 204
party politics in local councils 20–1
Passow, Shirley 253
Payne, Pamela 81
Peacock, Professor A. R. 34
peripheral development 42, 183
Perry, John 153–4
Pigou, A. 51, 244
Pilgrim's case 278
plan-making reforms 83–97, 228–30;
forward-planning process 83–4;
ad hoc decision-making 83–4;
central government and planning
process 85; changes in operation
85–6; case law 85; Planning

Advisory Group 86–91; 1967
White Paper 90; Town and
Country Planning Act, 1968 90–4;
duties of new local governments
93–6; grounds for inter-authority
disputes 95; second tier of plan-
implementing districts 96. *See also*
development plans, procedural
reforms *and* structure plans
Planner, The 153
Planning Advisory Group (P.A.G.)
76, 86–91, 94, 119, 151, 153, 188;
process of plan-making 87–8; two-
level proposals 88–9; 'action
areas' 89; national planning 89,
90; local decisions and regional
development 89–90
planning aid 115
planning appeals 9, 74, 90, 197;
Dobry recommendations 214–15.
See also planning permission
Planning Inquiry Commission, provision for 197, 234
planning permission 7, 42; refusals
and refusal appeals 11, 74;
increase of appeals 77, 86;
responsibility for 95
planning professionals and procedural changes 236–9
police 18–19, 54
politics and the control process
194–6, 227–8
pollution 3, 23
Poole, F. T. 206
Poulson affair 46
presentation meetings 158–9
press access to council meetings 46–
7; council committee meetings 47
Prest, A. R. 51, 56
procedural reform: importance of
230–6, 240–1; elected officials
and local planning officials 232;
rights of third parties 232–3;
advisory forums 234; local
advisory committees 234–5;
changes in considering plans and
planning applications 235–6; and
the planning professionals 236–9;
redefinition of the profession

303